Jim Black joined the Scottish *Sun* as chief sports writer in 1975 and spent twenty-four years there before becoming a freelance writer on football, boxing and golf. He has reported on several World Cup and European Championship finals tournaments.

JINKY

The Biography of Jimmy Johnstone

JIM BLACK

sphere

SPHERE

First published in Great Britain in 2007 by Sphere
This paperback edition published in 2010 by Sphere

Extracts from *Fire in My Boots* by Jimmy Johnstone, published by Stanley Paul,
reprinted by permission of the Random House Group Ltd.

A CIP catalogue record for this book
is available from the British Library.

ISBN 978-0-7515-3985-1

Typeset in Caslon by M Rules
Printed and bound in Great Britain by
Clays Ltd, St Ives plc

Papers used by Sphere are natural, renewable and
recyclable products sourced from well-managed forests and certified
in accordance with the rules of the Forest Stewardship Council.

Mixed Sources
Product group from well-managed
forests and other controlled sources
www.fsc.org   Cert no. SGS-COC-004081
© 1996 Forest Stewardship Council
FSC

Sphere
An imprint of
Little, Brown Book Group
100 Victoria Embankment
London EC4Y 0DY

An Hachette UK Company
www.hachette.co.uk

www.littlebrown.co.uk

To the memory of a truly great football player and his fellow Lions for the enjoyment and pleasure they gave to so many.

CONTENTS

JINKY

PREFACE

Jimmy Johnstone was an enigma all his life: a footballing maestro who played only twenty-three times for his country; a member of the first British team to win the European Cup, yet who worked as a lorry driver after he retired. This book could be a tragedy, the story of an athlete who fell victim to a disease that made him unable to use his body, a man who never quite found his place, yet whom fans voted as Celtic's greatest-ever footballer. It could be a tragedy, but it isn't, because Jinky's heart and mind, his indomitable spirit, would not allow it to be so.

Those of us who watched Jimmy Johnstone in action came away with images that we will never forget, images of speed, invention, mischief, more speed and more invention. Because Jinky on the wing was a sight to behold. At his peak and on his day he had few rivals anywhere in the world. His electrifying bursts of speed could take him past several defenders in one movement. Compact, self-contained and remarkably brave for one so small, he was virtually unstoppable by fair means. Jinky would signal his intent by dropping a shoulder and setting off on a crab-like run, swivelling his hips and turning defenders one way, then the other. Once into his stride, he displayed a varied bag of tricks, drawing defenders towards him and then skipping past them as if the ball were tied to his feet.

Opposing full-backs seeing Jinky's name on the team sheet must have groaned at the prospect of facing a player who could beat them two and three times over before releasing a killer pass to a team-mate or cutting inside to shoot. The accurate crosses he delivered were a handful for any defence, and he was extremely difficult to shake off the ball because of his control and ability to change direction. With his low centre of gravity, Jinky appeared to bounce off defenders.

It seemed at times as if his feet barely touched the ground or the ball while he floated along at breakneck speed. Yet Jinky was more than an entertainer and provider for others. He was a prolific goalscorer, whose timing enabled him to score spectacular goals from long range and seemingly impossible angles. His reflexes invariably put him one step ahead of opponents, and frequently his speed of thought and movement enabled him to outjump much taller opponents. For one so small, he scored a remarkable number of goals with his head.

If there was a criticism of Jinky it was that he was not a natural team player. He would often go off and do his own thing rather than pass the ball. But his manager Jock Stein recognised the showman in Jinky and encouraged the individual flashes of genius, in the knowledge that his team's most valuable asset was capable of turning a game in a few moments. Jinky's unpredictable temperament made him the player he was: the one thing you could expect was the unexpected. He may not have had the consistency of some of his Lisbon Lions team-mates, a fact that Stein also acknowledged, but like many world-class performers he could win a game almost single-handed. This made him unique.

Jinky was a non-conformist, he was incalculable. When in the mood he would switch the play at will, flicking the ball across the pitch instinctively. The trick was to let him be himself, and Jock Stein, more than anyone else, recognised this. Jinky needed to be a free spirit.

My grateful thanks to the many people without whose help this book would not have been possible. Special gratitude goes to Bryan

Cooney, Tom Duthie, John Greig, Susan McLaughlin, John Quinn, Jason Tomas, Robert Weir and the *Scottish Sun* newspaper.

To the Lisbon Lions, in particular Bertie Auld, Tommy Gemmell, Bobby Lennox and Billy McNeill, for being kind enough to give of their time to share cherished memories of their team-mate. Thanks, too, to those players of a bygone age who assisted me with their recollections of Jinky.

I am also indebted to my literary agent, David Luxton, and Iain Hunt and all the team at Little, Brown for their patience, guidance and support. A number of the photographs in this book were provided by Eric McCowat. James Williamson is responsible for the author's portrait. I thank them both.

Last but not least, my wife, Marian, for her forbearance, and my closest friends for their reassurances through the periods of self-doubt. To them and to everyone who helped in any way, I send my deep gratitude.

1

The Last Hurrah

They came in their thousands, from the length and breadth of Scotland and far beyond. The east end of Glasgow has never witnessed anything quite like it. Jimmy Johnstone's passing, on 13 March 2006, did not come as a huge surprise, for his health had been in steady decline for some time due to the ravages of motor neurone disease, the illness he had battled with such courage and determination for more than four years following his diagnosis in November 2001.

But the shock was no less all the same. It seemed inconceivable to his former team-mates, friends and family that Jinky was gone. To his extended family of thousands of Celtic fans the news was almost too much to take in.

Within hours of the announcement that Jinky had passed away at his Lanarkshire home at 6 a.m. that black Monday, the main entrance to Celtic Park was strewn with floral tributes, scarves and football jerseys bearing the number seven. Hundreds of messages of condolence – many penned by fans who had not even been born when Jinky was at the peak of his unique footballing powers – bore further testimony to the affection in which he was held by so many. Significantly, amid the sea of green and white, the colours of Celtic's greatest rivals, Rangers, were also to be seen.

As the mountain of tributes grew to the player voted the Greatest

Celt five years earlier, it effectively became a shrine to the wee man with the heart of a lion. Television and radio stations carried lengthy obituaries to the youngest Lisbon Lion, and the third of their number to pass away following the deaths of Bobby Murdoch in 2001 and Ronnie Simpson three years later. Many thousands of words in the national press recounted in great detail the life and times of arguably Scotland's greatest-ever footballer. For once, hardened sports writers could not be accused of cynically exploiting a tragedy for the sake of filling column inches. In most cases they had been frustrated by the constraints of the space allocated them.

In death, as in life, Jimmy Johnstone was big news. It would perhaps be stretching a point to suggest that Glasgow ground to a halt on the day when Jinky finally lost the fight to overcome a disease that claims more than 1,200 British lives a year. But time stood still in some parts of the city, at least for a brief period as those who had witnessed the skills of a player of conspicuous world class became lost in their memories.

Tears flowed again on the morning of Friday, 17 March – St Patrick's Day – when Jinky made his final journey to Celtic Park to receive one last standing ovation at the scene of his greatest triumphs. The sun shone and there were smiles, too. The solemnity of the funeral mass, at St John the Baptist Church in his native Uddingston, was lightened when Jinky's close friend, Willie Haughey reminded the packed congregation, to loud laughter, that if anyone had lent him money, 'The debt died with Jimmy.'

Joseph Devine, the Bishop of Motherwell, while declaring that football fans everywhere had been hit by a 'tidal wave of sorrow' and 'a river of sadness' at Jinky's passing, also introduced a light-hearted note when referring to the more outrageous aspects of the deceased's life, claiming that he had made more use of the confessional than any other Celtic player. He also recalled one particular game at Falkirk when Jinky had tormented the opposition's defence. 'An elderly supporter turned to me and said: "Father, please forgive the bad language. See the wee man. Is that not sheer bloody poetry" – although if memory serves me well, he used a rather stronger adjective than bloody.'

The Bishop added: 'Whoever can forget the sight of Jimmy skipping off the pitch after the trouncing of Red Star Belgrade with a 5–1 victory because Big Jock had promised him he wouldn't have to fly for the second leg because Jimmy didn't particularly like flying?'

Brian Quinn, the Celtic chairman, paid a glowing tribute. Jinky was 'magical', he said. He could stand alongside Pele and Maradona. There was not a single dissenting voice.

Billy McNeill, captain of the Lisbon Lions, and a man for whom Jinky had the greatest respect, bit back tears as he waxed lyrical about his former team-mate in a eulogy that came straight from the heart. 'The wee man was an incredible personality,' he said, 'and an incredible footballer. He had unbelievable ball control, was as sharp as a tack, as fit as anything, as a brave as a lion. Jimmy loved the fans because he was a fan himself.'

No better words could have been found to describe Jimmy Johnstone. In an age when the word 'great' is too often applied to ordinary mortals in a pair of football boots, Jinky was fully deserving of the accolade. It is a measure of the impact that Jinky had on the world stage that Real Madrid sent a telegram expressing, 'deepest condolences'.

Outside the church more than five hundred listened to the hour-long service as it was relayed over a PA system. Many wore Celtic tops and scarves. More than a few wept unashamedly. So too did several of Jinky's Lisbon Lion team-mates as he was borne from the church on the shoulders of his former brothers-in-arms, led by McNeill.

Such was the clamour by football dignitaries all over Britain to be present that Celtic opened the Kerrydale Suite at Celtic Park at 8.30 in the morning to serve breakfast to those arriving on flights from London, Manchester and Belfast. The club also hired a fleet of luxury coaches to transport the mourners to Uddingston. They included seven of the eight surviving Lions – Willie Wallace was the sole absentee, as it had been impossible for him to make the journey from his home in Australia – along with some of football's most famous names; Sir Alex Ferguson, Kenny Dalglish and Denis Law among them.

Earlier that same week Bobby Lennox – Jinky's closest friend among the Lions during the pair's playing days – had undergone surgery to have a pacemaker fitted. But Lennox refused to heed medical advice and stay away.

Tommy Gemmell, whose equalising goal in Lisbon all those years before had proved crucial to the outcome of the European Cup Final, was visibly upset. But Gemmell, bleary-eyed as a consequence of managing only a few hours' sleep after interrupting a holiday in Spain to be present, was also keen to relate tales of Jinky in his pomp, in an effort to ensure that his former team-mate remained uppermost in everyone's thoughts.

Former Celtic manager Martin O'Neill joined the current squad of players and his successor, Gordon Strachan, in the company of a host of Jinky's former Celtic and Scotland team-mates such as Davie Hay and Danny McGrain and, from Leeds, Peter Lorimer and Eddie Gray. O'Neill said: 'Jimmy leaves a big legacy behind, but for all his achievements he was also amazingly humble. You would talk about him and he always changed the conversation to you.'

Rangers were represented by manager Alex McLeish and three of Jinky's closest rivals, John Greig, Sandy Jardine and Davie Wilson. The then Scotland manager, Walter Smith, and coach Ally McCoist swelled the numbers from the football world.

Scottish parliamentarians also paid their tributes to the little winger, standing side-by-side with celebrities such as Rod Stewart and his fiancée, Penny Lancaster, and fellow singer Frankie Miller, who rose from a tough upbringing in the east end of Glasgow to conquer the American music scene.

Just a few months previously the streets of Belfast had been lined by thousands of ordinary men and women keen to pay their respects to another of the game's true legends, George Best, a friend of Jinky and another universally loved character. Yet few could have anticipated quite so large a turnout as the cortege made the slow and emotional six-mile journey from Uddingston to Celtic Park.

People came flocking to line the route: young and old, football fans and non-football fans; mothers with babies in pushchairs, workmen in overalls, pensioners with their heads bowed, youngsters who had taken an unofficial day off school to witness scenes that have already become folklore. Many wept quietly, others stood grim-faced, a few smiled at the memory of a player who was a true people's man. Most applauded.

The cortege reached London Road and a strange thing happened. The applause was replaced by chants of: 'Oh Jinky, Oh Jinky Johnstone, Oh Jinky Johnstone, He's on the way' in an adaptation of a cry that Jinky had grown used to hearing on so many of the great European nights at Celtic Park. While he was playing he might have been 'the wee man' or 'Jimmy' to most of his teammates, but to the fans he would always be 'Jinky', the name they gave him in recognition of his footballing talent.

There could have been no more fitting tribute to the man, but possibly even Jinky would have been taken aback at the numbers who had congregated outside Celtic Park to pay their final respects. Estimates of anywhere between twenty and thirty thousand were present to applaud, chant and cheer as the hearse stopped after being showered in scarves. Jimmy's widow, Agnes, his son James and daughters Marie and Eileen mingled with the fans for several minutes before the cortege set off for Bothwell Park Cemetery, where Jimmy Johnstone was laid to rest in his beloved Lisbon Lions blazer.

Seventy-five years before, ordinary Celtic fans had shown a similar outpouring of grief at the funeral of another iconic figure, John Thomson, when an estimated twenty thousand of them had walked the near sixty miles to Cardenden, in Fife, to pay homage to the young goalkeeper who died at the age of just twenty-two in September 1931, following a fatal injury suffered in an Old Firm match at Ibrox. But it is hard to imagine that Thomson's passing had a greater effect on the average man on the street than that of Jimmy Johnstone, father of three, grandfather of six, and great-grandfather to eighteen-month-old Paige.

Like his close pal Jim Baxter before him, Jinky succeeded in bridging the Catholic–Protestant divide that, regrettably, remains a blight on the west of Scotland. The Rangers fans may not have loved him, but the majority most certainly admired and respected him, for as Bishop Devine pointed out, Jinky eclipsed Old Firm rivalries and was loved by all supporters of the 'beautiful game'.

The following Sunday, at Hampden Park, CIS Insurance Cup finalists Celtic paid a further tribute to Jinky when each player wore the number seven on his shorts for the match against Dunfermline. The squad also had 'Johnstone 7' embossed on their tracksuit tops. But it was the one minute of loud applause just before the kick-off, which left many in the crowd with a lump in their throat, that would have appealed most to the subject of the ovation and brought a smile to his face.

In spite of his obvious disappointment at seeing his team beaten, 3–0, Jim Leishman, the Dunfermline manager, spoke for football fans everywhere when he said: 'The whole of Scottish football is delighted to be paying tribute to Jimmy Johnstone, a world-class player, whose strength was unbelievable.'

As the fans prepared to leave the stadium – the followers of Celtic to celebrate and those of Dunfermline to drown their sorrows – there was one final moment of raw emotion. The sound of Jinky's voice singing 'Dirty Old Town' in company with Jim Kerr, of Simple Minds fame, and a close friend, was almost too much for some. Lumps rose in many throats, and the tears flowed once again, as those closest to Jinky recalled that he had enjoyed nothing better than to belt out a song on the karaoke machine.

Agnes Johnstone and her son James smiled through their sadness. Thousands of hardened football fans swallowed hard as their thoughts returned to the sight of 'Jimmy Johnstone on the wing'– a chant which had rung out throughout the game. Outside Hampden a bunch of daffodils bore a moving farewell. The flowers spelled out: 'To the Lord of the Wing. Your moves were mesmerising.'

Neil Lennon, the victorious Celtic captain, struck a chord with those who had witnessed a mediocre yet emotional charged game when he declared: 'That was for Jimmy. I think he would have enjoyed it had he been here himself.'

Similar scenes were re-enacted at Celtic Park prior to Celtic's SPL fixture against Inverness Caledonian Thistle three days later when Agnes joined the Lisbon Lions clutching the CIS Cup won in what will for ever be known as the 'Jinky Final'.

It is hard to imagine any other player inspiring such powerful feelings, but Jimmy Johnstone always had a special relationship with the Celtic supporters because he was one of them – a man of the people. He may have stood just five foot, four inches tall, but out on the football field Jimmy Johnstone was a giant.

2

Crowning Glory

Would Celtic have won the European Cup without the flamboyant skills of Jimmy Johnstone? Who can say for sure? But one thing is certain: Celtic's opponents on the road to Lisbon would have slept a little easier in their beds had they not faced the challenge of a player who belonged on the big stage.

Jinky's part in Celtic's triumph can never be overstated. As well as scoring two of his side's eighteen goals in their Cup run, Jinky engineered at least another half-dozen, and his mere presence was enough to unnerve even the most skilled and accomplished defender. Tommy Gemmell, scorer of Celtic's equalising goal in the final against Inter Milan, stressed one aspect of Jinky's contribution when he recalled: 'If we were under pressure in a European tie, especially at Celtic Park, we had to try to get the ball to Jimmy to relieve the pressure because they always put two markers on him and that gave us a bit of space.'

Inevitably, Jinky's reputation preceded him, and from the moment Celtic launched their successful campaign against Swiss side FC Zurich, on 28 September 1966, he was a marked man. In the first leg, at Celtic Park, the powerfully built Swiss put the emphasis on physical contact, with Jinky the main target of abuse from cynical defenders hell-bent on stopping him at all costs. But in spite of Zurich's barely disguised intent to snuff out Celtic's most dangerous player by fair means or foul, Jinky refused to be intimidated and ended the game black and blue after being chopped down almost every time he set off on a run.

Celtic won comfortably, by dint of second-half goals from Gemmell and Joe McBride, scored in the space of six minutes, and Zurich gave Jock Stein no cause to believe that they had it in them to overturn the deficit in the return a week later. So although it was already customary for the away side in Europe to elect to defend a two-goal lead, Stein, a master tactician, elected to ignore conventional wisdom and give his players free rein in Zurich. The upshot was an even more emphatic win, this time by three goals.

With Jinky again singled out for special treatment, his teammates took advantage of Zurich's obsession with stopping him and had the tie won after twenty-two minutes when Gemmell opened the scoring to give Celtic a seemingly unassailable advantage. Celtic grew in confidence, and Stevie Chalmers's thirty-eighth-minute strike, followed by another by Gemmell, from the penalty spot shortly after the restart, simply confirmed the gulf between the teams.

French champions Nantes were expected to offer Celtic a stiffer test in the next round, but they too were no match for a team whose attacking philosophy was alien to most sides with a European pedigree.

In the first leg in France's fourth city, on 30 November, Stein kept his word that Celtic would not set out to play defensively, and the upshot of that bold approach was a 3–1 victory. McBride's twenty-fourth-minute goal cancelled out Nantes's opener after sixteen minutes and had the effect of demoralising the opposition. As the French wilted noticeably in the second half, Bobby Lennox and Chalmers scored two more to set Celtic on course for the quarter-finals.

The Celtic fans clearly shared that belief, for nine thousand fewer than the 50,000 who had attended the Zurich game turned out for the second leg the following midweek. Those who elected to stay away, believing the tie already won, had the misfortune to miss a virtuoso performance from the maestro. Jinky excelled, scoring the first goal, after thirteen minutes, and fashioning the other two with crosses in a repeat of the first-leg scoreline. The French press, suitably impressed by Jinky's tantalising touchline trickery, dubbed Nantes's tormentor-in-chief 'The Flying Flea'.

'Jimmy must have kept the ball for an hour that night,' observed Lennox. 'It was his European classic.'

Having demoralised Nantes by twisting and turning their defenders inside out, Jinky next focused his attention on the Yugoslavs of Vojvodina, a team considered, with good reason, to be a class above both Zurich and Nantes. For once, Celtic were forced to rely on their defensive qualities when they were pressurised almost without respite in the first leg, in Novi Sad, on 1 March 1967. The game in Yugoslavia turned out to be their toughest on the road to Lisbon.

Jinky had few chances to shine after being forced to join his team-mates in a rearguard action fighting for survival. In the end, Vojvodina – big and powerful and not lacking in skill – were probably entitled to feel a touch hard done by at having to settle for the narrowest of victories. A mistake by Gemmell, when he mishit an attempted pass to John Clark in the sixty-ninth minute, gifted Stanic with a simple opening that produced the only goal of the game.

With 75,000 crammed into Celtic Park for the return leg the following week, and Jinky in the mood to enhance his growing reputation among Continental fans, the stage was set for a show-down. While many teams found the pressure-cooker atmosphere of Celtic Park almost too much to handle, Vojvodina were so unruffled by their hostile surroundings that they had a chance to score after only five minutes and, had they taken it, might well have put paid to Celtic's European aspirations.

In the event, Celtic squared the tie thirteen minutes into the second half. Chalmers took advantage of a mistake by the goal-keeper and it appeared that Celtic would earn at least a replay in Rotterdam. But with less than one minute remaining, Jinky burst through on the right side to win a corner. Charlie Gallagher elected to take the resultant kick and flighted the ball perfectly into the heart of the goalmouth for Billy McNeill to rise and head a dramatic last-gasp winner.

Celtic's 2–1 aggregate success set up a semi-final meeting with the Czechoslovak Army team, Dukla Prague; formidable opposition, given that several of the side were survivors from the 1962 Czech World Cup final team beaten by Brazil, including their legendary captain, the outstanding half-back Josef Masopust. But Celtic were entitled to feel confident on the back of their victory over Vojvodina. They also had in Jimmy Johnstone a player whose soaring reputation now classed him as one of the finest wingers in Europe.

The semi-final draw favoured Celtic with home advantage for the first leg. But while Stein was convinced that his all-Scottish team, drawn from a radius of thirty miles of Celtic Park, was equipped to become the first British side to aspire to the heights of a European Cup final, that belief was not universal. At least one English commentator contended that only sheer luck had brought Celtic through the tie against Vojvodina: they were not good enough to achieve what had been beyond others in Britain, the outstanding Spurs double-winning team of 1961 included.

But while Spurs had an outstanding flying winger in Welshman Cliff Jones, Celtic had an even better one in Jimmy Johnstone, as Dukla were soon to learn. The tie was just twenty-seven minutes old when Jinky stamped his personal mark on it. Seventy-five thousand Celtic fans were suddenly ecstatic when he played a one-two with Stevie Chalmers and lofted the ball over the head of the advancing goalkeeper to score from six yards.

But Dukla were not a side to roll over, and Strune's equaliser on the stroke of half-time again had the doubters questioning Celtic's credentials. Not for long. Jinky's runs down the right side forced Dukla to detail two defenders to mark him, and Celtic took over the extra space this won them. Two superbly taken goals by Willie Wallace – signed by Stein from Hearts the previous year for £30,000 – brought a well-deserved victory. Indeed, Wallace, a bargain buy at the price, almost claimed a hat-trick when the ball struck the face of the crossbar in the seventy-second minute.

But would 3–1 be good enough to earn Celtic a place in the final? The Czechs' away goal might yet prove crucial in the event of a two-goal defeat for Celtic in the return in Prague thirteen days later, on 25 April.

Uncharacteristically, Stein chose to adopt an ultra-defensive approach for the return. Some have claimed since that his courage deserted him, but with a final of Europe's most prestigious football tournament just ninety minutes away, the decision to suspend his principles was understandable, much as he hated compromising his natural instinct to send his team out to attack. It showed how pained he was by going for safety that Stein rarely made mention of the game after declaring that Celtic would never again adopt such negative tactics. But to win 'playing ugly' made a lot more sense than sticking to a policy of attack at all costs that might win plaudits but not a lot else. No sides are faster forgotten than beaten semi-finalists.

In the event, Celtic played with one man up – Chalmers – and Jinky in a midfield role: even the free-flowing Jinky found himself adopting a defensive posture at times. But Stein's defensive tactics did their job. The end justified the means when Celtic secured a 0–0 result.

Lennox claimed later that Celtic had no option but to defend their corner. 'I spent most of the game standing next to big Tam Gemmell,' he said. 'We went out to play defensively, but not that defensively! We didn't have any choice.' The incomparable Masopust was so upset that he at first refused to shake hands with any of the victors. His reaction was one born of sheer frustration and the realisation that he would never again have the chance to play in a European Cup final. He later visited the Celtic dressing room to apologise.

It was a further week before Celtic learned who their opponents would be in the final at Lisbon's Estadio Nacional on Thursday, 25 May 1967. After the other semi-final, between Inter Milan and CSKA Sofia, ended in stalemate, the teams had been forced into a play-off, which the Italians won.

By then Celtic, already winners of the League Cup after beating Rangers 1–0 in the final the previous October, had achieved the second part of the domestic treble, the Scottish Cup, by dint of a two-goal win over Aberdeen just four days after disposing of Dukla. One week later, inspired by Jinky, whose two goals at Ibrox earned a 2–2 draw with Rangers, the league championship joined the growing haul of trophies. But the biggest prize of all awaited in Lisbon.

Celtic, and Jinky in particular, became immediate targets for the Italian media, who followed them everywhere. Who exactly were this bunch of working-class upstarts who had begun their glorious European run nine months earlier as rank outsiders? Inter were soon to discover that Celtic had earned their place in the final on merit rather than good fortune.

Celtic spent the week before the final at their favoured pre-match base at Seamill, on the Ayrshire coast. The hotel was besieged by Italian TV crews and most wanted to interview the flame-haired winger. He had impressed the Inter manager, Helenio Herrera, who had been present at Ibrox to witness Jinky's virtuoso performance on 6 May. The inventor of 'catenaccio', the mind-numbing defensive system that had justified its utter negativity by making Inter Milan the most successful club side in Europe, Herrera had privately expressed concern that Jinky posed a genuine threat to the Italians' chances of winning the European Cup, for a third time in four years.

But, publicly at least, Herrera, the highest-paid coach in the world, exuded an air of almost arrogant confidence. In truth, Jinky shared Herrera's opinion that Celtic were in danger of being utterly outclassed by a team with a huge reputation, and crammed with international players.

The sight of Jinky pictured standing alongside the elegant full-back Giacinto Facchetti on the eve of the final simply served to illustrate the sheer physical power of most of their opponents. It looked like a mismatch, Scottish flyweight versus Italian light heavyweight. But Facchetti wouldn't be the first to discover that what Jinky lacked in inches he more than made up for with skill and tenacity, not to mention the mischievous shifts of direction that gave him his nickname.

Herrera also made the mistake of believing that Inter would enjoy the support of the neutral locals, even going on TV to demand that the Portuguese back his team: as fellow Latins it was their duty to do so. This turned out to be a serious miscalculation on the part of the stony-faced Herrera. The Inter squad had arrived in the Portuguese capital ahead of their rivals but so, too, had thousands of Celtic fans, and they quickly won over the locals with their good-natured banter and friendly approach.

The Celtic players were heartened by the sight of waiters and hotel staff at their plush Estoril base sporting club badges. Jock Stein, Herrera's match when it came to outfoxing the opposition, also saw a way to win over their hosts, as Jinky recalled in his autobiography, *Fire in My Boots*. 'The Big Man knew that Continental footballers tend to move the ball very freely and seldom held on to it or give the kind of individual performance that has been a tradition of Scottish football,' he wrote. But that doesn't mean that Continental crowds wouldn't appreciate a bit of individual artistry. So he made my instructions loud and clear.

As early as possible in the game – in the first minute if I could do it – I was to gain possession and try to give a couple of those mazy runs of mine. I was to try to beat as many defenders as I could. It didn't matter too much if I lost the ball eventually so long as I wiggled and weaved my way past as many as I could.

The boss reckoned that the picture of a wee red-haired laddie having the guts, and the skill, to take on and beat world-class men like Facchetti, the famous international left back, and centre half Guarneri, would not only have an unsettling effect on the Milan defence itself but would greatly help to win over the support of the uncommitted among the Portuguese crowd.

Stein had had an insight into Herrera's psyche after accepting an invitation to study the coach's training methods several years earlier while manager of Dunfermline. It was an ideal opportunity to put into practice what he had learned. In particular, he realised the need to keep it simple. Jinky was instructed to play up at all times, on the right or the left, so long as he kept unsettling the Inter defence. Bobby Murdoch and Bertie Auld were expected to control the midfield and the full-backs, Gemmell and Jim Craig, were encouraged to join the attack on the overlap.

For all his meticulous planning, Stein was powerless to prevent the unforeseen when a traffic jam caused Celtic to arrive at the Stadium much later than intended. But perhaps the delay was a blessing, as it left less time for the players to dwell on the task ahead of them. Nevertheless, Jinky confessed to having been a 'bundle of nerves' as he stripped for the ultimate test.

However, his manner clearly told different story to the world at large, for Jinky later recalled:

People say we won the European Cup in the tunnel and that's probably correct. We noised them up and I remember Bertie [Auld] turning to one of their players and telling him to phone his ma because he was going to be home late that night. Bertie and I also led the rest of the lads in a chorus of the Celtic Song, which really threw the Inter players.

There they were, Facchetti, Domenghini, Mazzola, Cappellini; all six-footers with Ambre Solaire suntans, Colgate smiles and sleek-backed hair. They even smelt beautiful. And there's us lot – midgets! I've got no teeth, Bobby Lennox hasn't any, and old Ronnie Simpson's got none, top or bottom. The Italians are staring down at us and we are grinning back up at them with our great gumsy grins. We must have looked like something out of the circus.

When Celtic and Inter took the field in front of a capacity crowd of 55,000, the teams lined-up as follows: Celtic: Simpson; Craig, Gemmell, Murdoch, McNeill, Clark, Johnstone, Wallace, Chalmers, Auld and Lennox. Inter Milan: Sarti; Burgnich, Facchetti, Bedin, Guarneri, Picchi, Bicicli, Mazzola, Cappellini, Corso and Domenghini. The referee was Kurt Tschentscher of West Germany.

Almost at once, Inter paid Jinky the compliment of switching their full-backs in an effort to combat his obvious menace when Celtic swept straight into attack, as was their way. Inter were put

out by the instant offensive. They had clearly expected Celtic to
wait to get a feel for the occasion before unveiling their game plan.

Stein's foresight in instructing Jinky to run at the opposition
from the start was spot on. The Celtic players fed off the confidence injected by the palpable sense of anticipation in the crowd
every time Jinky got the ball. Then, after just seven minutes, came
the defining moment: Inter scored, very much against the run of
play, and made Celtic angry!

Craig brought Cappellini down in the penalty area and the
referee pointed to the spot. Mazzola took the resultant kick and,
with the minimum of fuss, stroked the ball past Simpson. Lesser
teams than the Lisbon Lions might have folded, told themselves
that it wasn't their day. Not Celtic. The penalty spurred them on.
They countered by drawing on Lennox's blistering pace and
Jinky's flair. But wave after wave of attacks was repelled. Inter held
on through a blend of good fortune – shots from both Gemmell and
Auld struck the crossbar – and outstanding goalkeeping by Sarti.

Yet there was no sign of despondency in the Celtic dressing
room during the interval. 'There were no angry words,' said Jinky.
'The boss simply told us to keep up the pressure. Attack was our
only possible strategy.'

But with Sarti having a great match and the game past the hour
mark, the thousands who had made the journey to Lisbon and millions more watching on TV began to wonder if the good fortune
that Celtic had enjoyed against Vojvodina was about to rebound
against them. Then it happened. The full-backs, Craig and
Gemmell overlapped, the former down the right side and the latter
up the left. Craig, sensing that Inter probably expected him to
cross, cut the ball back into Gemmell's path and, from around
twenty yards, the defender unleashed a viciously struck shot that
flew into the top right-hand corner of the net.

From that moment on the outcome was never in doubt. But
Celtic left it until five minutes from the end to claim a victory that
was thoroughly deserved. A move begun by Gemmell down the
left brought Murdoch into play and his low pass across the face of
goal was stabbed into the net by Chalmers. There was no way back

for Inter and the era of ultra-defensive football begun by Herrera was over.

Predictably, Inter shadowed Jinky for the entire ninety minutes, tracking his every move. It was a compliment, of course, but one he would happily have forgone as Burgnich stuck to him like glue. The frustrating tactic inevitably denied Jinky the opportunity to bring out his full bag of tricks, but not even the highly rated Burgnich could keep genius subdued all the time.

Jinky himself was disappointed with his contribution. He insisted that he had performed much better on other occasions. But by drawing Inter's fire he had freed his team-mates, and in Murdoch and Auld Celtic had the game's best players.

Jinky's initial feeling at time-up was one of almost numbness as thousands of delirious Celtic fans swarmed onto the pitch, eventually forcing captain Billy McNeill, who had to be given a police escort, to fight his way through the throng to collect the trophy on his own from the Portuguese President.

Jinky remained in something of a daze at the post-match banquet. Later, the players were joined by their wives for a party. But Jinky's wife Agnes was not among them. Just four days earlier, on 21 May, she had given birth to the couple's first child, Marie.

Next day the team flew home to a heroes' welcome at Celtic Park, where an estimated 60,000 gathered to proclaim the new champions of Europe in a remarkable show of emotion.

Winning the European Cup was the pinnacle of Jinky's career. It was also, he claimed, the greatest moment of his entire life. He named his new home 'Estadio' after the stadium that hosted the biggest achievement in Scottish football history.

Jimmy Johnstone was an integral part of that triumph, but the greatest credit goes to Jock Stein for the part he played in masterminding the conquest of Europe's finest.

'The one thing about Lisbon was how he had us all believing that we were every bit as good as Inter Milan,' said Jinky. 'There was no way he was going to allow us to take the field that day with any kind of inferiority complex.

'We went out of the dressing room singing the Celtic Song and I don't think the Italians knew what was happening. They thought we were all crazy, but the boss had us relaxed and ready for the game.

'The 1967 team was the greatest Celtic team there has ever been and ever will be.'

The European Cup completed the 'full set' for Celtic in a remarkable season lasting fifty-nine games in the four competitions they won. Jinky featured in fifty of those matches, scoring thirteen league and three cup goals. The following December, Europe's football writers paid tribute to Jinky's contribution to Celtic's remarkable success when they voted him into third place in the poll to elect the European Footballer of the Year (the 'Ballon d'Or'). Only Florian Albert, of Hungarian side Ferencvaros, and Sir Bobby Charlton, of Manchester United, were placed ahead of Jinky, who left such luminaries as Franz Beckenbauer and Eusebio trailing in his wake.

Recently, on a visit to Scotland in his role as president of Inter Milan, Facchetti, capped ninety-four times by his country, said: 'Jimmy was to me your Scottish George Best, that's the truth of it. The only player who matched him for natural skill was Best.

'More often than not in that game in Lisbon I had Bobby Lennox and not Johnstone as my rival. But when you were a defender you were happy you weren't facing him too often because he was simply one of the game's great forwards, so fast, and a master dribbler. Jimmy's close control during that match was something to see. It really was incredible.

'Jimmy Johnstone will for ever be one of those lions of Lisbon and he should always be remembered like that. He was a small player, but had a heart as big as a house.'

It was a fitting accolade to a truly great player, and some might argue that the judges got it wrong by not installing Jinky two places higher.

3

Birth of a Genius

James Connolly Johnstone arrived in the world on 30 September 1944, just a short distance from the scene of the Battle of Bothwell Bridge, where Covenanters fought their southern rulers in 1679. It was entirely appropriate that Jinky should have been born so close to a battlefield, for, despite his lack of inches, the youngest member of the Johnstone family was blessed with great courage. Centuries later, Jinky was to revel in taking on the English with a memorable virtuoso solo performance in a 4–3 defeat at Hampden Park in 1966 in one of the many skirmishes he took part in.

The Second World War was entering its final phase, with the Germans on the run throughout Europe, when the last of Sarah Johnstone's eight children was born. Like the vast majority of families at that time, the Johnstones were intent only on surviving as best they could. Rationing meant that there were few luxuries. In the bleak postwar years most had to make do with very little, and the residents of the council house in Old Edinburgh Road that was the family home in the Viewpark district of Uddingston were no different.

Viewpark at the time was a typical mining area, and Jinky's father, Matthew, toiled down the local pit to provide for Sarah – a gentle, caring woman with a generous nature – and his offspring. The arrival of another mouth to feed was an additional burden for them both, but, by all accounts, Jinky's childhood was largely happy, and the youngster never lacked love and affection in the close-knit North Lanarkshire community that had learned to pull together in adversity.

Jinky was happiest as a child when he was free to roam in the surrounding Bothwell countryside playing all manner of games with his friends. But it was football that dominated most of their free time. 'Times were hard and football I guess helped us forget and gave us plenty of laughs,' he recalled in an interview. 'We would play until our clothes were splattered with mud and our faces shone with exhilaration. By the end of the day some of the lads' shoes were hanging off their feet.'

They would amuse themselves by kicking around a plastic ball until it was punctured when landing on a railing or a hedge. Sometimes they had the luxury of an old-fashioned leather ball with an inflatable inner bladder. This involved constant breaks in play to re-inflate the ball. Even when they had no proper ball to play with, Jinky and his pals were never stuck. They would improvise by using a tin can or even a stone, using their jackets as goalposts.

A back garden or a tarmac road provided the pitch, and matches were often the first to score twenty-one goals, or even forty-two, depending on the time of year and the hours of daylight. Often, in summer, a match would last all day long, from breakfast time until dusk. Jinky described it as 'total football' before the term had even been coined. It was part of almost every Scottish lad's life. But he later claimed: 'Football was no big deal, not in the way it became with all the hype. We all played it all the time. You would just pick up a ball and practise kicking it against a wall and in no time at all a team would form around you and yet another match would start.'

The county had already sired other several football legends prior to Jinky's birth and, like Matt Johnstone, Matt Busby and Jock Stein knew what it was like to return from their daily toil at the coalface blackened by choking dust and with bones that ached from being bent double working for up to ten-hour shifts in painfully cramped conditions of wet and cold. Those who were born into such tough working-class areas knew little other than a life down the pit, and perhaps it was these conditions that inspired Stein and Busby to seek an alternative lifestyle.

Hardened by their own experiences, the pair found an escape route through football. Stein's prowess as a centre half did not match his subsequent achievements as a manager, but it was owing to his organisational skills and influence on the team that Celtic won both league championship and Scottish Cup honours in 1954 before a troublesome ankle injury forced him to retire two years later.

Busby, a more naturally gifted player than Stein, also enjoyed greater success when he hung up his boots to concentrate on management although he did achieve the distinction of playing in successive FA Cup finals for Manchester City, in 1933 and '34, losing to Everton in the first and beating Portsmouth twelve months later in the second of his Wembley appearances.

Busby outdid his close friend Stein by winning a solitary Scotland cap, against Wales. But it was Stein who was first to conquer Europe, with Jinky an integral part of the team christened 'The Lisbon Lions'. Manchester United's feat in replicating Celtic's success the following season, when they defeated Benfica in extra time at Wembley to become the second British club to win the European Cup, led to inevitable comparisons of the two men. Both had been reared in traditional miners' row cottages and learned the true value of comradeship and team-work, qualities that stood the pair in good stead when it came to dealing with a group of eleven individuals with diverse personalities and needs.

Stein, at times outwardly gruff and unforgiving, was also capable of displaying compassion and understanding. It was as well, for he never tired of pointing out that Jinky gave him more problems than the rest of the Lions put together – and just as much pleasure! Busby, much more quietly spoken and fatherly in appearance, also had to deal with the mercurial skills and behaviour of another of the game's great wingers, George Best, but was perhaps ultimately less successful in quelling the rebellious spirit in his particular 'problem child'.

Jinky's own father spent his entire working life down a pit. He was well known locally as a sprinter, who also enjoyed a kick-about with his mates. But it was Jinky's elder brother, Pat, to whom he was close, who had the greatest influence on a boy who grew up the youngest of five surviving children. In addition to Pat, Jinky had three sisters, Theresa, Annie and Mary. Three other children, twins and a boy, did not survive.

Pat, nicknamed 'Blondie', was highly regarded as a footballer, with speed and a powerful shot, and Jinky tormented his elder sibling by nicking his football boots and heading for a nearby public park to kick a ball about for hours on end. But for fate intervening, Pat might have become the first in the family to wear the Hoops. Celtic planned to send a scout to watch him play for his Boys' Guild team, but on the previous Saturday, while chasing a fifty-fifty ball, he pulled up at the last second and collided with the goalkeeper, suffering cartilage damage that effectively ended his burgeoning career.

Jinky was too young at the time to full understand the implications of what had happened, but he claimed later to have sensed his father's bitter disappointment. Being close to Matt, a quiet and thoughtful man, Jinky may have picked up certain vibes and subconsciously been inspired to fulfil his father's dream of one day seeing his son play for Scotland.

Ironically, when the dream became reality, on 3 October 1964, at Ninian Park, Cardiff, it was the start of a love–hate relationship that was to develop and increasingly deepen over the eleven years of Jinky's international career. But fifteen years earlier, in 1949, wee Jimmy Johnstone had other, much more series matters on his mind when he embarked on his schooldays at St Columbus RC School in Viewpark.

From day one, education was not high on Jinky's list of priorities. Indeed, along with a classmate, the new boy hatched an escape plan and, due to his natural ability to body-swerve opponents, Jimmy evaded all attempts at capture by the teachers and made it home. But it proved to be a short-lived span of freedom when his mother marched him straight back to the classroom.

Although never an outstanding scholar, Jinky did excel at one subject. His natural talent with a ball at his feet quickly came to the attention of his teachers, who spied the tiny red-headed lad darting about the playground during the interval and lunchtime breaks when he stood out from his pals with a ball at his feet. One of the 'spectators', John Crines, took a special interest in the eight-year-old and it was at his behest that Jinky was instructed by his class teacher to play a trial for the school team.

But Jinky didn't fancy the idea. A combination of acute worry about his height and the fact that most of the members of the team were three or four years older than himself caused him to decline the invitation. Fortunately, Mr Crines insisted and, much against his will, Jinky had his first taste of organised football. Who knows whether the world would ever have witnessed the sight of Jimmy Johnstone weaving his way past countless defenders had the teacher not stuck to his guns?

Around the same time that Jinky was improving the prospects of St Columba's school team, he suffered an unfortunate experience he never forgot. A skin ailment caused him to have his head shaved, and he was sent to school wearing a balaclava to hide his baldness. Jinky quailed when he entered his classroom and was ordered by his teacher to remove his headgear. When he refused to do so, the balaclava was forcibly removed to expose his lack of hair. He ran from the room and kept on running until he reached home, nor did he ever forgive the teacher for her callousness.

But while Jinky lacked inches he was not short of courage and regularly found himself involved in scraps, as a result of being targeted by playground bullies. Although he invariably came off second best, he would never duck a fight, for fear of losing face with his pals, and the painful experience of being left bruised and bloodied stood him in good stead when he was a regular victim of unscrupulous defenders, who, if they could not stop him fairly, resorted to foul means instead.

Soon, with Jinky tormenting the opposition, St Columba's were a team feared by their primary school rivals. Winning became a weekly occurrence. Before the age of ten, in the season 1953–54

Jinky was part of a team that had won every competition open to it. But Mr Crines was a stickler for discipline and insisted that each player's boots were polished until they shone. 'Woe betide the boy who hadn't put every ounce of effort into polishing his boots,' Jinky remembered.

Although St Columba's played on grass, many schools had ash pitches that left legs red raw when a player slid on the treacherous surface. According to Jinky, it was like running a scrubbing brush or a pan scourer down exposed flesh.

Success breeds jealousy, and when Jinky and his team-mates travelled to Holytown to meet Chapelhall Public in a schools' cup final the game quickly developed into a kicking match, resulting in a rare defeat for St Columba's. Jinky, however, was outstanding, much to the disgust of a few locals, who were keen to pay him back 'for him having dared to display such skills. Jinky was saved from a beating by the intervention of a bigger, stronger pal, but the team bus was stoned.

In other circumstances, it might not have mattered all that much, as no one was injured, but St Columba's were due to return to face the same team at the same venue just a week later in another final. It could have turned nasty. This time, however, the home fans were heavily outnumbered by several busloads of supporters from Viewpark, and when fighting broke out once again after St Columba's had gained revenge for their previous defeat, it was the locals who had to scatter for cover.

The experience helped harden Jinky to the realities of life in a mining community, but much worse was to come when it was time to leave St Columba's and begin life at St John's Secondary at nearby Uddingston. St John's was not for the fainthearted, and Jinky's size compelled him to assert himself, so much so that he once issued a foolhardy challenge to fight three fellow pupils at the same time, in an effort to impress a girl who had caught his eye. He put up a decent show, but failed either to get the better of his rivals or to impress the young lady.

Whereas St Columba's had won just about every competition they'd entered, the St John's school team at Uddingston wasn't up to much – until Jinky arrived on the scene. His rare talent transformed St John's prospects almost overnight. He also had the luck to encounter a physical education teacher who was every bit as passionate about football as his star pupil. Tom Cassidy was quick to recognise a youngster blessed with exceptional natural skills, and encouraged the boy to develop them.

But it was a famous Englishman who was the inspiration behind Jimmy Johnstone's rise to prominence.

4

Enter Sir Stan

Stanley Matthews, later knighted for his services to football, and regarded as the finest winger of his generation, entered Jimmy Johnstone's life by chance.

Jinky had become a key member of the local St John's Boys' Guild side, and it was on a trip to Manchester with the team that he first became aware of Matthews. The Blackpool wizard became his instant hero when he watched the 1953 FA Cup final on TV, and saw Stan inspire his team to produce one of the most famous comebacks of all time. They beat Bolton 4–3, despite trailing by two goals at one stage.

Having marvelled at the Matthews magic, Jinky wasted no time in obtaining a copy of the great man's autobiography, *Feet First Again*. Little did Jinky think at the time that one day critics would draw comparisons with the man who was arguably the greatest influence on his budding career. Indeed, Jock Stein expressed the view that at his peak Jinky outshone even the first professional footballer to receive a knighthood.

What interested Jinky was not so much how Matthews played the game, as how he lived his life. Matthews espoused a mantra of self-discipline and dedication. Alcohol and cigarettes were to be avoided at all costs. A good diet was essential, coupled to a strict training regime to improve physical and mental strength.

The pupil read and reread Matthews's words, resolving to follow them to the letter in an effort to build up a level of fitness that would compensate for his slight build and enable him to acquire the necessary stamina to run for ninety minutes. Each afternoon, after school, Jinky would lay out a collection of milk bottles that reached from the kitchen of his home into the hallway and spend two hours at a time dribbling his way round them in an effort to improve his ball control.

The exercise nearly drove his mother and the downstairs neighbour to distraction. The patient Sarah eventually snapped when she visited her neighbour, Mrs Watt, and heard for herself the din that her youngest made while practising. Sarah was appalled, and confiscated young Jimmy's ball. For a time, it was peace, perfect peace for Mrs Watt and her family. But Mrs Watt was intrigued by the calm, and when Sarah visited her neighbour a short time later she asked about it. When Sarah told her that she had confiscated her son's ball to spare her further suffering, Mrs Watt insisted that it be returned. If the boy was as keen as that, he deserved to be encouraged.

Years later, when he learned of Mrs Watt's kindness, Jinky expressed gratitude for her gesture in helping him perfect the skills that would one day achieve his dream of playing for Celtic.

After tea, Jinky began a second training session, returning to the school playground – he ran the two miles there and back to build his stamina – to practise short bursts of speed, at the same time wrong-footing imaginary opponents. He recalled: 'I much preferred to do this in the dark nights when nobody could see what I was up to. I didn't want them to get the idea that I fancied myself as a footballer.

'The darkness made the ball much more difficult to see, but it also forced me to increase my concentration. Even then I knew that concentration was one of the great assets to have if you were to be a successful footballer.

'Once in the playground I went through several other routines I had worked out. Once of them was to kick the ball against the school wall, kill it dead as it bounced back, and then imagine what to do as opponents came at me from all angles.

'Another game was to trap the ball and move all in the one movement. I penalised myself if I made mistakes. For a bad mistake, like missing the ball, or lifting my head, I had to run several times round the playground perimeter. I was my own teacher and pupil.'

Reading that Matthews wore heavy brogue shoes on his way to games so that his feet would feel light when he slipped them into a pair of football boots, and give him a greater feel for the ball, Jinky borrowed a pair of his father's old pit boots several sizes too big to improve his speed and dribbling skills. He also realised the importance of working on his upper body strength, doing press-ups and weight-lifting to ensure that he was harder to brush off the ball. The effort proved worthwhile in the long run.

He worked on the almost perfect balance that was to become a hallmark of his game by hopping on one leg round the two-inch-wide perimeter rail at the nearby Thorniewood Juniors ground, seeing how far he could get before falling off.

Around the same time as he was studying Matthews's words of wisdom, Jinky's rapidly burgeoning talents were brought to the attention of Celtic. His PE teacher, Tom Cassidy, happened to be a close friend of Sammy Wilson, the Celtic winger. Having listened to Cassidy rave about a star pupil for months on end, Wilson eventually arranged for Jinky to become a ball-boy at Celtic Park in 1958.

Jinky, who had been playing the game from around the age of five with jackets for goalposts, had occasionally been taken to games by his father on a local supporters' bus, and he was a spectator at Hampden in October 1957 when Celtic produced one of the biggest shocks of all time, humiliating arch-rivals Rangers 7–1 in the League Cup final. But although a Celtic fan for as long as he could remember, Jinky simply had no time to watch football for playing it. At first he was unsure whether to accept the offer of becoming a ball-boy because it meant sacrifices in terms of his own playing aspirations.

Now, for the first time in his life, he had the chance to rub shoulders with the big names he had read about: Bobby Evans, Bertie

Peacock, Bobby Collins. Changing in the boot room, Jinky would sneak a glance along the corridor in the hope of spotting the stars.

Jinky was also noticed. Billy McNeill remembered: 'During one game the ball ran out for a goal kick and this wee redhead started to play "keepie-up". It became almost embarrassing for the rest of us, he was so skilful.'

But while others were already marvelling at Jinky's skills, it was no big deal in the mind of the fledgling star. 'I was just one of a bunch of ordinary lads who never bragged about things,' he said. 'Times were hard and football was the biggest part of our lives, just like it was for the boys in Brazil and Spain. They lived in poverty like us, and that's where all the great players come from, the streets.'

After a year, Jinky gave up his ball-boy duties. He missed playing too much and decided to resume his career with the local Boys' Guild team. Soon after his departure, he travelled to Manchester for an annual game against a team from the area. It very nearly proved to be the moment when Celtic lost him. His brother Pat, by now married and living in Doncaster, travelled to watch the game and got talking to a fellow spectator, who told the elder Johnstone that he fancied the wee redhead.

The inquisitive stranger asked Pat if he knew who the lad was. 'He's my brother,' said Pat. 'His name is Jimmy Johnstone.'

'Well, my name is Wishbone and I'm a Manchester United scout,' his fellow spectator replied.

Wishbone was so impressed that he immediately informed Matt Busby that he had spotted a youngster blessed with exceptional talent. The Manchester United manager did not waste any time in making contact with the chaplain in charge of Jinky's Boys' Guild team to arrange a meeting. It was at that point that Jimmy Johnstone might have taken his first steps to a career at Old Trafford, but fate intervened in the form of Frank Cairney, a keen church worker and follower of the Guild team.

Cairney, who went on to run Celtic Boys' Club, had dreamed for some time of Jinky becoming a Celtic player and insisted on being present at the meeting to represent the youngster's interests. He told Matt Busby that Jinky was already pledged to Celtic: there was no point in United pursuing their interest any further. It was a white lie, of course, though, given that Jinky had already formed a strong affection for Celtic and that he didn't like being away from home, it's doubtful that he would have taken to life in Manchester anyway. But what football fan could fail to be intrigued by that brief possibility of a United team fielding Johnstone on one wing and Best on the other?

Having effectively thrown United off the scent, Cairney moved fast to inform Celtic scout John Higgins of the growing interest in the fifteen-year-old. Celtic responded by contacting Jinky and asking him to attend training two evenings a week.

Jinky had already started work at Glasgow meat market when he got the call. But lugging huge sides of meat did not appeal to the diminutive delivery boy and he quit to take up employment at a clothing factory near his home.

Life as a trainee star was far from glamorous. After work, Jinky would dash home for some dinner before catching a bus to Celtic Park for training. He did not even have time to change from his work clothes. Mindful of the precarious nature of a football career, those closest to Jinky encouraged him to take up a trade he would be able to fall back on in the event that he failed to make it at the top, and it was while attending day-release cases at Burnbank Technical College that his and Tommy Gemmell's paths crossed for the first time.

'I was serving my apprenticeship as an electrician and we used to have a kick-about at lunchtimes,' said Gemmell. 'My first memory of Jimmy was with a tennis ball at his feet giving everyone a doing. Even then he was exceptional.'

But Jinky's apprenticeship as a welder was short-lived. His naturally fiery temperament brought him into conflict with a lecturer at day-release classes. The classroom had never been Jinky's favourite place and when he was taken to task over a piece of work a terrific row ensued. It eventually resulted in Jinky attacking the lecturer and pinning him to the ground. Luckily a classmate, Benny Rooney (who later signed for Celtic), intervened and pulled Jinky off the startled teacher before the situation got completely out of hand. When Jinky's employer, unhappy at the amount of time he was taking off work, gave him the choice of work or football, Jinky chose the latter.

The following year, on 7 October 1961, Jinky starred in a 4–2 win for the reserves against St Johnstone's second string, scoring one and making his side's other three goals. Jimmy McGrory wasted no more time. That evening he signed the seventeen-year-old for Celtic, for fear that another club might try to lure the youngster away from Celtic Park with an offer of greater riches.

Gemmell was also offered terms on the same evening and signed for the princely sum of seven pounds a week wages plus three pounds travelling expenses, the same as Jinky. 'We signed what was known as provisional forms, which meant if you didn't make the grade at senior level you were free to return to the juniors,' he said. 'I remember the pair of us travelling home on the same bus because we lived quite close to one another.'

Around the same time Bobby Lennox first became aware of Jinky. It was a cold wet Thursday evening at Celtic Park and the part-timers were training in the concourse of the main stand because of the conditions when Lennox spotted a wee redhead out of the corner of his eye. At first, he thought the newcomer was a fan who had somehow managed to sneak into the ground.

'We were doing sprints when I first saw Jimmy and I thought to myself: There's no way he's a footballer,' said Lennox. 'But I quickly changed my mind when we switched to ball work. As soon as I saw Jimmy with a ball at his feet I knew he could play all right.

'We became pals more or less straight away. Willie O'Neill was also in our "gang". I think the fact that the three of us were quiet and shy brought us together. But whereas Jimmy was a worrier about the game, I was the exact opposite. That probably helped us get on so well because I would continually reassure Jimmy that everything would turn out fine.'

But if Jinky imagined that his elevation to part-time professional would lead, in turn, to a sprint through the ranks to the first team, he quickly learned different. His slight physique led some at Celtic

Park to question whether he would make the grade, and at the end of his first season he was farmed out for a year to the Junior club Blantyre Celtic, so that he could gain experience and, at the same time, hopefully develop in size.

As it turned out, Jinky's stay with Blantyre Celtic was relatively brief. His ball skills and ability to turn defenders inside out quickly got him noticed and he was chosen to play for Junior Scotland against Northern Ireland. He was watched by Jimmy Gribben, who had been instrumental in bringing Jock Stein to Celtic Park a decade before, and the scout recommended that McGrory recall Jinky from the Junior ranks without delay. So, shortly after making his international debut, Jinky was back at Celtic Park.

But it was to be another two years before Jimmy McGrory, a Celtic legend in his own right on the strength of scoring 410 league goals in 408 games and a British record 550 in all, including eight in a single game against Dunfermline, gave Jinky his head. The player's performances for the reserves would have earned him quick promotion to the first team at most other clubs. But McGrory's natural caution led him to refuse to rush young players, for fear of exposing them to the demands of first-team football too soon and risk inhibiting their development.

Sean Fallon, Jock Stein's trusted assistant, remembered the first time he clapped eyes on Jinky. 'He struck me as a nice boy and a quiet lad, although later on I had to reassess my judgement about him being quiet. Jimmy was like a young thoroughbred colt, and you didn't want to risk breaking him. I could see that he was special.'

Bertie Auld, who was to become a team-mate, was shocked by Jinky's size: 'He was a frail, frail laddie who must have felt completely out of place because of his shyness. I thought he had just been released from nursery and sneaked into the ground under a turnstile. But he had all the ability and trickery in the world. You would have thought the ball was tied to his laces. That was my first impression of the wee man.'

The postwar years had not been kind to Celtic. Overshadowed by their bitter rivals, Rangers, under McGrory they won the championship only once – in season 1953–54 – and the Scottish Cup and

League Cup twice before Jock Stein's arrival as manager in 1965. There had been that memorable highlight in season 1957–58, of course, when Rangers were thrashed 7–1 in the League Cup final at Hampden Park. But, by and large, the team from the south side of the city had dominated the championship, with only Hibs and Hearts capable of loosening Rangers' stranglehold on more than one occasion.

'The club was more or less in the doldrums when Jimmy arrived,' said Fallon. 'Most of the experienced players had retired and we were left mainly with youngsters.' Some said that McGrory was simply 'too nice' to be a successful manager of a top club; that he lacked the ruthless streak necessary to turn Celtic into the dominant force in Scottish football, and certainly his record would seem to give credence to that view. But simply to dismiss him as a great player who failed to cut it in management would be an insult to the memory of a thoroughly decent man, who had the foresight to sign an extraordinary talent. Beyond question it was one of the most inspired pieces of business McGrory concluded during his twenty years at the helm.

However, while McGrory was quick to recognise Jinky's outstanding potential, it took the wiles of his successor, Jock Stein, to harness all the talents of the player who was to be voted the Greatest Celt nearly forty years later.

5

Fledgling Star

Jimmy Johnstone's first-team debut, on 27 March 1963, offered no hint of what was to come. Indeed, those Celtic fans who had bothered to make the short trip to Kilmarnock to catch their first glimpse of the teenager must have regretted doing so. Celtic suffered the sort of defeat that can shatter a young player's confidence and set his career back months, if not years. Losing is bad enough at the best of times, but a positive shock to the system when the opposition scores six without reply.

Kilmarnock, who were to be crowned champions two seasons later, tore Celtic apart. Leading by two goals at the interval through Joe Mason, who scored as early as the eighth minute, and Davie Sneddon, the home side dealt out a football lesson to their rivals in the second half as Bertie Black and Andy Kerr each claimed a brace.

The teams that day lined up as follows: Kilmarnock: Forsyth; Richmond, Watson; Murray, McGrory, Beattie; Brown, Mason, Kerr, Sneddon and Black. Celtic: Madden; Young, Kennedy; McKay, Cushley, Price; Johnstone, Craig, Chalmers, Gallagher and Brogan.

Jinky had made his mark the previous year. A public trial match at Celtic Park in August 1962 put his talents on parade when the reserves beat the recognised first XI by four goals to three. One newspaper correspondent described him as: 'A right wing bomb who would explode on Scotland's defences right away', and his immediate opponent, Jim Kennedy, was forced to agree with that sentiment.

But seven months passed before Jimmy McGrory handed the up-and-coming star his big chance. Regrettably, Jinky had no real opportunity to justify his manager's decision to blood him after a series of outstanding displays for the reserves, largely because his team-mates were involved in limiting the damage as best they could in a rearguard action at Rugby Park. Only one of those who lined up alongside Jinky that day – Stevie Chalmers – survived to play a part in Celtic's European Cup triumph four years later.

Davie Sneddon, Kilmarnock's inside-left, recalled: 'I remember that game well, for obvious reasons. We had a very good side and gave Celtic a real going over. But I noticed the wee fellow on the wing and thought to myself he had a chance of doing something in the game, the way he controlled the ball and could dribble with it.'

Hardly surprisingly, Jinky was left out of the team for Celtic's next game, a 5–1 win over Partick Thistle at Firhill six days later. McGrory wisely decided to give his new recruit time to lick his wounds and recover fully from his trauma. But Jinky was back a month later, and this time he had reason to feel pleased with himself, even though Celtic lost again, this time to Hearts. In fact Jinky scored his first goal, to put Celtic in front after an hour of the game at Tynecastle. Unhappily, two late goals consigned Celtic to a 4–3 defeat.

Jinky had also done enough to convince McGrory that he should retain his place in the side for Celtic's biggest game for two years, a Scottish Cup final showdown with arch-rivals Rangers. It was seen as a gamble to play the youngster in such a huge match, given Jinky's lack of first-team experience. But, by the same token, the Celtic squad was not exactly overflowing with natural talent

The teams lined up on 4 May as follows: Rangers: Ritchie, Shearer; Provan, Greig, McKinnon; Baxter, Henderson, McLean, Millar, Brand and Wilson. Celtic: Haffey, McKay, Kennedy;

McNamee, McNeill, Price; Johnstone, Murdoch, Hughes, Divers and Brogan. The atmosphere was tense, with 129,527 packed into Hampden Park, but the newcomer didn't seem fazed. Despite being policed by a vastly more experienced full-back in Davie Provan, Jinky displayed a remarkable confidence for one so young and succeeded in troubling the Rangers defence and netting a 'goal' that was disallowed. Even so, his own view was that he had not performed particularly well.

Celtic held out for a 1–1 draw after Ralph Brand had given Rangers a forty-third minute lead and Bobby Murdoch had equalised on the stroke of half-time. But it was not a classic Cup Final and Celtic earned a replay, by dint of some outstanding goal-keeping by Frank Haffey and the hard work of central defenders Billy McNeill and John McNamee.

The replay was scheduled for eleven days hence, on 15 May. In the meantime Celtic played two league games and Jinky appeared in both, the first a 2–0 home win over Clyde, the second a three-goal defeat away to Dundee United just four days before returning to Hampden. It was hardly the ideal preparation for a match as important as a Cup Final.

McGrory, clearly not keen to risk exposing Jinky to another big game in the dawn of his career, left him out of the side for the replay. The decision still came as a surprise, given that Jinky had shown he was capable of pressuring the opposition's defence. It has to be said that omitting Jinky for the replay was typical of the constant chopping and changing McGrory indulged in. Celtic, in fact, fielded no fewer than eight outside rights that season.

The decision to drop Jinky after his darting runs had caused problems for Rangers was made all the more bewildering by the fact that McGrory replaced him with a sluggish veteran, Bobby Craig, who had been signed from Blackburn Rovers a short time before. Craig, as it turned out, was regarded as Celtic's poorest performer in the second game. But, with hindsight, it was perhaps a blessing that Jinky did not feature, for Celtic were humiliated 3–0 in the second game, played in front of another huge crowd of 120,263. Such was Rangers' superiority that they toyed with their opponents in the final twenty minutes as thousands of Celtic fans streamed from the ground in a state of shock and disillusionment.

The season finished with Celtic in fourth place in the Championship, thirteen points adrift of Rangers in top spot. But there was at least one bright spot for the Celtic fans to enjoy. The emergence of Jimmy Johnstone augured well for the future.

All the same, Celtic was still a club in limbo as they entered the 1963–64 season. Pat Crerand had departed for Manchester United the previous February and there were no obvious signs that the team would improve sufficiently to end the fans' quest for silver-ware. Celtic finished one place higher in the league after failing to qualify from their four-team section for the knock-out stage of the League Cup, and being beaten by Rangers at Ibrox in the fourth round of the Scottish Cup. But there was some solace to be had from an extended run in Europe. Celtic had qualified for the Cup Winners' Cup, despite finishing runner-up to Rangers in the previous May's Scottish Cup final replay, because the Ibrox side were participating in the European Cup as champions.

Jinky took his European bow, on 10 October 1963, against Basle of Switzerland. But there were only 8,000 at Celtic Park to witness the start of what was to be a twelve-year adventure full of many more highs than lows. The reason for the meagre attendance was the fact that Celtic led 5–1 from the first leg and had the tie as good as won. Jinky revelled in the scene, however, and within three minutes of the kick-off had claimed his first European goal after he took a pass from Bobby Murdoch and smacked a powerful shot into the net. Celtic went on to score four more to emphasise their superiority and secure their place in the second round on a 10–1 aggregate.

Just one month later, Jinky had the first of many brushes with authority when he was sent off playing against Partick Thistle in a Glasgow Cup tie at Firhill. He clashed with Ian Cowan, and both were dismissed following a scuffle. Keen to display his talents against a rival winger, Jinky beat Cowan, but, instead of pushing forward into attack, chose to drag the ball back in an effort to repeat his trickery. Cowan reacted by whipping the feet from Jinky, who was furious and dived on the Thistle player. Both tumbled to the ground and Jinky had his hand in Cowan's face, while his rival lashed out wildly with his feet.

The irony of the date of the set-to, 11 November, was not lost on observers. It was Armistice Day, and only Jinky could have marked the occasion in such a manner!

Years later, Jinky recalled: 'I often think that I might not have been the player I was without that level of aggression in me.' But he didn't try to glorify the trouble he got into and came to regret all of it. Moments after getting into a scuffle, like the first time he was sent off with Ian Cowan, he would calm down and become full of remorse. Jinky felt he needed the high tension level to bring out the best in him.

There were to be five more dismissals before Jinky's Celtic career was over, but Tom 'Tiny' Wharton, regarded as the top referee of his generation, said before his death in 2005: 'Although I had cause to send Jimmy off twice, he was not malicious. He had a short fuse and a lot tried to make him lose control.'

Having served his seven-day Scottish FA suspension, Jinky was back in the side when Celtic faced Dinamo Zagreb in the first leg of their second-round Cup Winners' Cup tie, on 4 December, at Celtic Park.

Celtic were much more imaginative than the Yugoslavs and built a commanding three-goal lead. When Bobby Murdoch scored, very much against the run of play, shortly before half-time in the return leg a week later, Dinamo faced an impossible task. But it still required some solid defending by Celtic to restrict their rivals to two goals before they booked their place in the last eight of the competition.

By now Jinky was an established first-team player who augmented his dribbling skills with a steady flow of goals that reached ten in his first full season, including six in the league and two in Europe in thirty-eight appearances.

Celtic's third-round opponents, Slovan Bratislav, attracted a crowd of 53,000 to Celtic Park on 26 February 1964 and they were treated to a demonstration of all-out attacking football by the home side, but a combination of poor finishing and bad luck restricted the hosts to a single-goal advantage. It was only in the closing stages of the game that Jinky began to assert himself, and by then his team-mates had grown increasingly frustrated by their failure to add to a Bobby Murdoch penalty kick goal.

The return, at the start of the following month, was a fraught affair. Several of the Bratislava side had been members of Czechoslovakia's 1962 World Cup squad and had played in the final against the eventual winners, Brazil. Celtic were forced to rely on their defensive wiles to see them through. But they enjoyed the undeserved bonus of a late goal from John Hughes, who ran half the length of the pitch to secure the side's passage through to the semi-finals on the back of a two-goal aggregate success.

Celtic, it has to be said, had exceeded their own and their fans' expectations by reaching the last four, and some felt that MTK Budapest might prove a step too far when 51,000 turned out at Celtic Park, on 15 April, for the first leg. But those fears proved unfounded as Celtic, inspired by Jinky's trickery, pace and finishing, overran their rivals. Jinky was everywhere, especially in the second half, and it was his goal after forty-one minutes – a powerful strike after he had weaved his way into a shooting position – that broke the deadlock.

Boosted by his goal, Jinky tore the MTK defence apart and was instrumental in the build-up play that brought Stevie Chalmers two more, giving Celtic a seemingly unassailable three-goal lead to take to the Hungarian capital a fortnight later. But MTK were a very different team in the return. 'They simply didn't play at Celtic Park,' said Jinky. 'But they could easily have scored six in the second leg. Mind you, I think we maybe took the result a wee bit for granted as well.'

Whatever the reason for Celtic's astonishing collapse, MTK ran amok. Sensing that they had nothing to lose, the Hungarians launched attack after attack from the start and clawed back a goal after eleven minutes. Just before half-time, Jinky and Hughes each had the ball in the net, but the referee disallowed both for offside. Perhaps if even one of the 'goals' had counted, MTK could not have faced recovering a second time. In the event they ran out easy 4-0 winners after scoring three times in the second half.

That same season, Jinky made his Old Firm league debut in the traditional New Year's Day derby, but in spite of his best efforts, the little outside right was unable to gee up his team-mates, and Rangers triumphed, by dint of a Jimmy Millar goal. Yet

Jinky did leave his mark on the game, which was played at Celtic Park. Indeed, had his ninth-minute left-foot shot found the net instead of striking the base of the post, with goalkeeper Billy Ritchie beaten, he might have inspired a very different outcome. As it was, he received generous praise from at least one reporter, who considered that Jinky had brought the game to life after seeing a lot of the ball.

The Celtic fans had grown used to such disappointments. But there were better times ahead. Jock Stein would transform the club's fortunes and end Rangers' dominance in a manner that could not have been foreseen. Stein would also transform the career of a player he had admired from afar for some time, in the belief that Jimmy Johnstone had the credentials to become one of the game's biggest stars.

But it was a measure of the level of disillusionment at Celtic Park in the years just before prior Stein's accession that shortly after his brush with Cowan, Jinky had given serious consideration to emigrating to America. Listening to an aunt and uncle, who had returned to Scotland for a holiday, talk of their attractive lifestyle in the States had stirred Jinky's imagination. But, thankfully for Celtic and Scottish football as a whole, he resisted the temptation to turn his back on the game he was to grace with such flair and distinction.

6

The Stein Factor

Jock Stein had the greatest influence on Jimmy Johnstone's career – and on his life. Without Stein it is extremely unlikely that Jinky would have reached the heights he did. Indeed, Stein claimed that his greatest single achievement had been in extending Jinky's career five years longer than it would have lasted left to the player's devices.

That Stein struck terror into the heart of the player who gave him more sleepless nights than any other is not in doubt. An imposing figure, he towered over Jinky, and he was never slow to use his size to intimidate those who dared to cross him. Threats of 'I think I'll have a word with your priest' were not uncommon whenever Jinky stepped out of line. Neither was the sight of Big Jock in hot pursuit of his number seven when he had been the butt of a cheeky retort.

But both men had deep respect for one another, and Jinky was the first to admit that he owed much to Stein, even though he wondered more than once if the manager was anti-Johnstone.

Stein himself always insisted that he had Jinky's best interests at heart and the highest regard for his ability, while at the same time believing that perhaps the player did not fully appreciate his importance to the team.

'On the occasions when I crossed swords with Johnstone it was for the good of Celtic and for the good of the player,' said Stein.

'Johnstone's path was not smooth. He was just that type of lad. He was not a bad lad. It was just that if there was trouble, or a problem, Jimmy seemed to be in the thick of it.'

The announcement that Stein would be replacing Jimmy McGrory as manager was made at the end of January 1965. But Stein's and Jinky's paths had already crossed. Their first encounter took place in a toilet at half-time in a reserve match against Hibs at Celtic Park shortly before Stein took charge. Stein was still manager of Hibs, and the scoreline was blank.

Jinky was in the process of relieving himself when the giant shadow of Stein appeared over him. 'What are you doing out there, wee man?' enquired Big Jock. 'You're too good for reserve-team football. You should be in the first team.'

Jinky's career as a club and international player was in a trough at the time. Disillusioned by Jimmy McGrory's refusal to give him his head and by the team's indifferent results, Jinky worried that the manager was having reservations about him and his form suffered accordingly. Indeed, Celtic as a club appeared to be going nowhere. One scribe remarked: 'They are being left so far behind Rangers there is no longer a race.' Another, Cyril Horne, of the *Glasgow Herald*, wrote later that: 'Jimmy Johnstone was at such a low ebb early in 1965 that it was probable that he would revert to junior football again – and sink without a trace.'

Jinky had, in fact, become so fed up with football that he asked to be dropped. But the encounter in the Celtic Park toilet was Jinky's first experience of Stein the master motivator. He was lifted at once by the comment, and promptly raised his game, scoring a hat-trick in the second half.

But Jinky had wondered if Stein fancied him as a player when he read a comment made by the manager some years earlier regarding the talents of his counterpart in the Dunfermline team, Alec Edwards, during Big Jock's reign as manager at East End Park, to the effect that Johnstone could not lace Edwards's boots.

On that occasion Jinky had been a victim of the Stein psychology. The comment had hurt all the same, and there would be many other occasions in future when the pair would clash.

'For a long time I honestly didn't think he liked me,' Jinky once confessed. 'But I know now he looked out for me more than any other player because he regarded me so highly.'

Following his outstanding second-half performance against the Hibs second string, Jinky was reinstated to the Celtic first team. But, by then, any hopes of the title had disappeared, and another barren season seemed likely.

Stein's first match in charge, against Airdrie at Broomfield, on 10 March, resulted in a highly encouraging 6-0 victory, with Bertie Auld scoring five of the goals. But only two of the remaining eight league games were won as Celtic slipped to eighth in the championship.

Celtic had not won any silverware for seven years, and their fans had grown increasingly disillusioned. But Stein's arrival breathed new life into the club. Having served a highly successful managerial apprenticeship with Dunfermline, whom he had guided to Scottish Cup final glory against Celtic in 1961, and Hibs, he set about transforming the club's fortunes. But he was clearly not entirely convinced that Jinky – utterly disillusioned by his own and his club's lack of progress under McGrory – would dovetail with his future plans. Indeed, it turned out later that Stein had been ready to transfer-list Jinky and fellow winger John Hughes, in the belief that neither had lived up to their true potential.

Stein's uneasy relationship with Jinky in the early months of his reign was demonstrated by his decision to drop the wee man for the Scottish Cup semi-final replay with Motherwell on 31 March. Jinky had had the ill luck to have a goal disallowed in dubious circumstances in the first game, which finished 2–2, but his overall performance had been indifferent and Stevie Chalmers was preferred for the replay four days later. Celtic beat Motherwell 3–0, with Chalmers scoring the first of their goals, and the striker retained his place for the final the following month.

Stein chose not to play Jinky in the final, on 24 April, and his belief that Celtic were more effective without him appeared justified when Billy McNeill headed the winner nine minutes from time to kick-start the Stein era, which was to be the most success-ful in the club's history. However, four days after the 3–2 victory at Hampden, Jinky was recalled to the side for the final game of the season, at Dunfermline, when the home side gained an element of revenge by winning 5–1 in a glaring reversal of fortunes.

In all he played thirty-nine times that season, scoring four goals, including Celtic's solitary strike in the League Cup final the previous October when they lost 2–1 to Rangers. Celtic had begun as favourites in that game, and Rangers were in danger of being over-run at one stage by Jinky's electrifying wing play. But Jim Baxter, in his role as captain, made the inspired decision to switch full-backs and the move took some of the sting out of Jinky's play.

While he remained uncertain about Jinky, believing that he was too much of an individualist and not enough of a team player, Stein was gradually persuaded by the sight of Jimmy totally dominating practice matches when none of the first-team regulars could dis-possess him. Stein was also impressed by Jinky's work ethic and the fact that he lived for football. So when Spurs made an approach for Jinky in September 1965 they were instantly rebuffed. 'Jinky could do things Matthews could never do,' Stein was later to state.

For all that Jinky and Stein did not always see eye-to-eye, Jimmy had the utmost respect for his manager, claiming: 'I don't think any other manager in football could have done as much for me as Big Jock did. I would have amounted to nothing but for him. I would have had no sense of direction in my career.

'Jock Stein never wasted words with you, but whatever he said was always the soundest advice you were ever likely to be given.

'Everything that Celtic became was down to him; he made the club what it is today. There's no doubt about that.

'Sure, there were good players when he arrived to take over as manager, but we were not winning things. He changed that, and when we won the European Cup, Celtic became a big name in world football. Before that we had been known in Scotland and down south, but no one bothered too much about Celtic on the Continent. He brought that extra fame and it still exists today because of him.'

According to Sean Fallon, Stein's assistant, the manager had a love–hate relationship with Jinky. 'We used to look upon him as a kind of little boy lost,' said Fallon. 'Off the record I'd have a word with wee Jimmy, or the Big Man would speak to him quietly, but all his brains were in his feet.

'The wee bugger would come in for training and you would know he had been misbehaving yet he would train as if he had been in bed at nine o'clock the night before. Then, when you were getting on at him he would look at you with those big eyes of his and you would feel sorry for him.

'But whatever problems Jimmy provided were usually forgiven because he had such marvellous natural ability. He would win games for you – dozens of games he won for us in those days – and the people would go to games just to see him play. There was a special feeling between Jimmy and the fans. He was with the club from the time he was a kid, and if he had had just a little bit more self-discipline there's no saying how good he would have been. He was one of the greats anyhow, but he had such ability.'

It didn't take long for Stein and Jinky to have their first major clash. It came the following season after a particularly uninspiring Celtic performance in a European Cup Winners' Cup tie in Denmark in November 1965, when a Joe McBride goal sealed the narrowest of wins over AGF Aarhus. Stein let rip at his players, but was especially annoyed with Jinky, telling his winger that he wouldn't be in the team for the next game. That was bad enough, but what followed shocked Jinky when he was informed by his furious manager that he would never again wear a Celtic jersey.

It turned out to be an empty threat. Stein later explained to Jinky that he had hit out in anger and frustration at the team's performance as a whole. But it was an example of Stein's volcanic temper, and a warning to Jinky that his manager didn't do things by halves.

Jinky's habit of shooting from the lip, his tendency to speak first and think later, led to several very public run-ins with Stein. Perhaps the most memorable of them occurred in October 1968, when Celtic played Dundee United at Celtic Park three days after accounting for St Etienne in the European Cup. Jinky, by his own admission, was not having the best of games when Stein decided to substitute him in the second half. But Jinky reacted angrily to being replaced by George Connelly, and as he made his way off the pitch he hurled abuse at Stein before also hurling his strip into the dugout.

Thousands of fans saw this happen, and Stein was furious at such a public show of ill-discipline. As Jinky made his way up the tunnel he could hear Stein's footsteps thundering after him. Terrified of what fate might befall him, it crossed Jinky's mind for a moment to bypass the dressing room and head straight out of the ground rather than confront his manager. But sense prevailed. He swallowed his feeling of dread, and faced his accuser.

For more than ten minutes, Stein berated his errant star in the ripest language. Even by Stein's standards it was a frightening experience, and it left the culprit in a state of shock. He was hit with a seven-day suspension and the loss of a week's wages. He was also forced to issue an apology to his manager through the press.

Stein's reasoning in substituting Jinky with half an hour to go was based on the knowledge that he seldom played two outstanding games back-to-back, and Jimmy had been brilliant against the French.

Jinky's suspension meant that he missed the 1–0 League Cup semi-final win over Clyde on 9 October. Stein also omitted him from the squad for the league game against Hearts at Tynecastle the following Saturday, when Celtic again triumphed by one goal. But it was a calculated gamble on the part of the manager, who felt confident Celtic could win both games without Jinky in their line-up.

A month or so later, Stein, with his repertoire of mind games, who knew exactly what buttons to press when it came to getting the best out of Jinky, tried a very different tack. Celtic were drawing 1–1 with Red Star Belgrade at half-time in the first leg of their second-round European Cup-tie at Celtic Park when Stein pulled a master stroke. He used Jinky's legendary fear of flying to his own and Celtic's advantage to inspire Jimmy to produce one of his greatest performances in the Hoops. Stein followed Jinky into the toilets to make him an offer he simply could not refuse – the chance to miss the return leg in Yugoslavia, provided that Celtic won the match by four clear goals!

Jinky became a man inspired. Buoyed up by the knowledge that he would not have to climb aboard an aircraft for the four-hour flight to the Yugoslav capital, he tore Red Star apart almost single-handed. Within two minutes of the restart Celtic were in front when Jinky turned the Red Star defence to score. From then on it was almost all one-way traffic as Celtic grew in confidence through the sheer brilliance of a player with a mission. Seeing that Jinky was on fire, Bobby Murdoch supplied him with a string of passes from which he twisted and turned the defence inside out.

But Jinky kept the best till last when he scored a wonderful solo goal nine minutes from time to seal a 5–1 victory. Taking a pass from Murdoch, he breezed like a whirlwind through the defence, weaving first this way and then the other, before lashing the ball into the net.

But his reaction to the goal further surprised his already bemused team-mates, who had been taken aback by Jinky's keenness to defend as well as attack, anything to ensure the result that would spare him the terror of another flight. Racing to the touchline, Jinky kept shouting: 'I don't have to go, I don't have to go.' His team-mates, who knew nothing of the deal, were mystified by what seemed like an overreaction. When they found out what caused it, they were also divided in their response to their manager's mind games.

But Billy McNeill recalled: 'Jimmy tore a superbly talented team apart. It was the most magnificent performance I have ever seen on a football park.' Inevitably, Stein essayed another ploy in an attempt to persuade Jinky to travel to Yugoslavia after all. He told him that he had received a special request by telephone from the Red Star president begging him to ensure that Jimmy Johnstone played in the second leg, so that the people of Belgrade would not be denied the chance to see the world's greatest footballer in action.

This time Stein's tactic did not work. A deal was a deal, and Jinky resisted all of Stein's blandishments. In the event, Celtic drew 1–1 to secure a 6–2 aggregate victory and a place in the last eight.

Jinky's fear of flying had developed over the previous two years following a flight from Toronto to Prestwick in the summer of 1966 when returning early from Celtic's close-season tour to Bermuda, the States and Canada. Jinky and team-mate Ian Young had been given special dispensation to leave the tour ahead of the main party as they both had weddings arranged. Half an hour into the flight the plane hit turbulence. At first, apart from the obvious discomfort, there didn't seem too much to worry about, but suddenly the aircraft shuddered and began to lose height at an alarming rate. Hand luggage tumbled from overhead lockers and terrified passengers clung to one another, fearing the worst.

An eternity later, the plane came out of its dive and steadied. The captain explained that they had hit an air vacuum, something that could not have been foreseen. The fuselage was strewn with baggage and personal belongs, according to Jinky, who completed the rest of the flight in a state of high anxiety, waiting for it all to happen again.

Jinky's experience left him feeling that he was not meant to fly, and for several days before a flight he would experience great difficulty sleeping. His appetite was also affected.

Before that taste of fear on the flight from Toronto, Jinky had suffered a bad experience when Celtic ran into difficulties on their return from Tbilisi six months earlier, in January 1966, following a 1–1 draw with Dinamo Kiev in the Cup Winners' Cup. A technical fault forced the pilot of the club's chartered Aer Lingus flight to land at Stockholm, where the aircraft began to ice up in extreme weather conditions. As the temperature dropped to well below zero, the pilot made two failed bids to take off, and was about to try a third time when the Celtic chairman, Sir Robert Kelly, mindful of the tragedy that had befallen Manchester United at Munich eight years earlier, ordered him to abort, for fear of a second disaster involving a British side.

The Celtic players spent the night in the Swedish capital, and eventually arrived back just fifteen hours before an important league match against Hearts at Tynecastle. A request to the Scottish Football League to have the fixture postponed because of the exceptional circumstances was rejected. Not surprisingly Celtic lost 3–2. A highly suspect landing at St Etienne a few weeks before the Red Star game did nothing to quell Jinky's increasing fears, and flying remained an ordeal of an ordeal for the rest of his life.

It was said that Jock Stein had spies everywhere, only too willing to report on the misdeeds of his players. That may or may not have been true, but Stein certainly had some watchers in place at strategic points such as the Noggin, Jinky's local in Uddingston, the area of his birth, and where he spent most of his life, apart from his brief spell in America and the two seasons he spent with Sheffield United.

Legend has it that Stein received a telephone call from a Celtic fan whose home overlooked the pub informing him that Jinky and Bobby Murdoch had been spotted entering the premises in their tracksuits during a lunchtime break in a pre-season double training session. Adopting a posh accent, Stein phoned the pub to enquire if there was a Mr Jimmy Johnstone at the bar. When Jinky was summoned to the phone all pretences were dropped and a menacing voice boomed: 'You get your arses back here, pronto!'

Stein, who, contrary to popular myth enjoyed the odd glass of wine, liked to give the impression that he was fiercely anti-drink. But at no time did he impose a blanket ban on his players taking a drink. What is fact is that Stein cultivated a wide network of contacts from all walks of life who kept him exceptionally well informed. Sports writers, well-heeled supporters, businessmen, bookmakers and 'football people' were among those who marked his card, so it was small wonder that he was able to keep such close tabs on straying players.

Yet the Lisbon Lions knew how to enjoy themselves. Indeed, it might be said that they would have given any of their rivals a run for their money in the drinking stakes! Stein sometimes turned a blind eye to these occasional excesses, but mostly he was aware of any illicit booze session taking place when the squad was billeted at their favoured pre-match base at Seamill, on the Ayrshire coast, or away on a foreign trip, and would nip it in the bud.

In an effort to evade Stein's eagle eye, Jinky was known to sneak out of the Seamill Hydro and head for the Galleon Bar just a few hundred yards up the hill, in the hope of sinking a couple of beers before his inevitable capture when his manager's large shadow hovered over him and he was escorted, maybe by the scruff of the neck, back to base pending yet another dressing down the morning after.

There was undoubtedly a drinking culture in Scottish football in the 1960s – Jim Baxter being a classic example – and Celtic's increasing success and status meant the players attended more social events. The Lions as a group enjoyed a drink and Jinky found it difficult to resist being part of that culture. It appears that most of his later problems stemmed from his inability to hold his drink. Jinky's tolerance for alcohol was limited. Nevertheless, according to his closest confidant among the Lions, Bobby Lennox, Jinky drank only in moderation for most of his Celtic career and it was only when he left the club in 1975 that alcohol loomed larger in his life.

'Jimmy started drinking gradually after we won the European Cup,' said Lennox. 'Up to that point he hardly ever took a drink. There is a famous photograph of the pair of us aboard the aircraft bringing the team back from Lisbon wearing sombreros and making out as if we are slugging bottles of champagne. The bottles were, in fact empty. The picture was stunted for the benefit of press photographers, but I can understand why some people might have formed the impression that we were boozing.

'Admittedly, drink became a bit of a problem for Jimmy in the early 1970s and it got worse after he left the club. But an awful lot of stories about Jimmy were exaggerated. I should know. Jimmy was my closest friend and I roomed with him all over the world.'

Tommy Gemmell also made the point: 'There is no way any of us could have been big drinkers and turned in the performances we did. We weren't angels by any means. We knew how to enjoy ourselves. But we weren't a bunch of alcoholics by any stretch of the imagination. I never touched a drink from Wednesday onwards before a match and I think that probably went for the rest of the lads as well. Wee Jinky was also a magnificent trainer.'

Stein's insomnia meant that he would sit long into the night in the reception area of the various hotels the team stayed at, and from where he could supervise all movements, often instructing his trusted lieutenants, Sean Fallon and trainer Neil Mochan to: 'Go and check on the players.'

It was said that Big Jock could detect the slightest movement in the ceiling directly above him when he was at his post by the side door at Seamill Hydro, the signal that mischief was afoot, and could hear a pin drop at one hundred paces. Most of the Lisbon Lions will testify to that.

Stein rarely stood still for long, and it was not uncommon for him to leave Glasgow at lunchtime to attend a game in Manchester, to arrive home in the early hours of the following morning, and still to be the first person through the front door at Celtic Park. It was as well that he was blessed with such energy, for often keeping Jinky out of trouble was a full-time job.

Billy McNeill said: 'No player gave Jock more headaches than Jimmy Johnstone. Jinky was the bane of Jock's life at times and the wee man fell foul of the manager on countless occasions. Jock was fond of Jimmy, though, and did everything in his power to protect Jinky from himself, often placing a protective arm round his shoulder and assuming the role of father figure.

'One example was the time Jinky was suspended and sent home for a breach of club discipline. In those days, when a player was suspended by his club, his wages immediately stopped. A couple of days later Jock approached me and revealed that Jinky had telephoned him several times, begging to be allowed to return. "What are you going to do?" I asked. "I've already sent him his wages," said Jock. "Fine, can I be suspended, too?" I retorted, tongue in cheek, but that incident demonstrated that there was a softer side to Jock that not a lot of people were aware of.

'To be honest, the Jimmy we knew as a footballer might not have emerged without Big Jock's influence.'

At the time, Jinky was earning a basic wage of about £80 a week. Bonus payments could boost that figure to £150, but that hardly compared to what the millionaire footballer earns. The leading Scottish players now earn as much in a week as the average spectator does in a year. In the 1960s, while Jinky and his team-mates enjoyed a lifestyle that was beyond most, the top players were not rich.

About Stein, Jinky himself confessed: 'I was undoubtedly more of a problem to him than his own children, and there were times when he must have felt like kicking my backside from here to yonder. But there was mutual admiration, too.'

Tommy Gemmell, who claimed that Jinky was terrified of Stein, pointed out: 'Big Jock did everything in his power to protect Jinky. He defended him and covered up for him because he knew he couldn't do without him.

'Most of Jimmy's misdemeanours were the result of daftness. We were all young and stupid and did the sort of things young men do. It was just that Jimmy did more silly things than the rest of us.'

While agreeing that Jinky had a remarkable capacity for attracting problems, Bertie Auld insisted: 'Jinky wasn't scared of anyone, but he did respect Big Jock.'

Bobby Lennox shared McNeill's view that Stein had a genuine fondness for Jinky. 'If Jimmy did something wrong he did it with a smile on his face and Jock would laugh about it afterwards,' said Lennox. 'Although the manager could be ruthless at times, he loved Jimmy. But, like the rest of us, Jimmy was in awe of Jock, and his word was law. But Jock was good for Jimmy. They were the best of pals – and the best of enemies!'

That Stein gave Jinky greater leeway than the rest of his squad there can be few doubts. When Jinky issued Celtic with an ultimatum over his contract in the wake of the 1970 European Cup final defeat by Celtic, rather than take any disciplinary action, Stein permitted him to miss the club's close-season tour to the USA and Canada because of his fear of flying and fatigue after a long, hard season – a decision that didn't go down well with some players.

John Greig, the former Rangers captain who played against Jinky many times, and who was also a Scotland team-mate, was another who admired Stein's ability to coax the best out of Jinky. 'Jock Stein's man-management skills worked superbly with Jimmy,' said Greig. 'Like everyone else, when Jimmy was going through a rough patch of form and not performing to his own high standards he would need someone to lift his spirits, and Jock did that by telling him he could play the other team on his own, and sometimes he did, particularly in European ties and against us.'

Stein, in fact, allowed Jinky much greater freedom on the pitch than any other player. Accepting that Jinky was an individualist who performed best when allowed to run at opponents in all areas of the pitch, the manager did not attempt to inhibit that unique flair. That readiness to give his problem child his head was illustrated during a team briefing at Seamill on the eve of a European tie. Jinky, desperate for the loo, asked to be excused. But Big Jock carried on regardless, telling the others: 'We might as well keep going. That little bugger never listens to me anyway. He just does his own thing.'

Stein was never a micro-manager. He knew when to give his players their head, and allowed his captain Billy McNeill a level of control on the pitch to make changes if he felt so inclined. At the same time he ran a tight ship and was quick to curb any perceived excesses of 'freedom'.

Yet Jinky was often encouraged to switch position to the left, or through the middle, if the right back lacked pace. It was a freedom denied to others.

Stein was also fond of saying: 'Jimmy is like the Grand old Duke of York. When he's up he's up, and when he's down he's down.' Often the cause of his own predicaments, Jinky struggled to mask his personal problems. Although Stein was sometimes driven to distraction by his player's sudden explosions of temper on the pitch, he could be much more understanding if he sensed Jinky had a problem unconnected with the playing side of the game, and was usually quick to intervene in an effort to assist in smoothing over such difficulties.

While he recognised that Jinky's sense of inferiority made him fly off the handle at times, Stein was also quick to concede that, more often than not, when Jinky 'blew' his reaction was born of frustration at being targeted by unscrupulous opponents who played on his notorious temperament and endeavoured to wind him up. Consequently, Stein became adept at using the good cop, bad cop routine, playing both roles himself.

Stein's was an almost parental influence, and it was a mark of just how successful he was in curbing Jinky's worst excesses that the player experienced most problems when he was outside his manager's control and sphere of influence at Celtic Park.

7

International Tensions

Jimmy Johnstone's was a God-given talent, and one that he worked at developing and perfecting to become one of those few Scots-born players who rated the verdict 'world-class'. Yet his country saw fit to honour him a paltry twenty-three times. Had he been born a Brazilian it seems perfectly reasonable to suppose that Jinky would have taken his haul of international caps close to three figures.

Various reasons can be offered for Jinky's failure to become an automatic choice for his country, not least the natural shyness born of a surprising inferiority complex for one so truly gifted. By his own admission, Jinky felt out of place in the company of his fellow internationals. 'I was in awe of greats like Jim Baxter, Denis Law and Billy Bremner,' he said. 'They were giants of the game and the way they handled themselves in company made me despair. They always looked so composed with the fans or eating in big fancy restaurants. I was still the little boy lost.'

But there was much more to it than that, principally the refusal of a section of the Rangers support ever to fully accept the sight of the Celtic star in a Scotland jersey at the expense of their own hero, Willie Henderson.

The keen rivalry that existed between the pair did not entail any personal animosity. Indeed, Jinky and Henderson became close friends off the field, and that friendship endured until Jinky's dying day. But while Jinky and wee Willie coexisted amicably, the continual taunts of a few embittered souls eventually became almost too much for the former to bear, culminating in a sickening experience at Hampden Park in 1967 when chants of 'Henderson, Henderson' rang out from the traditional Rangers end of the national stadium throughout a game against Wales.

It was a devastating experience for Jinky, and he later confessed to releasing the ball quickly in subsequent Scotland matches rather than be subjected to another such barracking from so-called Scotland supporters. For a player who thrived on being in possession of the ball and teasing opponents by jinking this way and that way, playing quick passes was completely alien to Jinky's style of play, and underlines why he so rarely shone in his country's colours.

Henderson said: 'I had quite a few caps before Jimmy came on the scene and I was difficult to dislodge at that time. I remember Billy Bremner suggesting to one international manager that he should play both of us in the same team, but the manager replied: "Unfortunately, there is only one ball!"'

John Greig, who captained the 1967 'Wembley Wizards' to a memorable victory over reigning world champions England – the first time Sir Alf Ramsey's side had been beaten since their triumph the previous year – could not recall Jinky complaining about his harsh treatment.

Greig said: 'I suppose back then there was a bit of anti-Celtic feeling among a section of the fans because there tended to be more Rangers supporters watching the international team. But the players certainly got on well with each other. Personally, whenever I played for Scotland I just tried to enjoy the occasion, and I was never bothered by an abuse or recognised that as a problem.

'We were blessed with a glut of outstanding wingers at that time. As well as wee Jimmy there was Willie Henderson, Tommy McLean, Willie Johnston and Alec Edwards.'

Bobby Brown, the former Scotland manager who now lives in quiet retirement in the seaside town of Helensburgh, recalled receiving letters from those claiming to be Rangers supporters reminding him that he should select his 'own kind', a clear reference to the fact that he had been a Rangers and Scotland goalkeeper of note himself.

'I also used to get the occasional letter from Celtic fans accusing me of favouring Rangers players over Celtic players, but that was complete nonsense,' said Brown. 'I chose each player on his merits, not the colour of the jersey he wore at club level, and I was fortunate to have two outstanding right-wingers at my disposal in Jimmy and Willie.'

There were other reasons, of course, for Jinky's dearth of Scotland appearances over an international career spanning eleven years. Some Scottish Football Association officials did not approve of his individualism, believing that he tended to dwell on the ball for too long and overdid his efforts to turn full-backs inside out. At that time SFA officials wielded considerable power when it came to team selection, and there was in fact an official Selection Committee in place to 'advise' the manager. Significantly, in most cases it comprised members with no direct experience of team-management, or indeed much detailed knowledge of the game, but the existence of such a group meant that certain players were often selected ahead of more worthy candidates, for political reasons rather than footballing ones. Jinky probably fell victim to this kind of narrow-minded thinking on more than one occasion.

To be fair, his cause was not helped by occasional bouts of indiscipline fuelled by alcohol. Indeed, but for Willie Ormond's refusal to bow to pressure, Jinky's career would have ended several games before it finally did in November 1974.

Bobby Lennox, who knew Jinky better than most, also offered the view that Jinky's shyness was a significant factor in his apparent nervousness when he was on international duty. 'Jimmy felt at home at Celtic Park,' he said. 'We were a very tight-knit bunch, so when he went anywhere else he didn't know the other guys so well and his natural bubbly nature when he was in the company of Celtic players deserted him. If any of us were on Scotland duty at the same time he always looked for us to sit with him.'

For all that his international career failed to match his achievements with Celtic, what wouldn't Scotland give to have a Jimmy

Johnstone in the squad today? Former international full-backs the world over will happily testify to a genuine sense of relief when they learned that they would not have to face Jinky in his pomp, for one reason or another.

Kevin Keegan, the former England manager who marvelled at Jinky's skills on more than one occasion during a career spanning sixty-three international appearances, spoke for the majority of those were given a chasing by the wee man when he said: 'Jimmy was a terrific dribbler. You thought you knew what he was going to do and the next thing you were chasing him. He ought to have earned a hundred caps. Jimmy gave the team width, he tricked defenders and reached the byline, and still looked like a cheeky kid who had just stepped off a bald patch of grass behind the house.'

It was a measure of just how highly Keegan rated Jinky that he included him in his all-time British 'Dream Team'.

Ian McColl was the first Scotland manager to recognise Jinky's value to the national team, handing him his debut against Wales at Cardiff's Ninian Park on 3 October 1964. He had just turned twenty and had made his first-team debut for Celtic nineteen months earlier. But, despite limited first-team experience, the newcomer was preferred to Henderson, who had won his twelfth cap in the previous game, a 2–2 draw with West Germany in Hanover five months earlier.

Scotland lost, 3–2, but Jinky emerged with credit from the game. The late Hugh Taylor, writing in the *Scottish Daily Record*, was effusive in his praise of the debutant, who was involved in the build-up to Leicester's Davie Gibson scoring Scotland's second goal when he began the move before releasing a pass to Denis Law. Taylor, who lambasted the established internationals in the side for failing to give greater commitment, wrote: 'Johnstone was no mere understudy for Henderson. He had a lively debut and delivered some dangerous corners and had a shot blocked by a defender. It was a refreshing performance by Johnstone, and I am sure he will be called on again.'

Jinky retained his place for Scotland's next match, a World Cup qualifying tie against Finland at Hampden eighteen days later. A highly satisfactory 3–1 home win was the perfect start to secure a place in the finals in England. But it was to be another eighteen months before Jinky had the chance to resume his international career. Part of the reason was the dismissal of the introverted McColl on the grounds that he was not sufficiently authoritative and lacked the full confidence of his players – so said the SFA.

Jock Stein, who had only recently taken charge at Celtic, was persuaded to succeed McColl on a part-time basis on the understanding that he would oversee the fortunes of the national side only temporarily. But Stein, while already an admirer of Jinky, did not feel that the player was quite ready for an extended run in the side, so Jinky did not figure once during Stein's seven games at the helm. Henderson was preferred by the Celtic manager for the first six before injury deprived him of a place in the last game of Stein's brief reign, a crucial qualifying tie against Italy in Naples, on 7 December 1965.

A catalogue of injuries had robbed Scotland of the services of several key players, most notably Henderson, Pat Crerand, Jim Baxter, Denis Law and Ian St John. As a result of the call-offs, Stein was forced to choose a makeshift side, with Liverpool centre half Ron Yeats fielded wearing the number nine jersey in an involuntary 6–2–2 formation. Inevitably, given the circumstances, Scotland lost, 3–0 and defeat brought the grim realisation that the World Cup would take place in England the following summer without the presence of the hosts' closest rivals.

The mood of the Scotland fans was not helped when England visited Hampden four months later and inflicted a 4–3 defeat. But the game was a personal triumph for Jinky, who tormented the full-backs, George Cohen of Fulham and Blackburn's Keith Newton, who was constantly troubled by his direct opponent running at him and weaving his way into the penalty box at every opportunity.

Fittingly, Jinky had a hand in all three Scotland goals, delivering the corner kick for Law to head home three minutes before the interval and scoring twice himself in the second half, the second a spectacular curling shot from Law's cross. Yet Jinky's international career continued in fits and starts. He made his fourth Scotland appearance in a 1–1 away draw with Wales two years to the month after his debut in Cardiff, but was subsequently omitted from the side that faced Northern Ireland, beaten by two goals to one.

Jinky's first major setback in international football c..me when injury denied him the opportunity to be part of a famous Scottish victory, the humbling of world champions England at Wembley on 15 April 1967, just a little over a month before Celtic were crowned champions of Europe. An injury he had picked up against Dukla Prague in the European Cup semi-final proved troublesome enough for neither club nor country to risk Jinky breaking down on the big stage. Ironically, Bobby Brown, who had succeeded John Prentice as Scotland manager, elected to play Jinky's team-mate, Willie Wallace, more accustomed to occupying a striker role, on the right flank.

Jinky was upset to miss such a key occasion, and Scotland's triumphant 3–2 win over the Auld Enemy simply added to his bitter disappointment. But worse was to follow.

Six months later, following a 2–0 home defeat by the USSR, Jinky earned his sixth cap, against Wales. It could just as easily have been his last, for he later admitted that the chants of 'Henderson, Henderson' that rang out at Hampden on the evening of 22 November 1967 as Scotland secured a 3–2 win led to his disillusionment about playing for his country.

Jinky revealed: 'After the Welsh match I became an even bigger fan of Denis Law.' His spirits low, Jinky was sitting alone at the post-match banquet in Glasgow's Central Hotel when Denis came up and slapped him on the back. 'Well done, wee man, you were brilliant,' he said. 'I knew otherwise,' Jinky said, 'but I will always be grateful to Denis for that gesture. I could have crawled into a hole and no one would have noticed that night, but Denis tried to buck me up. It was a terrific tonic.'

Jinky was due a change of fortune, but there seemed to be no respite in his troubles when, fully expecting to join the team to face England at Hampden the following February in a make-or-break

European Championship qualifier, he was left out by Brown. Charlie Cooke, the former Dundee player who had since gone on to enhance his reputation with Chelsea, was preferred on the right side.

Scotland had to win to qualify, while a draw would suffice to take England through to the finals. Brown took the view that Jinky was not mentally prepared for such a huge game because of ongoing problems he was having at Celtic. Although his club form had been impressive, Jinky had been involved in a couple of spats with Jock Stein, who been highly critical of him following his ordering off in a match against St Johnstone. But the press chose to believe that there had been a clash of personalities between the Scotland manager and the player – a suggestion that Jinky vehemently denied.

The former manager also gave short shrift to the lie. 'Jimmy was a great little player and a lovely fellow, whom I always got on well with,' said Brown. 'He had his problems from time to time but I never found him anything other than pleasant and courteous. But Jimmy was also a very shy lad. I remember on one occasion, prior to a game against England at Hampden, when he pleaded with me not to ask him any questions during the team talk in case it caused him any embarrassment. "Sir, please don't ask me anything," he said. He always called me Sir.

'But what a player. I suppose you could describe him as mercurial, but he had tremendous ability. He could beat his man inside-out and then do the same thing all over again in the manner of a true entertainer. He would take on the full-back, run to the byline, and cross the ball with accuracy. You rarely see that sort of wing play nowadays and more's the pity. Jimmy was a sheer joy to watch. He was truly one of the greats of our game.'

But while Jinky had no problem with the manager, he found it impossible to get along with Brown's assistant, Walter McCrae, a taciturn man who made little or no effort to endear himself to either players or the press. The pair clashed not long before a match against England when McCrae asked Jinky to act as a linesman in a practice game between the Scotland players and Celtic at Largs.

It appears to have been a deliberate attempt by McCrae to humiliate Jinky, and he responded by telling the coach where to get off.

Unfortunately, the press got hold of the story and assumed the bust-up had been between Jinky and Brown, fuelling speculation that they were at loggerheads. But Jinky got his revenge when, a short time later, Celtic hammered Kilmarnock, who were managed by McCrae, 6–0 at Rugby Park. As he left the field, Jinky allegedly shouted to McCrae: 'Not bad for a linesman, Walter.' There is no record of McCrae's response!

But Jinky's clash with McCrae was a storm in a teacup compared to the one that blew up the following year shortly before Scotland were due to face England at Wembley, in May 1969. Jinky had by then helped Scotland to a win over Austria and a draw with West Germany. But a period of SFA suspension, incurred as a result of collecting three cautions, meant that he had missed Celtic's four-goal Scottish Cup final win over Rangers and the home internationals against Wales and Northern Ireland. However, Brown was anxious to include him in his squad for the England game.

At first, Jinky wasn't keen to accept the offer, as he did not feel mentally attuned following his suspension. But after being advised by Stein to speak to the manager directly, he was talked into changing his mind by the persuasive Brown and agreed to join the squad at their hotel in Glasgow, where he headed minus his boots. Stein, who had been critical of his mercurial winger in the preceding period, agreed to deliver the boots to the hotel.

But that night Jinky began to feel unwell and soon developed a temperature. Because of their well-documented fear of flying, he and team-mate Eddie McCreadie, of Chelsea, had been granted permission to travel to London by train, but when Jinky was physically sick on the first leg of the journey from Glasgow to Edinburgh he contacted Brown to inform him and was advised to return home.

The problem was that no one bothered to inform Big Jock, who reacted with fury, thinking that Jinky had once again changed his mind without telling him after he had gone to the trouble of acting as 'delivery boy'. Stein was so enraged that he refused to listen to Jinky's explanation of events and went as far as releasing a statement to the press advising Brown not to pick his player in future as he clearly could not be relied on. Jinky again made the wrong sort of headlines, even though he was completely innocent. He was diagnosed as suffering from tonsillitis and confined to bed with a temperature of 100 degrees.

Despite all this, Jinky had cause to feel relieved that he had once again missed a game against England, whose 4–1 victory on the Saturday evening did not augur well for Scotland's World Cup prospects.

Scotland required a miracle to qualify for the finals in Mexico the following year when they faced West Germany for the second time in seven months, in Hamburg, on 22 October 1969. But if anyone was capable of pulling something special out of the bag it was Jinky, and Brown wisely recalled him for what was the wee man's ninth international appearance. Brown's choice was fully vindicated when Jinky scored after three minutes, from close in. But despite a stirring Scotland performance, and another goal from Alan Gilzean, West Germany triumphed, 3–2. Tommy Gemmell, Jinky's Celtic Park team-mate, was ordered off for kicking an opponent up the backside.

But the inconsistency of selection that dogged Jinky's Scotland career continued when he was left out for the team for the next three internationals – a defeat by Austria in Vienna, a win over Northern Ireland in Belfast, and a goalless draw with Wales at Hampden. He was back in the side for the England game the following April, an drab affair that lacked both goals and individual brilliance. Jinky retained his place for the next match, a European Championship qualifier against Denmark in Glasgow. Scotland beat the Danes 1–0, thanks to a John O'Hare goal, but Brown preferred Cooke and Henderson against Belgium and Portugal as Scotland's European Championship aspirations were hit by back-to-back losses in Liège and Lisbon.

Brown, under mounting pressure from his critics, recalled Jinky for the visit to Wembley on 22 May 1971, but a relatively raw

Scotland side was outplayed by England. Their 3–1 victory moved the manager ever closer to the exit door, which swung open in the wake of successive 1–0 defeats by Denmark and the USSR.

With Brown gone, the SFA turned to Tommy Docherty, a former Scotland captain and the sort of charismatic character desperately needed to reinvigorate the national side. His appointment, in September, was welcomed by the majority of the Scotland fans and the players, not least Jinky.

Just a month after picking up the reins from Brown, Docherty took charge for his first match, against Portugal at Hampden, a game Scotland had to win to restore national pride. One of the first things he did was to recall Jinky.

'Jinky was a great player,' said Docherty, 'truly world-class, and I had no hesitation whatsoever about recalling him. He was a genius, and there is no player in the current game to match him, in my opinion. Jimmy had his problems from time to time and the pair of us had our moments as well. But the only people who experienced real problems with Jimmy during my time as manager were opposition left backs.'

With Jinky restored to the right wing, Scotland won, 2–1. The following month the team headed for Aberdeen to face Belgium. It turned out to be a watershed in Jinky's fragmented international career. Scotland won 1–0 at Pittodrie, and it was from Jinky's cross that O'Hare scored the all-important goal, leaving him to reflect that it was his finest performance in a Scotland jersey.

'The sheer relief of playing away from Hampden Park inspired me that night,' Jinky explained. As a result he put on a terrific show, to the delight of the Aberdeen fans. They chanted his name constantly and, according to Jinky, 'there wasn't a boo-boy in sight.'

Docherty also smiled at the memory of an outstanding performance when he recalled: 'Jimmy turned to me at half-time and said: "Boss, you'll need to substitute me – I have run out of new ideas on how next to beat the left back."'

Jinky featured in Scotland's next game – a 2–1 defeat by Holland in Amsterdam – to notch up appearances in three consecutive games for the first time. The run was broken when Willie Morgan, of Manchester United, replaced him in a two-goal victory over Peru at Hampden, but Jinky was back for a 2–0 home win over Northern Ireland one month later, in May 1972.

Jinky's substitute appearance – in place of Archie Gemmill – against England the following week was his last under the Doc. However, his banishment to the international wilderness appeared to owe more to an incident off the park than his contribution to a single-goal defeat by the Auld Enemy. Around the same time, Jinky, in company with team-mate George Graham, unwisely staged a raid on Docherty's room during an international get-together at Largs and made off with two bottles of the Doc's favourite tipple, champagne. According to Jinky, Docherty blew his top when the pair were unmasked as the culprits and the wee man was convinced that this incident was at least partly to blame for Docherty never again picking him to play for his country.

Docherty's version is different. 'When I found out Jinky had nicked my champers I said to him: "Listen, wee man, you'll need to play the game here and replace it." He replied: "I know, boss. But don't worry; I'll get you a couple of bottles." He was as good as his word, but the wee so-and-so bought two of the cheapest bottles he could find!'

Jinky also tried the Doc's patience on another occasion when drink was again the reason. The squad was at its customary pre-match base at Largs prior to a match against Northern Ireland at Hampden. Peter Lorimer, a rival of Jinky's for the number seven shirt, remembered: 'We persuaded the Doc to let us have the evening off to go to the cinema. En route we called in at a local pub for a quick half and word quickly filtered back that a few of us were in the boozer. I was horrified to see the Doc's face peering through the glass in the pub door. Jimmy had just gone to the bar to get a round in and we frantically tried to attract his attention. But Jimmy didn't cotton on and reacted by giving the rest of us the thumbs-up. Next thing Doc is tapping Jimmy on the shoulder and, quick as a flash, the wee man looks at the manager and says: "What are you having, Tommy?"

'Needless to say we were ordered back to the hotel for a bollocking and told that we would be confined to barracks in future.

Next night we won 2–0, but Jimmy didn't play particularly well and I was sent on as his replacement. As he was walking off he said to me: "Listen, you'd better play well to get us out of this or the pair of us will be in big trouble."'

For all that their relationship did not always run smoothly, Docherty enjoyed Jinky's company. 'Although he was naturally shy, he was a lovely wee fellow, and popular with his team-mates,' Docherty recalled. 'He used to say to me: "You're some man, gaffer." But it was Jimmy who was some man. People talk about Wayne Rooney being a great player but he isn't in the same class as Jimmy Johnstone.

'If Jimmy was still playing today you would need to rob Fort Knox to be able to afford to buy him. He had everything – wonderful skill and flair, speed, courage and an ability to score goals. He was an entertainer in the same class as Garrincha, Tom Finney, Stan Matthews and George Best. There is no doubt in my mind about that.'

It is a fact, all the same, that Jinky did not feature in Docherty's remaining five games as manager. Indeed, he was absent from the international scene for two years before winning his eighteenth international cap, on 14 May 1974, against Wales at Hampden. It was the start of a four-game run under Willie Ormond and confirmation of Jock Stein's belief that Jinky was playing some of the finest football of his career at the time.

How ironic, then that just when it seemed Jinky had cracked it at long last, his life began to unravel again, and all because of a night on the booze and a dilapidated rowing boat.

8

A Bright New Dawn

By the time Jock Stein became manager of Celtic, Jimmy Johnstone had played over seventy first-team games for the club and scored a dozen goals. But Stein's initial doubts about whether Jinky's individual skills could be harnessed and made to work for the benefit of the team as a unit appear to have persisted for several months.

It may, of course, have been the case that the wily Stein was simply playing mind games with his most naturally gifted player by letting it be known that he had certain reservations concerning Jinky's 'free spirit', in the hope that the little mischief-maker would sit up and pay more attention. Reservations or not, despite his reported doubts concerning Jinky, the new manager was not slow to call on his talents. Jinky, in fact, made fifty-four appearances in Stein's first full season in charge, scoring fourteen goals, nine of them in the league, as Celtic secured their first championship title for twelve years. Only three players – John Clark, Tommy Gemmell and Bobby Murdoch – played more games.

Jinky's contribution to ending a frustrating wait for their fans was significant, for he scored in two of the last three league games to ensure that Celtic's destiny was in their own hands when they faced Motherwell, at Fir Park on 7 May 1966, requiring a single point to be sure of pipping arch-rivals Rangers at the post.

Jinky appears to have won Stein over during a series of games against Raith Rovers, Rangers, Aberdeen, Hibs, Hearts, Falkirk, and the Dutch side Go Ahead of Deventer, during the period between 15 September and 23 October 1965. Celtic won nine out of eleven, scoring a staggering forty-four goals for the loss of only twelve. Jinky was outstanding in the majority of these matches.

Raith Rovers had no answer to Jinky's high-speed runs and mesmerising skills in the League Cup quarter-final. First they were crushed 8–1 at home, when Jinky scored Celtic's third goal. Then he proceeded to torture his hosts all over again in the second leg the following week. A four-goal victory gave Celtic a 12–1 aggregate success.

One week after suffering a 2–1 defeat at Ibrox, on 25 September Celtic took their frustration out on Aberdeen at Celtic Park. The Dons were dumped 7–1, and Jinky scored two goals in the rout. The performance was the perfect rehearsal for Celtic's opening European Cup Winners' Cup tie the following Wednesday.

Go Ahead were not expected to trouble Celtic unduly, and so it proved, but their hapless players had not bargained for being so teased, turned and generally tormented as they were by Jinky in front of a spellbound Dutch audience of 25,000. Jinky's two goals contributed to a 6–0 victory, and such was the level of his performance that the locals applauded him throughout the second half.

Just a few days earlier Tottenham Hotspur had been rebuffed by Stein when they made an approach for Jinky. Clearly the manager had seen more than enough to convince him that Jinky had an integral part to play in his long-term plans for Celtic.

Incredibly, at the same time as he was endeavouring to turn things round at Celtic Park after years of steady decline, Stein somehow found the time and energy to manage Scotland for six months.

Just before they eased off against Go Ahead in the return leg, which they won 1–0, Celtic faced Hibs in the League Cup semifinal at neutral Ibrox. Celtic had reached the last four despite suffering two defeats in their qualifying section, to the Dundee clubs. But it required a Bobby Lennox goal in the dying seconds to force the tie into extra time after the sides had served up a cracking spectacle, as Jinky ran himself ragged on a stamina-sapping pitch. The replay was another story: this time Hibs were swept aside, 4–0.

The final, just five days later, on 23 October 1965, pitted Celtic against Rangers, but hopes of a classic were dashed by indiscipline. Five players were booked in an ill-tempered encounter, described by one reporter as 'a hard, grim game and it could be that some like their football that way; people who chew tobacco, bite their nails, eat razor blades'.

Celtic won 2–1, courtesy of two first-half goals scored by John Hughes, both from the penalty spot, the first when centre half Ronnie McKinnon had an aberration and inexplicably punched a free kick from John Clark. Full-back Davie Provan conceded the second when he brought down Jinky. But Provan felt aggrieved.

'I was playing against Jimmy Johnstone,' he said, 'and there is hardly any need to tell you that he was superb. Contrary to what Celtic supporters might say, I bet there was not one occasion when he went off the park having been deliberately kicked by me. The problem was when you are a big man like me playing against a wee fella like Johnstone, every tackle looked awkward. Anyway, Jimmy was weaving his way into the penalty area and I tackled him. To me it was no better or worse than any other tackles I had made on him earlier, but he went down flat and all I can remember is the referee pointing to the penalty spot. We protested about it, of course, but got nowhere.'

The victory earned Celtic their first success in the competition since 1957, when they had annihilated Rangers, 7–1. It was also a landmark occasion for Jinky, who collected the first of his nineteen winner's medals.

October also brought league wins over Hearts (5–2), Falkirk, who were beaten 4–3 at Brockville, where Jinky scored the equaliser after the home side had taken a 3–2 lead, Dundee (2-1), and Stirling Albion, thrashed 6–1 at Celtic Park. But a 1–1 home draw with Partick Thistle at the start of November left Celtic trailing Rangers by three points in the championship race.

A seven-game winning run, which included the successful nego-
tiation of a Cup Winners' Cup second-round tie against the Danes
of AGF Aarhus, meant that Celtic led Rangers on goal average by
the turn of the year. In three of those games – against St Johnstone,
Hamilton and Aarhus – Jinky scored to underline that he was more
than just a provider of chances. Morton's 8–1 defeat at Celtic Park
on Christmas Day also highlighted the flair and power of the Celtic
team as a whole.

Allan McGraw, one of the most prolific goalscorers in Morton's
history and subsequently a successful manager of the Greenock
club, said: 'I wish I could claim not to have played that day, and I
suppose I might as well not have, given the score. But it was obvious then that Jock Stein was in the process of fashioning an
exceptional side. Stein achieved the perfect blend because there
was no obvious weakness from defence through to attack.'

But every great team needs outstanding players, individuals who
stand out from the rest, and Jinky had already established himself
as Celtic's crown prince. Part of his attraction for the fans was that
you never knew just what was coming next.

At the age of just twenty-one, Jinky's great speed of movement
and wonderful balance had already established him as one of the
true stars of Scottish football. Defenders had also come to learn that
Jinky rarely went down and stayed down. He almost always
bounced straight back up. Over the years he took a lot of painful
knocks, but he was a hardy specimen who rarely complained about
his treatment, much though he might have cause to.

Jinky also risked sustaining physical damage at the hands of
team-mates on occasion. Full-back Tommy Gemmell recalled issu-
ing a threat to rearrange Jinky's features during a training session
when his team-mate pushed his luck a little too far.

'Jimmy loved to nutmeg opponents, even at training,' Gemmell
revealed. 'This day at Barrowfield he started doing it to me during
a practice match and I warned him: "Listen to me, wee man,
because I am only going to say this once, you only get away with
one more of those. Try another one after that and I am going to kick
f— out of you." Jimmy turned to Jock Stein and asked if he had

heard what I had said. Jock replied: "Yes – and it seems fair enough to me." So, Jimmy had his three nutmegs and that was it.'

It was on 3 January 1966 that Celtic had served notice of their aim to be Scotland's top club. Having welcomed in the New Year with a 3–1 away win against Clyde, they faced Rangers at Celtic Park two days later. A sudden cold snap put the fixture in doubt, but referee Tom 'Tiny' Wharton eventually passed the pitch playable – a decision that was to have far-reaching consequence for Rangers, who were overwhelmed 5–1.

Celtic won their next game, against Dundee United at Celtic Park, by 1–0, but then suffered their first defeat since losing to Rangers four months earlier when they travelled to Pittodrie to face an Aberdeen team thirsting for revenge for having been hammered 7–1 earlier in the season. Perhaps there was a reaction to a three-goal midweek win over Dynamo Kiev at Celtic Park, but whatever the reason, Celtic failed to turn their overall dominance into goals, and lost 3–1.

Over the next six weeks Celtic's and Jinky's form fluctuated alarmingly. The demands of chasing success on three simultaneous fronts made it hard to stay consistent on all three.

A narrow win over Motherwell was followed by a 3–2 defeat by Hearts. In fairness, Celtic's run-up to the Tynecastle match was farcical. Horrendous travel problems on the return journey from Kiev, involving an unscheduled overnight stop at Stockholm because of a problem with the aircraft, caused the Celtic players not to arrive back in Glasgow until late on the Friday evening. The Scottish Football League's refusal to postpone the fixture meant that they had only a few hours' sleep before facing Hearts, as Stein had ordered his squad to undertake a midnight training session in an effort to counter jet lag.

Celtic bounced back by taking four goals off Stranraer in the first round of the Scottish Cup and six off Falkirk the following week. But the Falkirk result proved to be no more than a temporary return to the form Celtic had displayed earlier in the season. A Scottish Cup win at Dundee was immediately followed by the biggest upset of the season, a 1–0 defeat by lowly Stirling Albion.

The result put Rangers back in pole position in the title race, on goal average. The Ibrox side also had the cushion of a match in hand.

Two days after the Stirling defeat, Celtic again beat Dundee, this time by five goals to nil, and a 3–1 Scottish Cup win over Hearts on 9 March, after a 3–3 draw in the first game, helped further boost morale. Jinky scored the first of Celtic's cup goals in front of a crowd of 72,000, a record attendance for a midweek game at Celtic Park.

These successes were followed by wins over St Johnstone and bottom-of-the-table Hamilton, pulverised 7–1 at Douglas Park. Jinky, back to his sparkling best, scored twice. Rangers, meanwhile, had suffered a major form slump, losing to Falkirk and drawing with Hearts and Kilmarnock to throw the championship race wide open once again.

A 2–2 draw away to Partick Thistle on 21 March might have put paid to Celtic's title aspirations but for the fact that Rangers lost that same evening, to Dundee United. Wins over Kilmarnock and St Mirren, twice, in the league and Dunfermline by 2–0 in the Scottish Cup semi-final, set Celtic up nicely for their Cup Winners' Cup semi-final against Liverpool at Celtic Park on 14 April.

The Liverpool tie was one of seven games Celtic played in seventeen days in April, when the fixture congestion strained their resources to breaking point. In addition to the demands of club football, the trio of Jinky, Tommy Gemmell and Bobby Murdoch were also in the Scotland team beaten 4–3 by England at Hampden on 2 April when Jinky scored twice.

But for all that their legs ached from the demands of such run of games, Celtic did themselves credit against Liverpool at Celtic Park on 14 April, and were unfortunate not to win by more than just Bobby Lennox's fifty-first-minute strike. However, when they returned to action less than forty-eight hours later, against Hibs at Easter Road, they were feeling the strain, and it showed. A goalless draw enabled Rangers to regain a share of the lead at the top of the First Division, thanks to a 5–0 win over Morton at Cappielow.

Celtic at least had the advantage of a game in hand over

Rangers, but the players' already fragile confidence was further dented by two shattering defeats in the space of four days. Jock Stein believed that his team was capable of reaching its first European final, but Liverpool had other ideas. Celtic survived sustained pressure for an hour on a heavy Anfield pitch, but goals by Tommy Smith and Geoff Strong in the space of five minutes were lethal blows. Even so, Celtic very nearly forced the tie into extra time in the final minute, when Lennox scored a perfectly good goal only to be ruled offside. After watching film of the game Belgian referee Josef Hannet had the good grace to concede that he had made a mistake.

A Scottish Cup final meeting with Rangers only four days later did Celtic no favours. In the event, it was, by all accounts, a drab spectacle dominated by defences. The match ended goalless and required a midweek replay – the last thing Celtic needed at that stage.

But Jinky, who for tactical purposes had been left out of the second leg at Anfield to enable Stein to field John Hughes, in the belief that Hughes's strength and power would unsettle the Liverpool defence, found the inspiration to light up Hampden the following Wednesday. Jinky played a brilliant game, and turned Rangers' left back Davie Provan inside out, but he could not prompt a victory. For all that they were generally outplayed, Rangers destroyed Celtic's dream of a domestic treble when Kai Johansen hit a speculative drive to score an unexpected winner in the seventieth minute.

Lesser sides would have folded. Celtic had stumbled, and they desperately needed a spark of inspiration. It was Jinky who provided it. The games against Morton and Dunfermline were defining moments in Stein's first full season and Jinky rose to the challenge all the way.

Jock Stein's effort to exude an air of confidence could not disguise his own growing unease. He could sense the edginess in his players, whose nerves were not calmed by the knowledge that Morton, locked in a relegation battle with local rivals St Mirren, still had one last chance to avoid relegation.

Celtic were tentative at first, and when Morton were awarded a penalty after half an hour it seemed that a season which had held so much promise just weeks earlier might be about to unravel. But fate intervened: the Celtic players and their worried fans breathed a huge sigh of relief when Fleming Neilsen's kick flew over the crossbar. Jinky had been the one to concede the penalty, for a push on Allan McGraw.

Even after all these years, McGraw cannot for the life of him understand why Jinky was playing so deep at the time. 'I was actually coming out of the penalty box when he pushed me,' McGraw recalled, 'and I never understood why it happened. Jinky had a tendency to be roaming all over the park but it struck me as strange that he was back playing a defensive role. It wasn't as if I posed a threat at the precise moment either. In fact, my back was more or less to goal.'

McGraw was Morton's elected penalty taker, but Neilsen, for some reason, insisted on taking the kick. Had Morton scored, Celtic might well have crumbled. Jinky atoned for his rush of blood by breaking the deadlock almost exactly on the stroke of half-time. His cross struck a defender and the ball flew past goalkeeper Erik Sorensen. Having grabbed the game by the scruff of the neck, Jinky put the seal on an outstanding performance by engineering Celtic's second goal in the final minutes of a tense encounter. He outpaced the defence before delivering a pinpoint accurate cross for Bobby Lennox to head past Sorensen.

But Celtic were not yet across the finishing line. Dunfermline and Motherwell lay in wait. Rangers had kept up the pressure by beating Dunfermline 2–1 at East End Park. But the Jinky–Lennox partnership, which had proved so effective at Cappielow, again provided the key to unlocking a victory after Alex Ferguson, later to manage Aberdeen and Manchester United, had given the Fifers the lead. Again, a lesser team might have cracked, but Celtic's strength of character shone through. Dunfermline, who were themselves chasing a European spot, led for only five minutes before Lennox delivered the equaliser nine minutes from half-time. But it was Jinky who sent 30,000 Celtic fans into raptures in the fifty-ninth minute when a shot by Lennox was blocked and he pounced on the rebound to net the winning goal from close range.

The significance of the narrow win over Dunfermline was made clear by Rangers' 4–0 success against Clyde, which enabled them to match Celtic's points tally of fifty-five. But Celtic's vastly superior goal average meant that they would have had to lose by several goals at Motherwell on Saturday 7 May in the only outstanding fixture. But in the last minute of the last game on the last day of a momentous season, Lennox scored for the third game in a row to ensure that Celtic were crowned champions.

Willie Hunter, the former Motherwell inside forward, played in the game. He said: 'Bertie Auld was the motivator in midfield and he made them tick. But it was Jimmy's wonderful flair and balance that was the key. But I have often felt that Jimmy might not have become the player he did had it not been for Jock Stein. Big Jock pointed Jimmy in the right direction, and he needed guidance, in the sense that he was prone to going off and doing his own thing with the ball.'

Hunter had witnessed at first hand Jinky's habit of 'doing his own thing' in an Under-23 Challenge Cup match at Fir Park a few years previously. Hunter was playing outside-left and yet kept seeing Jinky's back: so intent was he on dribbling past one player after another that he actually ended up back in his own penalty box!

By aspiring to the level of league champions, 'The Kelly Kids' – so dubbed because they were a product of the youth policy established by the chairman, Bob Kelly, several years earlier in the hope that the club could replicate the success enjoyed by Manchester United's 'Busby Babes' – came of age. But it had taken Jock Stein to harness the talents of such as Jinky, Jim Craig, Tommy Gemmell, Bobby Murdoch and Bobby Lennox and turn them into winners.

Much credit was also due to Stein's assistant, Sean Fallon. It was Fallon who had shown the foresight to sign Bertie Auld from Birmingham for £11,000 even before Stein took over from Jimmy McGrory. The Irishman had also been responsible for bringing aging goalkeeper Ronnie Simpson to Celtic Park, paying Hibs £2,000 for his services. Stein, in fact, had been on the point of letting Simpson leave Easter Road to become player-manager of Berwick Rangers when Fallon made his move.

Stein's first signing was Joe McBride, from Motherwell, in June 1965, for £22,500 – £2,500 less than Dunfermline had been prepared to pay for the striker. Such was McBride's desire to play for Celtic that he accepted a £1,000 signing-on fee from Stein compared to the £5,000 Dunfermline had offered. Stein's faith in McBride was repaid with forty-three goals in season 1965–66 before injury cut short his career.

Stein, always forward-thinking, was only partially satisfied with his team's achievement in winning both the league title and the League Cup. He had made clear his belief that success in the European Cup Winners' Cup was attainable, and was vexed by the manner of Celtic's defeat by Liverpool. But long before the season was drawing to a close, Stein drew up plans for an ambitions summer tour to Canada and the United States to commence four days after the title was won.

The first stage of the 20,000-mile, thirty-five-day tour involved a stop-off in Bermuda to allow the players to recharge their batteries after the rigours of a non-stop ten-month campaign. Stein insisted that the group travel first class and stay at the best hotels to combat the effects of jet lag and humidity. The players were given time off to swim and play golf, but it was certainly no holiday. The manager also drew up a demanding programme of games against Tottenham Hotspur, Bayern Munich, Bologna and Atlas of Mexico, in addition to practice matches against local sides. Celtic played eleven matches in all and emerged undefeated, winning eight of them, including beating Spurs twice.

It was during these five weeks that much of the planning for the following season was conceived and perfected. Stein gathered information on his players and experimented with various formations. One of the key outcomes was his decision to move Auld into the middle of the park to play alongside Bobby Murdoch, a pairing who would be vital to the team's success in the forthcoming European Cup campaign. Stein also encouraged his full-backs to push forward in preparation for facing tightly packed European defences.

But it was off the pitch that most improvement happened. The squad came together and began to develop the belief that they were unbeatable. It was self-confidence bordering on cockiness, and Jinky, for all that he displayed shyness in the company of relative strangers, responded better than most. Nowadays we would call it an exercise in bonding. Sean Fallon said: 'The club had started to look as if it was going places but we needed someone to motivate the players and Jock was that person. We used the 1966 American Tour to mould the team and judge how to get the maximum out of each player. We also worked on set pieces and laid the groundwork for the success that followed.'

Captain Billy McNeill agreed that the tour played a significant part in the team's subsequent successes. He pointed out that prior to Stein's arrival Celtic had lacked a leader. 'We had a team full of talented young players but no real leadership,' he said. 'Big Jock provided that.'

But while McNeill conceded that Stein had been the most influential figure, he pointed out that Celtic could not have aspired to the heights they did had they not possessed the talents of such as Jinky: 'Jimmy needed a good team to play in and we were a good side. Equally we needed that little bit of individual talent and flair and Jimmy had that in abundance. Jimmy had this exceptional talent. His greatest asset was his ability to run at people and take defenders on. He could eliminate defenders quite easily. It still amazes me just how talented he was, the way he took people on.'

Bobby Lennox concurred. 'It was on the American tour when we were away together for five weeks that we all became really close. We played eleven games and were unbeaten, winning eight of them. Jock had a big influence over all of us, but probably more so on Jimmy because the Big Man would sort you out if you needed sorting out, which, in Jimmy's case was not as often as people tended to think. Jimmy was a good professional.'

Lennox, who remembered Jinky as a very generous man, added: 'He was great and gifted but he worked on his gifts and got better and better. He also had great fitness. He loved training.'

Most of the surviving Lisbon Lions are in agreement that the seeds of their future success were sown in that summer of 1966. They could sense a growing *esprit de corps*. Stein knew instantly what was best for his players and did his utmost to ensure that they toed the line.

Jinky told the author in 1998: 'Junk food was banned. With Big Jock constantly watching what we did, chips were out when he was supervising mealtimes. Things like puddings and ice cream weren't allowed. Jock would let us have a starter and a main course but no sweet. But when Jock wasn't watching we would go through the card and eat what we fancied.

'Personally, I never worried about my diet and I don't think it did me any harm. My pre-match meal was steak and toast while most other guys had beans on toast, or eggs, or a piece of chicken, nothing too heavy. But when I was at home I ate what I liked, including chips, which I love. I also ate eggs in all forms and I don't recall them making me ill, or having been blown off course as a result of eating beans.

'But it was great to get away with Scotland out of Big Jock's road because there were no restrictions at mealtimes. Don't get me wrong. Times have changed and it has been proved that a more balanced diet is beneficial for health. But our diet didn't seem to do us any harm, considering Celtic managed to win the European Cup.'

Stein may have won most arguments with his players, but his plea to Jinky to postpone his wedding for a week fell on deaf ears. Jinky was scheduled to return to Scotland before the end of the American tour to marry Agnes Docherty, the girl he had met at Viewpark Youth Club and fallen in love with at the age of seventeen.

On the eve of Jinky's departure from Toronto, Stein tried hard to persuade him to stay. Injuries had been piling up and Celtic still had two games to play. Jinky refused, but before very long he would wonder if Stein had had a premonition of sorts, given what happened next day when he suffered the mid-air ordeal that was to leave him with a permanent fear of flying.

9

The Untouchables

Celtic sent shock waves through Scottish football before they had even set out on the first of their fifty-nine domestic and European fixtures in the greatest season in the club's history.

Manchester United, boasting the talents of England World Cup heroes Bobby Charlton and Nobby Stiles, Irish genius George Best, and Scotland stars Denis Law and Pat Crerand, who had left Celtic in 1963 to seek pastures new at Old Trafford, were swept aside almost with contempt in a pre-season friendly. The 4–1 scoreline at Celtic Park by all accounts flattered the team that was to be crowned English champions eight months later. For once, Best was completely upstaged by another world-class winger by the name of Jimmy Johnstone. Not for the first time, and certainly not for the last, Jinky was in his element performing on the big stage in the company of international stars.

Rangers were similarly dealt with in the Glasgow Cup, trounced 4–0 at Ibrox, where Billy McNeill scored the opening goal and Bobby Lennox claimed a hat-trick. The victory represented revenge for Celtic's Scottish Cup final defeat the previous April when they had completely outplayed Rangers yet lost to a Kai Johansen goal.

By the time Celtic played the first of thirty-four league games, against Clyde at Shawfield, on 10 September 1966, they had scored a further twenty-three goals – thirteen of them from Joe McBride – for the loss of only six in their League Cup qualifying section, recording double wins over Hearts, Clyde – hit for six at Celtic Park – and St Mirren, thrashed 8–2, also at home. Clyde, who were to finish third in the championship, fared little better in the league encounter, losing 3–0. Four days later Dunfermline were brushed aside in the League Cup quarter-final first leg, eventually losing the tie 9–4 on aggregate.

It was a wonderful time to be a Celtic fan, and the conviction that Celtic were capable of winning the 'treble' grew when Rangers suffered their second Old Firm defeat in the space of a month, by two goals to nil at Celtic Park, where Bertie Auld and Bobby Murdoch struck in the first four minutes of a one-sided match.

Following a 2–1 victory over Dundee at Dens Park, Celtic again went on the rampage when they entertained St Johnstone on 1 October. Jinky scored the second of sixteen goals in fifty appearances that season when he gave Celtic an eleventh-minute lead before also claiming a second and Celtic's third in a resounding 6–1 win. Jinky had got off the mark the previous month when scoring Celtic's fifth goal in a 6–3 League Cup quarter-final first-leg rout of Dunfermline.

One week later a highly talented Hibs side, containing several internationals, was beaten 5–3 at Easter Road, and even at the early stage in the season Pat Stanton, the Hibs captain, could sense that Celtic were building towards something special. 'We had some outstanding players ourselves,' he remembered, 'guys like Arthur Duncan, Jimmy O'Rourke, Peter Cormack, Colin Stein and Allan McGraw, but despite playing well that day we couldn't tie wee Jimmy down. He was everywhere, and if my memory serves me correctly he had a hand in at least a couple of Joe McBride's four goals.

'That Celtic team was outstanding, but Jimmy was exceptional – supremely talented, fast, tricky and brave. He was a tough little guy who never shied away from a challenge and very rarely moaned to referees when he was the victim of a particularly heavy challenge, which was often.'

Players were much less prone to 'diving' than they are today. When they went down and stayed down it usually indicated a genuine injury. But there was generally less fuss made when a player sustained an injury that finished his season, or even one that threatened his career, because the player's value and wages were very much lower. That said, Jinky's value to Celtic could not be overstated.

By the time Celtic faced Rangers in the League Cup final at Hampden, on 29 October, having taken out Airdrie in the semi-final twelve days earlier, they had extended their advantage over second-placed Kilmarnock to three points. A 3–0 home win over Airdrie was followed by a 5–1 defeat of Ayr United, also at Celtic Park, when Jinky claimed another couple.

Celtic won their first trophy of the season, thanks to a first-half goal by Lennox. In truth, fortune favoured the victors, for Rangers played well enough to deserve a second bite at the cherry, but despite outplaying Celtic for much of the match, they could not fashion scoring chances.

A week later Celtic dropped their first league point of the season. They were held 1–1 at home by St Mirren after an emphatic 7–3 victory in the previous fixture against Stirling Albion, where Jinky's name again figures on the score sheet. But three straight wins, against Falkirk, Dunfermline and Hearts, quickly repaired any damage done by the team from Paisley.

Celtic's 5–4 win at East End Park, on 19 November, proved to be the most thrilling league game of the entire season. Celtic, inspired by Jinky's mazy runs as he twisted and turned past the flailing feet of desperate defenders, three times came from two goals down to snatch a dramatic last-gasp victory when Joe McBride slotted home an eighty-ninth-minute penalty. Jinky claimed his sixth goal of the season when he notched the second.

Alex Totten could still recall the encounter in clear detail. The Dunfermline left back on that day, Totten, who is now commercial director of Falkirk Football Club, faced the thankless task of playing in direct opposition to Jinky.

'It was one of the best games I was ever involved in,' Totten remembered. 'There was a crowd of nearly 25,000 and they witnessed a marvellous spectacle, one full of great football and non-stop excitement. Jinky was everywhere orchestrating moves.'

Dunfermline led 2–0 after thirty-three minutes with goals by Hugh Robertson and Pat Delaney. Bobby Murdoch pulled one back for the visitors one minute after Delaney had struck, but Bert Paton quickly restored Dunfermline's two-goal advantage. Now enter Jinky, two minutes from the interval, when his clever run and shot brought a second Celtic goal.

When Alex Ferguson made it 4–2 three minutes after the restart the game seem lost, but the massive self-belief that Stein had instilled in his players shone through when first Bertie Auld and then McBride pounced to level the match at 4–4.

Had it finished all-square Celtic would have had no grounds for complaint, but Dunfermline lost to virtually the last kick of the game after Roy Barry had pushed a shot from Murdoch over the crossbar. The referee, Tom 'Tiny' Wharton, did not spot Barry handling the ball and awarded a free kick. Then he changed his mind after consulting a linesman and pointed to the penalty spot instead. McBride's nerve held and his eighty-ninth-minute goal proved decisive in the championship.

The defeat was a sickener for the Dunfermline players, for they had been promised a £100-a-man bonus if they beat Celtic – the equivalent of three weeks' wages. It came as little consolation for Totten, who revealed that Jinky had a habit of chatting away to opponents during a game, when Stein remarked that he had played well in spite of facing an opponent at the top of his form.

According to McBride it was his best-ever game for Celtic and the most exciting of his career. The match had superb finishing, excitement, very skilful football – and Jinky, of course.

Earlier, Celtic had begun their triumphal European Cup run with a comfortable five-goal aggregate win against FC Zurich and had also added the Glasgow Cup to their trophy haul when beating Partick Thistle 4–0. But while Celtic had created an aura of invincibility they were not infallible, as was highlighted when they could only draw with Kilmarnock and Aberdeen before losing 3–2 to Dundee United at Tannadice on the last day of the year.

By then Celtic had advanced to the quarter-finals of the European Cup on the back of 3–1 wins, home and away, against Nantes when Jinky added to his goals tally in the success at Celtic Park.

The signing of striker Willie Wallace from Hearts was also highly significant. Nicknamed 'Wispy' by his new team-mates because he was so quietly spoken, Wallace contributed twenty-one goals in thirty appearances in his first season. His arrival coincided with the loss of Joe McBride just before Christmas. McBride, whose Celtic career was curtailed by a knee in jury, had scored thirty-five goals when he was forced to undergo surgery on his damaged cartilage.

The late cancellation on 3 January 1967 of the traditional New Year Old Firm encounter because of frost proved a bigger blow to Rangers, given that Celtic had won only two of their previous five games. It turned out to be Celtic's rockiest spell of the season and Rangers viewed the postponement as a missed opportunity to apply further pressure to their bitter rivals. Their sense of frustration redoubled when Celtic set off on a six-game winning run, in a rich vein of form enhanced by Jinky at his scorching best. He scored in four of these games, including two against St Johnstone in a 4–0 win at Muirton Park on 14 January. Significantly, that was also the day when the Lisbon Lions appeared together for the first time as a unit.

There was no containing Jinky, and his manager drew the obvious conclusion. The late Bobby Murdoch recalled one pre-match tactics talk when Jinky, concerned that he had been given no specific instructions, asked Stein: 'What about me, boss?' Big Jock turned, patted Jinky on the cheek, and replied: 'You? You just do whatever the f— you want.'

It was little wonder that Bertie Auld maintained that you could see the fear in the eyes of opponents when Jinky was on song. But life rarely ran smoothly for Jinky for long. Two outstanding performances against Vojvodina in the European Cup quarter-final were immediately followed by another fall from grace.

Having succeeded in keeping his fiery temper in check for the best part of two years, Jinky once again erupted on 11 March, in a Scottish Cup third-round tie against the amateurs of Queen's Park at Celtic Park. A defender, keen to make a name for himself, stuck to Jinky like glue, suppressing his skills by any means he could manage. Eventually, Jinky could take no more. After having the feet whipped from him for the umpteenth time, he sprang back up and in a moment of blind fury made as if to head-butt his tormentor. The referee failed to spot the incident, but Jock Stein did and Jinky was hit with a seven-day suspension.

Celtic won, 5–3, but his club ban caused Jinky to miss the next match, a home win over Dunfermline by the odd goal in five as Rangers hovered menacingly in the background just two points off the pace. A surprise draw at lowly Stirling the previous month had offered a chink of light for the Ibrox side, who were themselves chasing European glory in the Cup Winners' Cup.

Increasingly, it appeared that the rearranged Old Firm match, scheduled for 6 May, would turn into a title decider, and when Celtic could only draw at home with Aberdeen on 19 April, following wins over Falkirk, Hearts, Partick Thistle and Motherwell, the tension rose. But Celtic maintained the upper hand when they faced Dundee United at Celtic Park on Wednesday 3 May.

By then the second part of the domestic treble had been secured. Celtic, who had already seen off Arbroath, Elgin City and Queen's Park, booked their place in the Scottish Cup final by beating Clyde, 2–0. Celtic had been held to a goalless draw in the first match although they had a strong claim for a penalty kick turned down four minutes from the end when a shot by Jinky appeared to be elbowed away by defender Davie Soutar.

Celtic's opponents at Hampden on 29 April were Aberdeen and the sides lined up: Celtic: Simpson; Craig, Gemmell; Murdoch, McNeill, Clark; Johnstone, Wallace, Chalmers, Auld and Lennox. Aberdeen: Clark; Whyte, Shewan; Munro, McMillan, Petersen; Wilson, Smith, Storrie, Melrose and Johnston.

Jinky was handed a free role by Stein, who switched him from the right wing to inside forward to act as a double spearhead with Wallace. It proved to be an inspired move. Ally Shewan, the

Aberdeen left back, had been primed to try and contain Jinky, and Stein's tactical switch caused havoc in the opposition ranks. Shewan was left in two minds whether to follow Jinky or to switch his attention to Stevie Chalmers, who had been instructed to play wide on the right. Celtic took full advantage of the Dons' confusion, and with Jinky revelling in the freedom he was afforded Celtic were never seriously threatened.

Jinky later said: 'Big Jock would never hesitate to stick me in the middle of the attack, or switch me over to the left, if he thought it would produce goals. He wasn't so much a great tactician as a superb motivator with the remarkable gift of making you feel like the best player in the world.'

Wallace scored both Celtic goals, the first after forty-two minutes and the second four minutes into the second half when Jinky – performing like the best in the world – finished off a clever run on the right and squared the ball to his unmarked team-mate.

With the League and Scottish Cups in their possession, Celtic were expected to wrap up the championship four days after their Hampden triumph, but a surprise 3–2 defeat at the hands of Dundee United – the only team to beat them twice that season – renewed Rangers' hopes of preventing Celtic from completing a clean sweep. Celtic had a one-point lead and a superior goal difference. They also had a match in hand, against Kilmarnock at Celtic Park. But Rangers were entitled to feel that if they could inflict a defeat on their rivals they might yet snatch the title, given that Celtic were coming under mounting pressure with the European Cup final only nineteen days away.

Celtic's 3–1 aggregate victory over Dukla Prague had made them the first British club to reach the final of Europe's premier tournament. Jinky scored the opener at Celtic Park, but his team was forced to adopt an ultra-defensive stance in the return to hang on for a goalless draw in Czechoslovakia just four days before facing Aberdeen and were undoubtedly feeling the strain of such a taxing schedule of big games.

But Rangers' hopes of bringing Celtic down at the penultimate fence were dashed at a rain-sodden Ibrox by the smallest man on the pitch. Jinky revelled in the difficult conditions and scored both Celtic goals in a 2–2 draw. As a consequence of drawing the game, the match against Kilmarnock at Celtic Park on 15 May was of no great significance, other than enabling Stein to flummox Inter Milan's spies by playing Billy McNeill at inside right instead of in his customary role at the heart of the defence. Celtic still managed to win, though, by 2–0, to put the seal on a magnificent championship campaign.

The final piece of the jigsaw fell into place in Lisbon ten days later when Celtic contrived to produce a performance worthy of winning the European Cup in any season and achieved the greatest result in the history of Scottish football by beating Inter Milan 2–1.

Remarkably, considering the demands made on them, Celtic fielded a hard core of just fifteen players. Five others made a total of six appearances between them. Two of the Lisbon Lions, Tommy Gemmell and John Clark, played in all fifty-nine competitive games, of which forty-eight were won and eight drawn. Only Dundee United, twice, and Vojvodina managed to inflict defeat on the most successful team in Celtic's history, one which averaged more than three goals a game – 201 in all in a total of sixty-five matches, including Glasgow Cup ties and friendlies.

But Jinky always insisted that there was no secret formula behind the Lions' success. 'Big Jock held the reins like a champion jockey,' he said. 'Football was in the players' veins and he made it flow. We approached every practice game like a cup final. We treated every team with respect and our attitude was always right. Jock wouldn't have it any other way. That helped us in Europe because they were just another series of games which had to be won.

'The atmosphere among the players was also exceptional. Consistency of choice worked perfectly. We were such a tight-knit bunch. Even for training games we had two regular sides. Sure, there were times when we were at each other's throats, but any disputes remained private within the confines of the dressing room. We never aired our differences publicly. We also socialised as a team and we knew how to have a laugh. That was crucial.'

Stein's habit of taking is players to Seamill, on the Ayrshire coast, to prepare for big games was a key factor in bringing his players closer together and building team spirit. Bobby Lennox, who hails from nearby Saltcoats, recalled that the trips to Seamill were crucial in the 'bonding' process. They were also occasions for Lennox and Jinky to get up to all sorts of mischief.

'We were the youngest in the squad and sometimes we behaved like kids,' Lennox admitted. 'We did daft things like sneaking into the hotel restaurant prior to meals and tampering with the cruet sets, so when the other lads used them the tops came off and they ended up with their food covered in salt and pepper.'

Lennox, an accomplished golfer after taking the game up later in life, also confessed to collaborating with Jinky to cause havoc when their team-mates took to the links. 'Jimmy and I weren't golfers at that time and we would suddenly start talking loudly when the others lads were about to play a shot or hide their balls in bushes. Sometimes we even hid in a bunker and popped up just when someone was about to putt.'

The other Lions largely tolerated the antics of the mischievous pair, but they drew the line at allowing them to disrupt their regular card schools. 'They would do their best to keep the venue secret, but we usually managed to find out which player's room they had gone to and then drove the rest of them mad by interrupting their game,' said Lennox.

Stein also acted as a father figure, according to Jinky. For the player, it was essential that he could go to the manager if he had a problem. Jinky admitted: 'I had a few in my time and Big Jock helped me out when I had difficulties that were unconnected with football.'

For all that he spent much of his time living in the lap of luxury, staying at top hotels and enjoying the finest cuisine, Jinky was happiest among his own folk in his native Viewpark. He also developed a passion for hunting and shooting. Jinky found roaming the hills and woods of Lanarkshire the perfect antidote to the inevitable stress associated with playing football at the highest level.

A close friend, Alex Goldie, taught Jinky how to bag a steady supply of rabbits and ducks. But Jinky's talent for landing in hot water inevitably brought him into conflict with the law when the police twice charged him with poaching. He was convicted on both occasions after he and Goldie were caught illegally hunting game on the nearby estate belonging to the late Sir Alec Douglas-Home, the former Conservative Prime Minister. Jinky admitted to several other narrow escapes.

10

Olé, Olé

Real Madrid rolled out the red carpet for Alfredo di Stefano a fortnight after Celtic's Lisbon triumph, but it was Jimmy Johnstone who performed with a majesty entitling him to walk down it.

It may be stretching a point to suggest that Jinky upstaged the Great Man, but 120,000 Spaniards were moved to chant, 'Olé, Olé' every time Jinky took control of the ball and began yet another of his serpentine runs. The Bernabeu Stadium has rarely witnessed a more magical performance than the one that Jinky conjured up.

As champions of Europe, Celtic had been invited to provide the opposition for di Stefano's testimonial match on 7 June 1967. It was an offer the club simply could not refuse, despite having played sixty-four games in the space of ten months. The sixty-fifth turned out to be arguably the finest of Jinky's career.

The Bernabeu was filled to capacity, but those who came to pay homage to the man nicknamed 'The White Arrow' were denied the chance to see the Lisbon Lions in all their glory. Jock Stein replaced goalkeeper Ronnie Simpson with his understudy, John Fallon. Stein reasoned that if Celtic lost no one would be able to claim that Real had beaten the European champions.

The manager need not have worried. Celtic beat their illustrious rivals 1–0, courtesy of a goal by Bobby Lennox – Celtic's 201st of the season in all competitions and challenge matches – scored midway through the second half. But while it was Lennox who earned the plaudits for sealing a famous victory, it was Jinky who was the architect of Celtic's triumph. Almost inevitably, the goal was set up by Jinky when he split the defence and slipped an angled pass for Lennox to run on to. When di Stefano took his final bow after a quarter of an hour, the way was clear for Jinky to grab centre stage, and he did so, with both feet!

Eventually, the Real defenders, who had no answer when Jinky ran at them, were reluctant to commit to challenging him, for fear of being made to look stupid as he baffled and bemused them all over the pitch. Jinky, socks round his ankles, was virtually unstoppable. His opponents swapped desperate glances, as if to seek guidance on coping with the menace in their midst. The few occasions when Jinky's threat was nullified came about when defenders brought him down with heavy challenges, happy to concede a free kick in the process.

The match may have been tagged a 'friendly', but it was played in a fiercely competitive spirit, instanced by the fact that midfielder Bertie Auld was ordered off, along with Amancio, for trading punches. Auld, who revealed that the Celtic players were paid just £100 each, effectively had a ringside seat following his dismissal in the first ten minutes of the match, and he has never regretted landing that right hook, for it gave him the chance to watch a master at work.

'I had a fabulous view of what I consider to be Jinky's finest performance for Celtic,' said Auld. 'That evening Jinky became an all-round player. He suddenly grew in stature. He was more than just a trickster, the way he drew opponents to him and hit twenty- and thirty-yard passes.

'Di Stefano's testimonial led to Jinky becoming the complete footballer and by the latter stages of his career he had a part of everything in his game. In addition to combining bravery with skill, he also became stronger. He was like a light-middleweight boxer in build and he was very clever; very aware. He had the capacity to absorb knowledge quickly and the pace and vision to exploit situations.

'Jinky could go past people or stop and put his foot on the ball before hitting it into space. He was also a prolific goalscorer and it was quite remarkable how many of these goals came from headers, given his height.'

It was a measure of the impression Jinky made on di Stefano that the Argentine legend sought him out at the post-match banquet and asked him to pose for a souvenir photograph alongside Puskas, Gento and Santamaria, winners of half a dozen European Cup medals each. It was confirmation that di Stefano recognised Jinky as being in the same class as his Real Madrid team-mates.

Seven years previously, Jinky had stood as a fifteen-year-old on the Hampden Park terraces, on an April evening in 1960, marvelling at the skills of perhaps the greatest club side there has ever been. The occasion was the European Cup final when Real, with di Stefano, Puskas, Gento and Santamaria in their line-up, completely destroyed a very competent Eintracht Frankfurt side, 7–3. Puskas scored four of the Real goals, di Stefano the other three.

Jinky was later to say: 'The match remained the biggest single influence on my career. It was like a fantasy staged in heaven. I had never seen football like it, nor would I ever again. I'll recite the names of that Madrid forward line till the day I die.' He could not have imagined then that one day he would himself grace one of the great football stages and earn glowing accolades from the men who had thrilled him and left such a lasting impression.

Billy McNeill, the Celtic captain, recalled in a newspaper article: 'Our win in the Bernabeu summed Jimmy up. We had just won the European Cup, but still he had the hunger to play his greatest game on one of THE stages. That night Jinky did everything and what's often forgotten is he wasn't a wee fly you could swat away. He was such a powerful little player and Real discovered that.'

Jinky, the consummate showman, could not recall having produced a more complete display of trickery and skill, or a game when he had not put a foot wrong, or, indeed, one he had enjoyed more. Significantly, he kept a video recording of the match, describing it as his all-time favourite archive.

Yet Jinky's preparation had been far from perfect. His wife

Agnes, who had missed the European Cup final because she was in labour with the couple's first child, Marie, was invited to fly to the Spanish capital as a guest of Celtic to make up for her disappointment. But a severe thunderstorm broke just before her plane was due to land, and Jinky was so concerned at the thought of his wife in the air in such atrocious conditions that he became noticeably distressed. But his fears proved unfounded. Agnes arrived safely, and it may have been his sense of relief that contributed to an emotional Jinky playing the game of his life.

But off the field, Jinky refused to take any unnecessary risks. The following day he and Agnes set off for a fortnight's holiday in Benidorm – by taxi! The 250-mile journey took more than a day to complete, but anything was preferable to stepping aboard an airliner, if such an ordeal could be avoided.

We will probably never know if Real Madrid tabled an offer for Jinky, but several of his team-mates are convinced that Madrid did approach Celtic in an effort to introduce fresh young blood to their aging team, and that Jock Stein somehow managed to suppress details of the bid.

Far from being out of place in the company of such soccer luminaries as di Stefano, Puskas and Gento, Jinky would have slotted in perfectly. Bobby Lennox said: 'I have no doubt whatsoever that Real came in for Jimmy. They must have done after that performance. Over the years others must also have tried to persuade Celtic to part with him. But Jimmy only ever wanted to play for Celtic. We were a very good side ourselves and Jimmy was happy with the company of his team-mates and being part of a winning team.'

Bertie Auld was in complete agreement, but he added: 'It would not have mattered what sort of money Real Madrid or any other club had offered to buy Jinky. He would never have agreed to a move.'

AC Milan certainly did make a move to sign Jinky. His performance against their city rivals, Inter, encouraged Milan to offer Celtic £100,000 for Jinky's services, a bid that was dismissed out of hand by his employers. Jock Stein allegedly replied: '£100,000? That's a lot of cash for just one game!'

While the match against Real Madrid was memorable for all the right reasons, the next time Celtic faced Latin opposition, in the form of Racing Club of Argentina, four months later, in the so-called World Club Championship, the atmosphere was hostile.

Ten of the Lisbon Lions were in the line-up. The omission was Stevie Chalmers, whose place was taken by John Hughes. Celtic: Simpson; Craig, Gemmell; Murdoch, McNeill, Clark; Johnstone, Lennox, Wallace, Auld and Hughes.

Lisbon had been a triumph. South America turned out to be a disaster as the cynical Argentines shamed football in a way that made the national team's disgraceful behaviour in the World Cup the previous year seem tame by comparison. Celtic won the first leg, at Hampden Park, in front of 90,000 spectators, on 18 October 1967. Billy McNeill's sixty-ninth-minute header, when he rose above the defence in spite of the Racing defenders' best efforts to impede him, gave Celtic a slender advantage for the return in Buenos Aires a fortnight later.

But Racing's blatant disregard of the Spanish referee and their brutal tackling and cynical approach did not augur well. Jinky had been a prime target. No Celtic player suffered more. Defenders simply ran into him and obstructed him and he was kicked, punched and spat on by ruthless opponents hell-bent on intimidation.

'South American internationals are normally fantastic players, but their club players are animals,' he recalled in an interview with the *Scottish Sun* newspaper.

Given the level of cynicism displayed by their players in Glasgow it came as no surprise when Racing stooped to new depths of thuggery in the Argentine capital on 1 November. The 120,000 fans were caged behind wire fences but still somehow managed to inflict an act of violence before kick-off. Goalkeeper Ronnie Simpson was struck on the back of the head by a missile and was left bleeding from a gash so nasty that John Fallon had to replace him in goal. There were two other changes from the first leg, Chalmers and Willie O'Neill replacing Auld and Hughes.

Jinky remembered: 'I spent all three games having lumps kicked out of me. In the first game I was spat on, stamped on, and had players run their studs down my legs, but we made the mistake of thinking it would not get any worse in Argentina. How wrong we were.'

Jinky had made history by becoming the first player to be released, temporarily, from domestic suspension to play in the second leg following his dismissal against St Johnstone the previous month. But he later confessed that the SFA had done him no favours, given events in South America.

'We were frightened,' he admitted. 'We had thirty policemen with us the whole time. On the Sunday, we went to a Catholic church and they came with us. The only place they didn't go with us was the toilet.'

Celtic had flown into an atmosphere of hatred and violence and Jinky was quickly singled out for a grim warning. On the team's arrival at the Avellaneda Stadium, an official handed him a box containing the strip of the player who had literally marked him at Hampden. Perhaps, on reflection Jinky's cheeky act of nutmegging one of Racing's hit squad at Hampden had been a bad idea, even if it was his intention to show the opposition that he would not be intimidated by their tactics. But it was a sight to behold all the same.

Celtic were not helped either by the fact that tensions were running high all over the country. The Argentine nation as a whole had been deeply offended the previous year when Sir Alf Ramsey labelled the national team 'animals' in the wake of the brutal World Cup quarter-final at Wembley when the Argentine captain, Rattin, was sent off against England, and they were not in a mood of forgiveness. There was a ferment of anti-English feeling, and the locals were either unaware of the subtle differences between England and Scotland, or simply refused to acknowledge the distinction, choosing to ignore the facts on the basis that Celtic was a British team.

When the second game eventually kicked off, Celtic did their utmost to play football and even managed to take the lead midway through the first half when Jinky was rugby-tackled by the goalkeeper and Tommy Gemmell scored from the resultant penalty kick. But the writing was on the wall for the Scots when Jinky was denied a goal for no good reason. Racing, with the connivance of the Uruguayan referee, won 2–1, with goals by Carlos Raffo, who was offside, and Juan Carlos Cárdenas to square the tie, necessitating a third game to decide the destination of the World Club Championship.

Hindsight is a wonderful thing, and wise counsel would have advised the Celtic party to abandon their attempts to strike a blow for Europe. But while the chairman, Sir Bob Kelly, was in favour of returning home without further delay, the manager, Jock Stein, thought otherwise. Sean Fallon, Stein's assistant, recalled: 'When the third game was ordered the chairman wanted to come home straight away. But Jock wanted to play. He didn't want it to look as if Celtic would not fulfil their obligations as the European representatives. He didn't want to be accused of running away. It was the only time that Bob Kelly and Jock had a serious difference of opinion about the way the club should go about things.'

So Celtic crossed the River Plate to prepare for a 5 November date in Montevideo, capital of Uruguay – and walked straight into a riot disguised, though clumsily, as a football match.

The bizarre sight of photographers racing on to the pitch in Buenos Aires and brushing Celtic players aside to photograph the celebrations when Racing scored was an almost laughable detail compared to what Celtic had coming in part three of an Argentinian ordeal.

Celtic had been forced to stay at a third-rate hotel in Buenos Aires. Their accommodation in Uruguay was little better. Situated in a square in the centre of the city, the hotel became a target for thousands of Racing fans who had made the short trip across the River Plate, and they kept the players awake singing and chanting at two in morning.

Having stuck with their fateful decision to play a deciding match, Celtic lined up: Fallon; Craig, Gemmell; Murdoch, McNeill, Clark; Johnstone, Lennox, Wallace, Auld and Hughes.

While the Uruguayans in the Centenario Stadium were happy to side with Celtic against their traditional bitter rivals from Argentina, the presence of an estimated 15,000 Racing fans was sufficient to create another hostile atmosphere. All hell broke loose in a match that shamed football. Statistics from the brutal and bloody encounter state that six players – four Celtic and two Racing – were ordered off and that baton-wielding police were sent in to restore order on the pitch. But, for all that some Celtic players lost the plot, the facts became garbled by the selective vision of certain journalists – most of them English – who chose to overlook the level of outright intimidation that the European champions were subjected to.

In the event, only three Celtic players took the walk of shame. The fourth to be sent packing, Bertie Auld simply refused to go, telling the referee, Rodolfo Perez Osorio, of Paraguay, who no longer had an atom of control, to get lost. Gemmell too should have been consigned to an early bath, for blatantly kicking a Racing player up the backside, but Big Tam's indiscretion went unnoticed by the overwhelmed official.

From the outset, the Racing players had only one thought in mind – stop Celtic, and Jimmy Johnstone in particular, from settling into any sort of rhythm.

The match was barely fifteen minutes old when Jinky was sent crashing to the ground by Alfio Basile. It was a brutal challenge, but Basile escaped censure by Osorio. So too did his team-mate, goalkeeper Augustin Cejas, when he walked almost the entire length of the pitch to take a kick at Jinky as he lay on the ground receiving treatment. But one keen-eyed policeman spotted the incident and promptly whacked Cejas with his baton.

The grotesque nature of the match was graphically illustrated by Bobby Lennox's ordering off in the first half for an offence that no one saw because it never happened.

Juan Carlos Rulli, the instigator of much of the trouble in all three games, committed conspicuous fouls on several Celtic players, who surrounded the referee to protest. Lennox was not among them. An innocent bystander, he was standing some yards away from the incident when the harassed referee pointed to him and gave him his marching orders.

Jinky was next to go, early in the second half. Already black and blue from head to foot, he lashed out at a defender who had attempted to pull him down and was sent to join Lennox on the sidelines, presumably for violent conduct.

Jinky's recollection of events was somewhat different. 'I was sent off for raising my hand, for retaliation. But there is a limit to what you can take, and the referee from Paraguay was not protecting us. My hair was soaked in spittle because their players kept spitting on me all the time.

'As I was running upfield to collect a short pass from Bertie Auld I saw the defender, Martin, coming at me and I had no doubt about his intentions. He was going to scythe the legs from me. So I slipped the ball quickly to Bertie and left Martin flat-footed. But as I made to run past him he grabbed the front of my jersey and attempted to pull me down. Instinctively, I tried to shake myself free and in doing so I lightly touched his forehead.

'The Racing trainer added to the circus-like performance by putting a plaster on Martin's "head wound". We were awarded the free kick, but the next thing I knew the referee was signalling that he was ordering me off. I stood in disbelief for a second but quickly realised that there was no point arguing against the decision. The referee seemed to be looking for an excuse since I was regarded as one of the main dangers to Racing's ambitions. Even Argentine officials came up to me afterwards and apologised.'

Lennox and Jinky were the victims of squalid refereeing. But when John Hughes became the third Celtic player to be dismissed, 'Yogi' had no excuse. His action in blatantly punching goalkeeper Cejas in the stomach could have only one outcome.

Racing won the 'game' with a goal from Cárdenas ten minutes after the restart. But, in truth, the result was a near irrelevance, given the mayhem that dogged the deciding match. Regrettably, the second battle of the River Plate attracted almost as many newspaper headlines as the first. That had been fought nearly twenty-eight years earlier when the pride of the German navy, the pocket battleship *Graf Spee* was scuttled by its captain after being left trapped in the middle of the river off Montevideo.

The *Graf Spee* had been hounded by a trio of British warships in a day-long battle. Celtic were hounded by cynical Argentines. But whereas the captain of the *Graf Spee*, Hans Lansdorf, behaved with honour before committing suicide no honour belonged to those who were responsible for turning a football match into a war.

The Celtic players were each fined £250 by the club for their part in the undignified brawl, but, in reality, Celtic simply withheld the bonus payment promised prior to the ill-fated trip to South America. Hughes, who had deserved to be sent off, and Auld, who simply refused to obey the referee's instruction, were fined an additional £50 each by the SFA, while Jinky was severely censured by the Association.

Jinky and his team-mates were partially vindicated some years later when Cejas revealed in an interview with *Soccer Monthly* that the Racing players were under instruction to take whatever measures they deemed necessary to stop Celtic from winning by provoking their rivals beyond endurance.

'I remember the play-off in Montevideo,' Cejas recalled. 'I was given a "specific" role. I didn't have to hit anybody, just be goal-keeper. But suddenly, Basile really hit the red-headed Johnstone with a hell of a foul, one of the worst I have ever seen, and the referee sent him off. I started walking casually out of my goal with my hands behind my back, and made my way slowly towards Johnstone. He was still on the ground when I arrived, so I kicked him as hard as I could for getting my team-mate sent off.'

What an admission! But it came as no surprise to Jinky. 'They knew all the dirty tricks in the book,' he recalled. 'If they kicked you they came over and made out as if they were apologising. They would pat you on the head, as if to say sorry, but they were really pulling your hair or administering a sly slap. They were really callous and cynical. I was lucky to be alive after playing three games against these guys.'

The tragedy, from a sporting perspective, and the fact that Celtic's dream of being crowned World Champions turned into a nightmare, did not come about because they failed to reproduce the stunning football they had displayed on the European stage. They lost, and their reputations suffered, because they encountered a bunch of footballing thugs who were prepared to sink to even greater depths than the *Graf Spee*.

11

Dominance

Jinky was on top of the world when the 1967–68 season kicked off. The Racing Club debacle was still to come. Celtic were European champions and the wee winger was buzzing. His winning goal, scored against Dundee United in the ninetieth minute in Celtic's opening match of the season – a League Cup tie – simply served to underline that everything in the garden was rosy. Or at least so it seemed. But, true to form, just when it seemed that life was running smoothly for Celtic's incident-prone number seven, Jinky self-destructed once again.

When Celtic prepared to face St Johnstone in a home game on 23 September, they had already qualified for the knock-out stages of the League Cup. But their defence of the European Cup was looking decidedly shaky following a 2–1 home defeat by Dinamo Kiev three days earlier. Perhaps it was the disappointment of losing to the Russians, complicated by worries about the new home he had bought and was in the process of renovating, that led to Jinky imploding. Whatever the reasons, or reasons, an act of retaliation against St Johnstone's Kenny Aird cost him dear.

Aird, frustrated at being made to look silly yet again as Jinky attempted to dribble round him for the umpteenth time, whipped the legs from under his opponent. Most times Jinky would simply have picked himself up and got on with the game, but on this occasion he reacted with fury and punched Aird full in the face. Aware that his sudden flash of temper could have only one outcome, Jinky turned at once and set off on the lonely walk to the dressing room.

Jock Stein was furious that his team had been reduced to ten men as a result of one player's indiscipline, even though Bobby Murdoch's equaliser earned Celtic a point, but the manager's reaction was nothing to the SFA's. When Jinky appeared before the Association's disciplinary committee he was hit with a twenty-one-day suspension. The timing of the ban had the effect of ruling him out of the League Cup final the following month.

The loss of wages and the disgrace of his third ordering off were bad enough, but it was missing out on the chance to collect another winner's medal when Celtic beat Dundee 5–3 at Hampden that hit Jinky hardest. What made exclusion all the more galling was that Jinky had scored twice in a 6–2 quarter-final win over Ayr United, and again when Morton were trounced 7–1 in the semi-final. In fact he scored five goals in total to set Celtic up for the first part of a domestic double.

Celtic's European Cup campaign was already over by the time they secured their first honour of the season. A 1–1 draw in Kiev, after the hosts had snatched an equalising goal in the final minute, ended one of the shortest European reigns on record. One month later the World Club Championship showdown with Racing Club of Argentina added to Celtic's and Jinky's misery, which was compounded when they were beaten in the play-off in Uruguay and he was sent packing for the second time in the space of just six weeks.

With the League Cup back in the Celtic Park trophy room and the doors back into Europe slammed shut in their faces, the Celtic players focused their attention on retaining the championship. But by mid-February, Stein, stung by a Scottish Cup first-round exit at the hands of Dunfermline, was concerned enough to call a meeting of his players to try to impress upon them the need to achieve a greater level of consistency. They trailed league leaders Rangers by two points and, having fulfilled both fixtures against their closest rivals – a 1–0 defeat at Ibrox and a 2–2 draw at Celtic Park – Celtic were dependent on them slipping up.

So the timing of Jinky's return to form at the start of the following month could not have been better. Willie Wallace scored four goals against Kilmarnock in a 6–0 win on 2 March, but it was Jinky who stole the show. He treated Rugby Park as his stage and proceeded to dismantle the home defence, roaming at will and taking considerable satisfaction at witnessing Kilmarnock coach Walter McCrae's distress following the pair's earlier spat while on duty with the Scotland squad at Largs.

Jinky shone again when Celtic took another six goals off St Johnstone at Muirton Park three weeks later. This time Bobby Lennox scored four goals, but again Jinky, who claimed his side's fifth, was the principal architect of a victory that stoked up the pressure on Rangers. Five days later it was Dundee United's turn to suffer. Jinky scored the opening goal in thirteen minutes, when he twisted and jinked past several defenders before finishing off a mesmerising move. It was later claimed that at least one defender had shied away from challenging Jinky rather than risk committing himself and being subjected to further humiliation. United copped a five-goal thrashing.

Not for the first time, Jinky maintained his scoring sequence in Celtic's next game, a 2–0 win over Hearts at Tynecastle to raise his season's tally to ten goals. But it was Jinky's general play in the closing months of the season that proved decisive in taking Celtic past Rangers when their rivals hit a sudden slump in the run-in. Draws with Dundee United and Morton and a home defeat by Aberdeen on the last day of the season – Rangers' first in the league – saw Celtic crowned champions by just two points.

Jinky had further cause for celebration on 2 May 1968, when the second of his three children, Eileen, was born. The demands and responsibilities of parenthood may have had a calming influence on him for a time, According to those who knew him best, Jinky enjoyed the role of doting dad and was regularly seen changing nappies or pushing the pram. But the peace and tranquillity were not to last.

Yet many observers consider that the following season, 1968–69, was Jinky's most outstanding in terms of his standard of play. He maintained a remarkably high level of consistency in all competitions as Celtic clinched their second treble of league championship, Scottish Cup and League Cup and sixth league and cup double. The only disappointment lay in a quarter-final exit from the European Cup.

But, inevitably, it was not all plain sailing. Jinky's well-publicised clash with Stein, when he threw his jersey at him after being substituted against Dundee United in October, led to speculation that he was unhappy at Celtic Park and might seek a transfer. Certainly, Stein's very public condemnation of Jinky's behaviour and his decision to hit him with a seven-day club suspension, in addition to axing him for two matches, showed how sorely his patience was being tried. All the same, it seems unlikely that there was ever much real chance of Jinky's Celtic career being brought to a premature end.

But Jinky's mercurial nature meant that Stein could not rely on him as surely as he did on others, although the circumstances of the suspension that led to him missing the 1969 Scottish Cup final were open to question. Jinky was a victim of the SFA's system of punishing any player who amassed three cautions. On that occasion he was given a fourteen-day ban, one that cost him several hundred pounds and the chance to participate in one of the most one-sided Old Firm games of all time.

Jinky attempted to explain his temperament by pointing out that he came from a very nervous, highly strung family which had suffered a few quite serious nervous breakdowns. By his own account, he could never be fully at peace with himself. He had always to be doing something, even if it was only biting his nails.

The least thing could set him off, it seemed. The most trivial cause might trigger a reaction. Something most others would shrug off often became a major incident for concern for Jinky, and spark his inner tensions to erupt.

Perhaps it had something to do with being a redhead, for most associate red hair with a quick temper. He certainly seemed to be built for rapid, and often quite needless, responses, at least in his early career.

But while Jinky did strive to control his temper, it should be remembered that like most gifted ball players of his generation he was sorely tried by the crude challenges of defenders he outclassed and outwitted.

Jinky's height, or rather lack of it, also clearly played a part in determining his complex personality. It left him with a sizeable inferiority complex, bound up with a belief that he was ugly and unattractive to women. It was as if he always had something to prove to himself and others. He went as far as to seek professional medical help in an effort to curb his temper.

Billy McNeill admitted that Jinky was a complex personality but also stressed that he was without malice. 'Jimmy was intelligent,' said McNeill, 'but he had a short attention span and was always looking to be up to some sort of mischief. But for all that he was a wee rascal at times, he was never malicious. You could see when he wasn't entirely focused, and that led to him becoming bored, and that in turn would result in him getting up to nonsense of some sort.'

On one occasion Jinky was found hiding from Jock Stein behind a pile of coats in the cloakroom at Seamill Hydro after the manager had conducted a detailed search of the premises in an effort to establish the whereabouts of his winger – Jinky had sneaked off to join in some wedding festivities being held in the hotel's function suite. When he was eventually discovered, Jinky was giggling away merrily to himself.

For all that he was never completely at ease with life, Jinky enjoyed the trappings of success. By his mid-twenties he owned a plush bungalow and drove a top-of-the-range Jaguar. He even ventured into the pub trade in 1969 when he became mine host of the Met, a popular watering hole near Hamilton. The name of the pub was changed to the Double J, but the business eventually failed, largely because Jinky devoted too little of his time to the venture.

But while Jinky posed no sort of threat to the business world, he continued to have few equals on a football pitch, and nothing could overshadow his contribution to Celtic's success in season 1968–69. As well as scoring nine goals in forty-eight first-team starts and another two appearances as a substitute, Jinky's remarkable level of consistency enabled Celtic to maintain a powerful challenge on all fronts. One sports writer was moved to comment: 'Jimmy Johnstone is playing the best football of his career with such consistency that a powerful case can be made for suggesting that he is the most exciting player in the world right now.'

Certainly, Jinky's performance against Red Star Belgrade at Celtic Park on 13 November was regarded by several of his teammates as his finest ever. Spurred on by the promise from Stein that he would not have to travel to Yugoslavia for the European Cup second-round, second-leg match if Celtic won by four clear goals, Jinky shredded the Red Star defence, scoring two of the goals in the stunning 5–1 victory.

Celtic's European aspirations were blunted by AC Milan in the next round when the Italians had the foresight to assign West German World Cup star Karl-Heinz Schnellinger the onerous task of marking Jinky. Having been held at home, Milan snatched a 1–0 victory at Celtic Park when Schnellinger produced an outstanding performance to blunt Jinky's menace. Schnellinger was one of the few who succeeded in putting out the fire in Jinky's boots.

Although beaten twice by Rangers, Celtic finished five points clear of their rivals in the championship race to claim a fourth successive league title, with Dunfermline back in third place.

Alec Edwards, the former Dunfermline and Hibs winger, who Stein once famously claimed during his time as manager at East End Park was a more complete player than Jinky, still holds the view that Celtic would not have won so many trophies without Jinky. Edwards said: 'It was Jimmy who would come up with something special when the team required a spark of inspiration. He wasn't just a brilliant entertainer, he was also a match-winner. We had a good team at Dunfermline and were always capable of beating Celtic, but Jimmy frustrated us on a lot of occasions.'

Very few left backs got the better of Jinky, but Erich Schaedler did better than most. The Hibs defender could handle the threat posed by Jinky as most others could not. This may have been because Schaedler was smaller and stockier than the average defender and was also very quick. Jinky preferred playing against tall full-backs like Davie Provan of Rangers, who always found him a handful due to their size and the fact that they were always in danger of conceding a free kick when he ran at them. Sometimes when the big defenders tried to take the ball off Jinky, if they made the slightest contact he would go spinning and the challenge would be made to look worse than it really was.

Hibs could have done with Schaedler in their line-up when they faced Celtic in the League Cup final on 5 April 1969. The final had been put back six months due to a fire at Hampden Park, but it was Hibs, boasting several international players in their line-up, who were well and truly burned. The teams were: Celtic: Fallon; Craig, Gemmell; Murdoch, McNeill, Brogan; Johnstone, Wallace, Chalmers, Auld and Lennox. Hibs: Allan; Shevlane, Davis; Stanton, Madsen, Blackley; Marinello, Quinn, Cormack, O'Rourke and Stevenson.

Hibs might as well have not turned up. Celtic performed brilliantly, à la Lisbon. Chris Shevlane, the Hibs left back who was to later become a team-mate for a very brief period, was given a torrid time by Jinky, who, while not managing to share in the six Celtic goals, constructed a number of them. Celtic were unstoppable and led 6–0 before two late goals repaired some of the damage to Hibs' pride.

Flushed with success, and with a three-figure weekly wage packet boosted by bonuses, Jinky looked forward with relish to the start of the 1969–70 season. But when the crash came it was accompanied by a resounding bang. Having been stopped by traffic police near his home in Lanarkshire, Jinky was charged with driving under the influence of alcohol and subsequently fined £50 and given a one-year driving ban. Jock Stein's response was predictable. The furious manager left Jinky out of the squad for a pre-season friendly in France and also axed him from the first three

games of the season, League Cup ties against Airdrie, Rangers and
Raith Rovers.

Speculation was rife that Jinky was on his way out, and press
reports claimed that Stein had been involved in talks with several
English clubs with a view to selling his prize asset for £150,000.
Doubtless, Stein was the source of these rumours in an effort to
shock Jinky into the realisation that he was not prepared to tolerate
what he considered a flagrant breach of self-discipline. Jinky
reacted by announcing that he had reached a crossroads in his
career and would need to discipline himself both on and off the
field – or risk putting his career at Celtic in even greater jeopardy.

Jinky, his penance completed, was recalled to the side on 20
August 1969 for the Old Firm return at Celtic Park, a match Celtic
won 1–0. Celtic topped their qualifying section by a single point,
but when they lined up against Ayr United in the semi-final, on 8
October, after disposing of Aberdeen in the previous round, Jinky
was again absent. An ear infection forced him to withdraw and
Celtic struggled without him, held to a 3–3 draw after extra time.
However, with Jinky back in action they won the replay, 2–1, to
reach their sixth successive League Cup final. But when Celtic
and St Johnstone faced each other twelve days later at Hampden
Jinky was again missing.

Jinky, Billy McNeill and Tommy Gemmell had played for
Scotland in a 3–2 World Cup qualifying defeat by West Germany in
Hamburg three days earlier, and Stein, mindful of the need to con-
serve his players' energies in a team now campaigning on four
fronts, decided to drop Gemmell from the cup final team and
demote Jinky to the substitutes bench. In Gemmell's case it was
punishment for being sent off in Germany, for kicking Helmut
Haller on the backside. Stein's decision to 'rest' Jinky was less
clear-cut. Jinky eventually featured in the match, as a replacement
for Stevie Chalmers, as Celtic ground out a 1–0 win.

The following midweek Jinky scored the fourth of eleven goals
in forty-four appearances that season when he equalised
Aberdeen's second goal in a 3–2 win at Pittodrie. He had already
netted in a 2–1 defeat by Hibs and been on target twice when

Celtic overwhelmed Raith Rovers, 7–1. His form dipped briefly after he had claimed another 'double', in a 4–2 win at Ayr, and he was substituted in a 3–0 win over Morton at Cappielow on 29 November. But less than three weeks later Jinky was back to his scintillating best. Dundee United paid the price of the revival. Jinky tore them apart in spite of atrocious weather conditions of sleet and snow to engineer a breathtaking 7–2 victory.

In the intervening period Celtic had reached the last eight in the European Cup. They also led Rangers by two points in the league at the turn of the year. That lead eventually extended to twelve points, the greatest winning margin of any of Celtic's nine consecutive championships.

Rangers also suffered at Celtic's hands in the Scottish Cup, going down 3–1 when the teams were drawn together in the third round. Celtic were then expected to go on to retain the trophy, but instead they ran up against an Aberdeen team bristling with youthful talent and self-belief. They lost 3–1 just four days before beating Leeds United at Hampden, on 15 April 1970, to clinch their place in the European Cup final.

With the championship and the League Cup already won, defeat by Aberdeen was far less of a blow than it might normally have been, for Stein, his players and their fans were convinced that all that Celtic need do to be crowned champions of Europe for a second time was turn up at Milan's San Siro Stadium on 6 May.

But Feyenoord rewrote the script, and defeat had far-reaching consequences for Celtic and Jimmy Johnstone. Heartbroken, disillusioned, and with a clear sense of his true worth to clubs of the calibre of Spurs and Manchester United, Jinky dropped a bombshell two weeks later by slapping in a transfer request, to the consternation of his manager and the amazement of his army of fans.

12

Old Firm Memories

Like all great entertainers, Jimmy Johnstone performed best on the big stage, in front of a large audience, and games against Rangers provided the perfect setting to flaunt his outrageous talents.

Some players have been reduced to quivering wrecks by the intimidating atmosphere of an Old Firm game. Jinky revelled in it. It was as if they had been created with the little winger in mind. The baying taunts of the Rangers fans acted as a spur, while the roars of approval from the Celtic supporters that greeted the sight of Jinky tormenting the opposition drove him to reach for higher peaks of brilliance.

'I loved Old Firm games,' he said. 'They are great occasions and the greatest club game in the world. They have everything. But I never slept the night before. In fact, I used to have to change the bed sheets because I sweated so much anticipating what lay ahead. But what a feeling. The tension was unbearable and often victory was more of a relief than a reward, but there is not an atmosphere like it.'

For more than a decade Jinky frustrated and often tormented a succession of Rangers defenders. His habit of beating his man and then repeating the feat all over again just because he could left lost of them cursing his very existence. Jinky was on the winning side in twenty of his forty-three Old Firm games, excluding the Glasgow

Cup and the short-lived Drybrough Cup ties, scoring ten goals in the process. Rangers won sixteen, with the remainder drawn. But the statistics tell only part of the story.

Lesser mortals would have shied away from the constant physical, sometimes brutal challenges of opponents, who, if they could not stop him fairly, were never loath to attempt to do so by foul means. Yet, Jinky would seldom complain. More often than not he picked himself up, dusted himself down, and simply got on with the game. It was an attitude that won him the admiration of his rivals and even of some Rangers fans, who could not help but marvel at his skills, for Jinky had a big bag of tricks.

John Greig, voted 'Greatest Ever Ranger' in 1999, was a contemporary and played in opposition to Jinky in many of those Old Firm encounters. A powerfully built player blessed with both skill and a razor-sharp football brain, Greig, who captained club and country with great distinction, was an uncompromising defender who never held back in a challenge.

By his own admission, Greig left his mark on opponents, Jinky included. But there was never any malice between the pair. Indeed, he remembered with fondness their many duels. 'I played against Jimmy at left back only a few times,' Greig recalled. 'But I don't suppose it mattered very much who was in direct opposition to him because he was one of that rare breed of player who could change the course of a game single-handedly.

'Jimmy wasn't only supremely talented, he was also remarkably strong for a wee guy, and he didn't lack courage. He regularly got clattered by opponents but that never put him off, or stopped him trying to beat his man, because he was brave. No matter how many heavy tackles he was subjected to, unlike the modern-day player, Jimmy bounced straight back up and you never heard him complain. As soon as he was back on his feet he was demanding the ball so he could try to beat you again.

'If the full-back was booked for a challenge on Jimmy, Jock Stein used to tell whoever was taking the resultant free kick to pass the ball to the wee man so he could take on the defender again and force him to commit to another tackle, in the knowledge that he would have to tread warily, for fear of falling foul of the referee for a second time.'

Jinky's habit of wanting to beat defenders two or three times in the same movement led to dire warnings from Greig that he would be forced to deal with him in an uncompromising manner rather than risk further embarrassment

Opponents had no time to stand back and admire Jinky's skills as they were invariably too busy trying to stop him doing further damage. Jinky's ability to dispossess an opponent and beat one man after another created space for his team-mates. The way he could take players out of a game is something the modern game has lost. But one suspects that the way teams are organised nowadays it would be much harder for Jinky to make his mark. Players are no longer encouraged to be individualists. It's more about passing the ball and making runs, and you have two choices, you either go with the ball or the man.

But Greig lamented the passing of the 'tanner ba' players of yesteryear. 'Tanner' meaning sixpence, a 'tanner ba' was a six-penny ball, a tennis ball which youngsters bought and played with in the streets. 'Football misses guys like Jimmy Johnstone,' he said. 'He was an entertainer who demanded the ball, and took people on and, while he was in the process of beating his opponent, or opponents, he took players out of the game and created additional space for his team-mates.'

In spite of the intense rivalry between the Old Firm, the bitterness that prevails among sections of the rival supports did not extend to the players of Jinky's generation. It was not uncommon for Celtic and Rangers players to chat to one another on the pitch before and during the game, often kidding each other on about the reactions of the fans.

There was humour, too, one Saturday afternoon in January 1970 when Jinky ended up resembling Worzel Gummidge. Celtic Park did not have undersoil heating in those days and the pitch had been covered in straw in an effort to protect it from the frost. But it was still bone-hard when the match kicked off with the pitch surrounded by bales of straw.

Tom 'Tiny' Wharton, who stood six foot, six inches tall, was referee and gave the players extra leeway to compensate for the conditions underfoot. Greig took full advantage of the fact that 'Tiny' was being more lenient than usual and kept on inadvertently bumping into Jinky, who landed in a heap among the straw several times. When he left the pitch at half-time Jinky had bits of straw sticking out of his hair, his ears and his jersey. He looked ridiculous, but even he could see the funny side and his face lit up with a smile.

On another occasion, Jinky displayed his sharp wit when he was subjected to a couple of heavy tackles by Greig in quick succession. He picked himself up after the second, which had been worthy of a booking, looked the Rangers captain straight in the eye and asked: 'Greigy, are you trying to intimidate me?'

Greig will never forget the impact Jinky had on the game in an age of outstanding players. He maintained that: 'If Jimmy was playing in the present day others would be in awe of him. I think he felt a certain responsibility to entertain the fans. But to keep reproducing such a high standard of skill week in, week out, takes a bit of doing and, don't forget, there were some seasons when he played fifty games or more.'

Jinky recalled his many jousts with Greig, joking: 'I still have the bruises to prove it.' Yet while he considered the Rangers player to be an aggressive opponent, Jinky also thought him fair. He certainly did not view Greig as malicious.

Whenever they lined up on opposite sides Jinky would take great pleasure in making it difficult for Greig. In a game on New Year's Day in the 1970s Jinky remembered giving him a particularly torrid time. The defender was not helped by the conditions. After heavy rain the pitch was slippery, 'the sort of day big defenders dread'. The little winger 'skinned' Greig three times and was fouled every time as he went by. Despite ending up in a heap the referee Bobby Davidson ran up to Jinky and admonished him to 'stop clowning around and get on with the game'.

Jinky recalled: 'Both of us had a job to do and there was no quarter asked or given. But I think John holds the unofficial record for keeping me up with his boot while I was in the air after a tackle. Most defenders got two touches but Greigy often managed three!'

Jinky was handed an Old Firm baptism of fire on 4 May 1963 when he was selected to play in the Scottish Cup final in only his third first-team game in a Celtic XI of Haffey; McKay, Kennedy; McNamee, McNeill, Price; Johnstone, Murdoch, Hughes, Divers and Brogan. Rangers were represented by: Ritchie; Shearer, Provan; Greig, McKinnon, Baxter; Henderson, McLean, Millar, Brand and Wilson.

The match finished goalless and Jinky was dropped for the replay, which was won 3–0 by Rangers. Jinky had to wait until the following year to savour the sweet taste of victory.

Three Old Firm appearances in season 1963–64, in the league, League Cup and Scottish Cup, all ended in defeat without Celtic even managing to score a goal. But it was a case of fifth time lucky on 5 September 1964, when the teams lined up: Celtic: Fallon; Young, Gemmell; Brogan, Cushley, Kennedy; Johnstone, Divers, Chalmers, Gallagher and Hughes. Rangers: Ritchie; Hynd, Provan; Greig, McKinnon, Baxter; Henderson, McLean, Forrest, Brand and Wilson. The diminutive Jinky thrilled the home support in a 58,000 crowd at Celtic Park when he outwitted the Rangers defence time and again on a rain-sodden pitch to emerge as the architect of a 3–1 win. Celtic could even afford the luxury of a missed Charlie Gallagher penalty.

Seven weeks later Rangers extracted revenge in the League Cup final and Jinky's first Old Firm goal – scored from close range in the sixty-ninth minute – was little more than a token gesture.

Celtic were beaten again just over two months later when a first-half Jim Forrest goal was all that separated the teams at Ibrox on New Year's Day. Celtic squandered the chance to share the spoils when Bobby Murdoch sent his penalty kick over the crossbar after John Hughes had been brought down by Ronnie McKinnon six minutes from time. By then Celtic were playing with ten men because Jinky had been sent off by referee Tom Wharton, for the second time in his career. A red mist had descended when Rangers'

Icelandic inside forward Tottie Beck, not for the first time, charged into him. Jinky, who could never quite explain to his own satisfaction why he was prone to such sudden fits of temper, ran straight at Beck. It was little more than a full-blooded body check, but Beck went down and made the most of his fall.

Jinky was hit by a fourteen-day SFA suspension, but he was convinced that the Rangers players were favoured by referees, who were intimidated by the atmosphere generated by the Rangers fans at Ibrox and tended to overlook some offences as a result. On the occasion of his sending off he claimed that Jimmy Millar, the Rangers centre forward, had got away with murder, hacking and kicking his way through the game to set an aggressive tone.

It seems reasonable to also assume that Jinky was suffering from a deep sense of frustration during that phase of his career, as his own form had been erratic, due in part to self-doubts stemming from the team's indifferent league form, which culminated in Celtic finishing eighth in the championship.

The following season – 1965–66 – Rangers drew first blood when they won the opening league encounter, on 18 September, by two goals to one at Ibrox. But when the sides resumed hostilities on 3 January, Rangers were humbled. Jock Stein, in his first full season in charge, was on his way to fashioning the team that would go on to win the European Cup seventeen months later, and with Bobby Murdoch, who passed the ball with inch-perfect precision, supplying Jinky with plenty of ammunition, Celtic ran riot in front of 65,000 fans at Celtic Park.

As it happened, Rangers scored first, through Davie Wilson after just ninety seconds, and held the lead until four minutes after the restart. But this only served to rile their hosts, for once Stevie Chalmers had equalised the floodgates flew open. Celtic poured forward, Chalmers claimed two more for his hat-trick, and Charlie Gallagher and Murdoch added two more. Celtic were inspired by Jinky, who gave left-back Kai Johansen a torrid time. Jinky missed out on a sixth goal when his effort struck a post.

In the intervening period Celtic had won the League Cup, beating their arch rivals 2–1 at Hampden, on 23 October 1965. This was an untidy, ill-tempered game, further marred when thousands of Rangers fans streamed on to the pitch in an effort to prevent the Celtic players from parading the trophy, and the SFA subsequently banned the winning team in cup finals from doing a lap of honour.

The teams on the day Jinky collected the first of nineteen winner's medals were: Celtic: Simpson; Young, Gemmell; Murdoch, McNeill, Clark; Johnstone, Gallagher, McBride, Lennox and Hughes. Rangers: Ritchie; Johansen, Provan; Wood, McKinnon, Greig; Henderson, Willoughby, Forrest, Wilson and Johnston.

Celtic again dominated the fourth and fifth Old Firm meetings of the season, the Scottish Cup final, on 23 April 1966, and the replay, following a nil–nil draw, four days later. Yet Celtic were denied. Rangers scored with a snap shot out of the blue after seventy minutes for the only goal of the game.

'We were on form that day and did everything right,' Jinky reflected. 'To be honest, we could have scored ten goals, but the ball simply would not run kindly for us. Then Kai [Johansen] hit one out of nothing and that was it.'

The following season, as we have seen, Celtic retained the League Cup, when Bobby Lennox scored the only goal of the game in the nineteenth minute, on 29 October 1966; and the previous month Rangers had lost the league encounter at Celtic Park, 2–0.

But it was in the third and final Old Firm clash of a momentous season for Celtic that Jinky produced one of his finest performances in the Hoops. Sandy Jardine, who was to become a Scotland team-mate, was handed an Old Firm baptism of fire, on 6 May 1967, in the fixture postponed from 3 January. It should have been a treasured memory for the former Rangers defender when he scored, but Jardine was upstaged.

Jinky struck twice to secure the 2–2 draw and ensure that Celtic retained the league title. Jardine's delight at crashing home a twenty-five-yard shot via the underside of the crossbar in the forti-eth minute was short-lived when Jinky equalised less than one minute later after goalkeeper Norrie Martin had failed to hold a shot from Willie Wallace. The ball ran free to Bobby Lennox on the six-yard line, his effort struck a post, and Jinky, following up, converted the rebound from close range.

Jinky's second goal was a mark of sheer brilliance. Taking a throw-in from Stevie Chalmers, Jinky made for the penalty area, avoiding a challenge by Ronnie McKinnon, veered left as other defenders closed in, and unleashed a viciously struck left-foot shot from twenty-five yards that flew into the corner of the net. It was a fantastic goal.

For all that relations between the Old Firm rivals were generally cordial, Sir Alex Ferguson recalled the occasion of his Old Firm debut in 1967 when Jinky welcomed him with a kick on the ankle and the comment that he was 'a big blue-nosed bastard'.

Honours were even the following season, with a win apiece and two draws in the four Old Firm games. In the last of them – the 2–2 draw at Celtic Park, on 2 January 1968 – Jinky excelled, torturing the opposition's defenders with a superb display of his dribbling skills, despite being singled out for some rough treatment.

For all that Celtic became the dominant force in Scottish football during the Stein era, the gap between them and Rangers was not wide. Indeed, the championship often stayed undecided until virtually the last kick of the season, which was just as well from Rangers star Willie Henderson's perspective.

According to Henderson, who competed with Jinky for the right-wing berth in the national team: 'The bonus for winning was always a lot more in an Old Firm game, and you always worried about collecting because the extra cash came in very handy at a time when footballers were earning a pittance compared to today's top players.

'The problem from our point of view was that Jimmy could turn a game in the blink of an eye with the fantastic skills he had. We also knew that there was a very good chance that whichever side won the Old Firm game would be sitting top of the league, and in with a tremendous chance of winning the title.'

It was a similar story in the subsequent campaign when the clubs were again drawn in the same League Cup qualifying section.

Celtic won both League Cup encounters, but lost both league games.

The fifth meeting of the season – effectively a rubber match – came in the form of yet another Scottish Cup final featuring the country's top two clubs, on 26 April 1969. But there was one notable absentee from the big stage – Jimmy Johnstone. Yet another suspension deprived him of the opportunity to star in a ridiculously one-sided affair. A series of defensive blunders contributed largely to an embarrassing 4–0 defeat for Rangers, their first in a Scottish Cup final for forty years. Jinky was forced to watch the action from a seat in the Hampden stand after being clobbered by the fourteen-day suspension from the SFA for accumulating three cautions, one of them for speaking back to the referee and two for tackles deemed to be unacceptable.

The suspension ran from 22 April, and George Connelly, an immensely gifted player who experienced huge difficulties handling the pressures associated with celebrity status, and eventually quit the game after staging several walk-outs from Celtic Park, took Jinky's place, scoring the third goal on the stroke of half-time to enhance Celtic's second domestic treble and sixth league and cup double.

Amazingly, Celtic's second Old Firm success of the 1969–70 season, the 1–0 win on 20 September 1969, was also the first time they had managed to win at Ibrox for twelve years. They triumphed thanks to a Harry Hood goal, despite being reduced to ten men when Jim Craig was ordered off following a tackle from behind on Willie Johnston. The sides had met twice a month earlier in the League Cup, when Jinky missed the first match, a 2–1 win for Rangers at Ibrox, but featured in the second when Celtic beat their rivals 1–0 to top the qualifying section.

An uninspiring and goalless New Year match, played in treacherous underfoot conditions on a frost-bound pitch, was followed by the Scottish Cup third-round clash (and also the quarter-final) on 21 February 1970, at Celtic Park. Rangers scored first when Jim Craig gifted them an own goal after five minutes, but Celtic hit back to equalise in the thirty-ninth minute with a shot from Bobby Lennox that deflected off goalkeeper Gerry Neef into the net. Davie Hay effectively won the tie for the home side five minutes from time, but, to make absolutely certain of a semi-final place, Jinky added his contribution in the dying moments, racing through the defence before shooting home to make the score 3–1.

It was a nasty affair, full of bad feeling and provocative incidents, such as a Rangers player congratulating the unfortunate Craig on his own goal. One player, Alex MacDonald of Rangers, was ordered off, and others were fortunate to escape similar punishment. The SFA was so concerned by the field indiscipline and the level of crowd trouble following complaints by the city's magistrates that they felt compelled to summon the rival captains, Billy McNeill and John Greig, to appear before them, along with the managers and chairmen of both clubs, to express their disquiet.

Although Celtic's dominance of the Scottish game continued almost unabated in the early 1970s, Rangers were invariably capable of matching their rivals at least some of the time, and the Ibrox club's success in the first League Cup final of the new decade emphasised the point.

When the teams emerged to the roars of 106,263 at Hampden on 24 October 1970, Rangers counted among their number a raw sixteen-year-old by the name of Derek Johnstone. Virtually no one in the crowd had heard of the teenager just a few months earlier, let alone knew much about him. But Johnstone was about to overshadow his much more famous namesake and become a household name himself in the space of ninety minutes. The young Dundonian stunned Celtic by rising to head the winning goal in the fortieth minute to once again underline the unpredictable nature of Old Firm games, for Celtic had gone into the final as clear favourites on the back of a two-goal win over their rivals in the league at Celtic Park six weeks earlier.

The defeat also marked Celtic's third loss in a major final inside six months, and it is a fact worth remarking that the Celtic line-up included only five of the Lisbon Lions.

Celtic: Williams; Craig, Quinn; Murdoch, McNeill, Hay; Johnstone, Connelly, Wallace, Hood and Macari. Rangers: McCloy;

Jardine, Miller; Conn, McKinnon, Jackson; Henderson, MacDonald, Johnstone, Stein and Johnston.

Willie Johnston, Rangers' charismatic left-winger, recalled sitting on the ball at one point in the match at Hampden and incurring Jinky's displeasure. 'Jim Craig, the Celtic right back, kept standing off me and I became fed up running at him with the ball inviting him to try to take it off me,' said Johnston. 'So I suddenly stopped and sat on the ball. Wee Jimmy was livid. He came running across to me threatening all sorts and I swear to God I could see the veins in his neck standing out. I just laughed and that made him even angrier.'

When Celtic travelled to Ibrox on 2 January 1971, the result of a football match meant nothing in the shadow of the awful disaster that led to the deaths of sixty-six spectators in the greatest tragedy to befall Scottish football.

Jimmy Johnstone had seemingly sealed victory for Celtic in the eighty-ninth minute when he headed home after Bobby Lennox's shot struck the crossbar and rebounded into his path. But when Colin Stein equalised with virtually the last kick of the game hundreds of Rangers supporters, who had been making their way down stairway number 13, turned and attempted to clamber back into the ground to celebrate. They were met by a wave of supporters sweeping down uncontrollably on top of them. The resultant crush left 145 injured and 66 dead, most of whom suffocated under the mass of bodies. The official inquiry refused to accept that the tragedy had been caused by the returning fans but was unable to offer a more plausible reason for the steel barriers giving way.

In the absence of a satisfactory explanation, many persist with the view that the tragedy occurred because of the unavoidable rush of bodies from opposite directions. Whatever the cause, the disaster had far-reaching consequences for Scottish football as a whole.

There was a major overhaul of regulations to do with stadium construction, attendance limits and crowd control. Rangers were also convinced of the need to carry out massive reconstruction work at Ibrox (to the extent that the current stadium bears little resemblance to the old one).

The country was united in grief and the manner of the two clubs' handling of the tragedy in the ensuing days, when players bridged the great divide to attend the funerals of the deceased, further convinced Jinky of the absurdity of the bigotry that continues to blight the Old Firm. Although the victims had all been Rangers fans, Celtic contributed £10,000 to the Ibrox Disaster Fund and participated in a match between a Rangers and Celtic XI and a Scotland-select team at Hampden to help the families of the victims. The game was watched by more than 81,000 spectators.

Yet Jinky felt that hatred and bigotry would never completely disappear because of deep-rooted religious differences. A devout Roman Catholic, he condemned bigotry as utterly pointless and in later life highlighted the warm welcome he received at various Rangers supporters' clubs.

At both Celtic and Rangers, founded at a time when Irish immigrants, from the north and south of the country, were flooding into the west of Scotland in their tens of thousands, religion was in the club's roots. The majority of newcomers settled in Glasgow, the Roman Catholics favouring the east end and the Protestants the south side. By the time Celtic Football Club was formed in 1888, with the express purpose of caring for the poor children of the east end, Rangers had been in existence for fifteen years.

Rangers themselves drew considerable support from the shipyards of the Clyde, where Orangeman from Belfast and the North of Ireland made up a sizeable percentage of the workforce. But it was not until the turn of the twentieth century that the divisions widened. The bitterness intensified following the death of Celtic goalkeeper John Thomson in September 1931.

Thomson's fatal head injury, when Rangers' Sam English accidentally caught him with his knee as the young keeper dived to make a save at the centre-forward's feet, sparked further resentment. English was completely blameless, but the death of a player from an injury he suffered in an Old Firm game resulted in increased crowd trouble at matches.

While Jinky was playing, the troubles in Northern Ireland fuelled old rivalries and led to a further upping of tension. This culminated in the disgraceful scenes at Hampden in May 1980 when fans of both clubs staged a pitched battled. Mounted police had to restore order in the city for the first time since the General Strike of 1926.

Not surprisingly, the atmosphere was sombre when Celtic and Rangers resumed their rivalry on the pitch four months after the Ibrox disaster, on 8 May 1971, in the Scottish Cup final. The match finished 1–1, with goals from Bobby Lennox and Derek Johnstone. Jinky had performed ordinarily, by his own high standards, in that first encounter, but in the replay the following Wednesday it was he held the key to unlocking a twenty-first Scottish Cup final win for Celtic.

Jinky was listed at number seven but was given a roving role by manager Jock Stein, who asked him to play at inside right in a Celtic XI of: Williams; Craig, Brogan; Connelly, McNeill, Hay; Johnstone, Macari, Hood, Callaghan and Lennox. Rangers: McCloy; Denny, Mathieson; Greig, McKinnon, Jackson; Henderson, Penman, Stein, MacDonald and Johnston.

Rangers could not blunt Jinky's menace. His tricks and darting runs enabled Celtic to grab the initiative. Rangers' gamble of fielding Jim Denny for his debut in place of Alex Miller at right back, who had been injured in the first game, also backfired spectacularly.

Jinky had been out of sorts most of the season following the European Cup final defeat in Milan. Now he woke up. He gave Denny a torrid time, and carved up the helpless youngster almost at will. But it was not just Denny who struggled to try to contain the rejuvenated opposition winger. Jinky toyed with his rivals in a style he had not shown for some time.

The final was effectively won in the space of two minutes midway through the first half. Celtic's Lou Macari scored after twenty-four minutes, and just sixty seconds later, Jinky, whose bobbing and weaving had increased Rangers' sense of frustration, won a penalty kick when he was brought down by centre half Ronnie McKinnon. Exasperation as much as anything had provoked McKinnon's moment of imprudence.

Harry Hood converted the spot kick, and although Rangers were given a glimmer of hope when an own goal by Jim Craig reduced the leeway early in the second half, Celtic, with Jinky still orchestrating promising offensive moves at will, continued to dominate the play. Celtic eventually won 2–1.

Jinky maintained his welcome return to form at the start of the following season, scoring in the first competitive fixture of 1971–72, against Rangers in his side's opening League Cup tie at Celtic Park. His constant probing brought its reward in the sixty-seventh minute when he got on the end of a corner from Lennox and his shot found a gap in the defence. A young Kenny Dalglish, who made his Old Firm debut that evening, scored a second goal, from the penalty spot, three minutes later. Celtic were even more dominant in the return at Ibrox a fortnight later, winning 3-0 to top the qualifying section.

On 11 September the teams met for a third time in the space of one month, but the outcome was no different. Celtic's 3–2 success at Ibrox came courtesy of a Jinky match-winner, scored with his head in the eighty-ninth minute when he somehow outsoared a posse of defenders, each of whom stood several inches taller than him.

Jinky's scoring streak in Old Firm games continued on 3 January 1972, again with a feat of aerial prowess. Harry Hood's flighted cross found the little winger standing unmarked after jinking his way in behind the defence so that he was able to stoop and beat Peter McCloy with a close-range header.

The rapid emergence of Dalglish provided Jinky with a foil, and the double act was rarely more effective than on 16 September 1972 when the first Old Firm fixture of the season was staged at Hampden to facilitate reconstruction work at Celtic Park.

Jinky had been left out of the side for Celtic's first two league games – a 6–2 win over Kilmarnock and a two-goal victory against Morton at Cappielow – but was recalled as outside right. In spite of wearing the number seven, he was instructed to play down the left side. Not that it mattered. Jinky was simply irrepressible. Within two minutes of the kick-off he set up the opening goal for

Dalglish. McCloy had come for Macari's cross but missed it, and
Jinky headed the ball over the goalkeeper for Dalglish to prod it
into the net.

With seventeen minutes played, Dalglish and Jinky again com-
bined to prise open the defence, Dalglish cutting the ball back
from the byline towards his team-mate. Jinky's initial effort to
gather the pass landed him on his backside, but he somehow managed to stick out a foot and make contact at the second attempt to
score and set up a 3–1 victory.

There was a notable absentee when the Old Firm next crossed
swords, at Ibrox on 6 January 1973. Jock Stein had been admitted
to hospital over New Year complaining of chest pains and was diagnosed as having suffered a heart attack. It was no great surprise that
Stein's health should suffer as a consequence of the long hours he
spent at Celtic Park, and his habit of motoring down to England to
watch games, and returning immediately afterwards. His explosive
temper and frequent outbursts of rage must also have played heir
part. But, having insisted on listening to the game on radio, his
condition could not have been helped by Alfie Conn heading the
winner in the final minute

Although they had lost the previous Old Firm game, 2–1, Celtic,
with Stein back in charge after only the briefest of recuperation
periods, were favourites going into the Scottish Cup final against
Rangers on 5 May when the teams lined up: Celtic: Hunter;
McGrain, Brogan; Murdoch, McNeill, Connelly; Johnstone, Deans,
Dalglish, Hay and Callaghan. Rangers: McCloy; Jardine,
Mathieson; Greig, Johnstone, MacDonald, McLean, Forsyth,
Parlane, Conn and Young.

Rangers triumphed 3–2, thanks to an untidy winning goal
scored by Tom Forsyth on the hour mark when he prodded the ball
into the net after Derek Johnstone's header had struck a post and
shot along the goal-line. For a moment it looked as if Forsyth,
caught by surprise, would miss from point-blank range. But there
might well have been a different outcome. Shortly after George
Connelly had made it 2–2 from the penalty spot, Jinky scored what
appeared a perfectly legitimate goal when he latched on to a pass

from Dalglish and lobbed the ball over the goalkeeper's head. Referee John Gordon called the effort offside.

Jinky's remarkable habit of scoring against Rangers with headers continued in the first league encounter of the following season. The only goal of the game came in the sixty-ninth minute when Jinky headed a low cross from Davie Hay under McCloy. As things turned out it was his final goal against Rangers.

But by then Jinky had suffered the indignity of being ordered off in an Old Firm game the month before. One week after helping Celtic to a 2–1 League Cup win over their oldest rivals, he 'walked' for the sixth time in his career on 25 August 1973, in a 3–1 defeat at Celtic Park.

Jinky was involved in an incident with Alex MacDonald when he grabbed the Rangers midfielder and a scuffle ensued. MacDonald fell to the ground as if poleaxed and referee Tom Wharton sent Jinky off. He was subsequently fined £150 by the SFA and also suspended for fourteen days. But Jinky was adamant that McDonald had 'conned' the referee.

Jinky, whose form was indifferent at the time, was listed as a substitute for the League Cup semi-final meeting between the clubs on 5 December 1973, at Hampden, but had no opportunity to play a part in Celtic's 3–1 victory.

The following season, Jinky's last at Celtic, saw him feature in two Old Firm games, a 2–1 defeat at Celtic Park on 14 September 1974, and the 4 January encounter at Ibrox. The teams in Jinky's final Old Firm game were: Rangers: Kennedy; Jardine, Forsyth, Jackson, Greig; McDougall, Johnstone, MacDonald; McLean, Parlane and Scott. Celtic: Hunter; McGrain, McNeill, McCluskey, Brogan; Glavin, Hood, Murray; Callaghan, Dalglish and Wilson.

Jinky replaced Harry Hood in the second half but was unable to influence the result, a 3–0 win for Rangers. It was an inglorious ending to more than a decade of teasing the opposition, but Rangers were no doubt glad to see the back of their tormentor-in-chief.

13

A Game Too Far

Terry Cooper was regarded as one of the best left backs in Europe – until he ran into Jimmy Johnstone twice in the space of fifteen days in April 1970. Cooper would go on to play for England in the World Cup finals in Mexico a few months later, and he won twenty caps for his country, but no winger ever gave him more problems than Jinky.

In excess of 180,000 spectators witnessed at first hand two of Jinky's finest performances for Celtic, while millions more tuned in to the spectacle on TV as Britain's leading clubs did battle in the semi-final of the European Cup. The regret must be that Celtic and Leeds were drawn to meet at the penultimate stage of the competition, for they would have graced the final itself and captured the public's imagination in a way no other two teams could have done.

The games between Celtic and Leeds were effectively the final before the final, and the victors paid a high price for their exertions at Elland Road and then at Hampden Park. By the time Celtic travelled to Milan three weeks later to face Feyenoord much of their passion had been extinguished. Having given so much for 180 minutes against Leeds at the end of another demanding season, the players no longer had quite the same spring in their step and their legs had grown visibly heavier.

But Celtic's failure to win the European Cup for the second time in four seasons could not detract from the scale of the team's achievement in beating a side that was sweeping all before it in its own domestic competitions. This was the equivalent of Scotland versus England, and the Scots triumphed.

As custom dictated, the rival managers, Jock Stein and Don Revie indulged in ritual mind games in the build-up to the first leg at Elland Road. The former insisted that Celtic were the underdogs, while his counterpart, also with a black belt in gamesmanship, complained that his players were 'tired and jaded' as a consequence of their pursuit of honours. But it was Stein who played the trump card.

Sensing that Jinky was Celtic's potential match-winner, Stein, as he had done so often in the past, threw himself into the role of psychologist and set about convincing the little winger that he had no equal among the opposition's players. Stein constantly interrupted his pre-match team talks to announce that Jinky was going to destroy Leeds. This had the effect of boosting Jinky's often fragile confidence to a level so high that he believed he was bound to prove what his manager predicted.

Revie had also played into Stein's hands by fielding weakened sides in league games against Southampton and Derby, losing both to virtually concede the league championship to Everton. Stein, never slow to spot an opening, leapt on Revie's apparent uncertainty and declared: 'Leeds have shown us so much respect that it has cost them the league. But they must chase the game because supporters expect victory at home and they won't allow them too long to score.'

But it was Celtic who drew first blood on the evening of 1 April when the teams lined up: Leeds United: Sprake; Reaney, Cooper; Bremner, Charlton, Madeley; Lorimer, Clarke, Jones, Giles and Gray. Celtic: Williams; Hay, Gemmell; Murdoch, McNeill, Brogan; Johnstone, Connelly, Wallace, Lennox and Auld.

The match was barely one minute old when George Connelly struck with a shot from twenty yards. Connelly was unfortunate to be denied a second goal, for offside, after Jinky had done the spadework following a superb run. Jinky ran Leeds ragged that day, shattering the confidence of the most secure defence in England with his incredible dribbling at speed, sometimes floating past four or five opponents at a time.

Celtic had switched the return leg to Hampden to make more room for their fans, and the 136,505 who turned up on 15 April set a new European Cup attendance record for the unofficial Championship of Britain. Stein made only slight alterations to his team, Hughes, who had come on as a substitute for Connelly in Leeds, replacing Willie Wallace in the starting XI. Leeds recalled Norman Hunter in place of Paul Reaney, who had suffered a broken leg.

As in the first game, Jinky was on song, teasing and tormenting the luckless Cooper and company and causing continual havoc. Leeds scored first, after fourteen minutes, but skipper Billy Bremner's spectacular thirty-five-yard shot was not sufficient to subdue Celtic's fighting spirit.

Two goals in the space of five minutes at the start of the second half sealed Leeds' fate and booked Celtic's place in the final. John Hughes claimed the first with a header, and Bobby Murdoch the second, after fifty-one minutes. Jinky provided the pass for the match-winner after he had once again ripped the defence to shreds and dragged several defenders towards him before squaring the ball to Murdoch. Leeds's Welsh international goalkeeper, Gary Sprake, had been injured in a collision with Hughes and had to be replaced by substitute David Harvey, who was to go on to earn sixteen caps for Scotland. But Harvey's first action was to pick Murdoch's shot out of the net.

At one stage in the second half both Hunter and Cooper formed a pincer movement in a vain attempt to contain Jinky. They did so more in hope than expectation, and found themselves left flat-footed and red-faced when Jinky continued to dart past them.

Jinky and his ecstatic team-mates were able to celebrate in the final period of the match by staging an exhibition of their skills, such was their superiority. The best team in England had been humbled by the best in Scotland, and Feyenoord were placed on red alert to the danger Jinky posed to their European Cup ambitions.

Cooper, meanwhile, prayed that he had seen the last of the little Scottish pest. But Cooper, for all that Jinky drove him round the bend, never lost his respect for a player who, he said, had few equals.

'Jimmy had everything you could wish for in a winger,' said Cooper. 'He had such a low centre of gravity and it was so difficult to stop him. Unless you took him by unfair means it simply wasn't going to happen. Jimmy was a bit like George Best. That's the best compliment I can give him. But at Elland Road and Hampden, especially the game in Glasgow, I wasn't looking to pay him any compliments.'

Celtic had John 'Yogi' Hughes on one flank and Jinky on the other, and he was on fire. Leeds had a reputation as a very intimidating side, but they could not intimidate Jinky. He simply kept coming back at them. Cooper confessed: 'I would love to have kicked Jinky, but I couldn't get near him! I remember Norman Hunter turning to me at one stage and saying: "Kick that little Scots bastard." I replied: "I would – if I could catch him." I reckon I had good anticipation but I could do nothing to take the ball off Jinky.'

The late Billy Bremner claimed: 'That was one of the greatest exhibitions I have ever seen. Jimmy had one of these games where he was unstoppable. He destroyed us on his own and I remember turning to Terry Cooper at half-time at Hampden and saying to him there was no point in him going out for the second half.'

Sean Fallon, Stein's assistant, said: 'Leeds was just one of his great games. He really turned it on that night. They were so confident about the first leg down there. Not that Don and his people were shouting about what they would do. It was the English newspapers who were doing that. But still Don and the rest of them were quietly confident that they would get a result to bring with them to Hampden. We surprised them, and no one had more surprises for them that night than wee Jimmy.'

Celtic's route to Milan took them by way of Basle, Lisbon and

Florence. Only once did they stutter badly before sweeping Leeds aside, losing 3–0 to Benfica in Lisbon.

In their opening European Cup tie, on 17 September 1969, away to Basle, Celtic produced a competent enough performance, and a goalless draw virtually ensured that the return a fortnight later would be relatively straightforward. Goals from Harry Hood, after one minute, and Tommy Gemmell midway through the second half provided safe passage through to the second round.

Benfica, winners of the European Cup in 1961 and '62 and runners-up on three other occasions, most notably against Manchester United at Wembley two seasons previously, were guaranteed to prove much tougher opposition. But you would have been forgiven for thinking that their best days were behind them when Celtic destroyed their opponents – Eusebio et al – at Celtic Park on 12 November in an utterly one-sided encounter.

Celtic were simply devastating and Benfica were forced to withdraw Eusebio at the interval so as to switch to a defensive formation in an effort to contain their rampant rivals who were in danger of scoring half a dozen goals. In the event, Celtic settled for three, and it appeared that the contribution from Gemmell, Wallace and Hood would suffice to secure a place in the last eight.

Celtic took a trip down memory lane when they returned to Lisbon by staying at the Hotel Palacio in Estoril, their headquarters before the final two years earlier.

But in a complete reversal of fortunes, Benfica regained their magic in the return leg. Eusebio's goal after thirty-six minutes sparked a shock revival, and when Graca scored another four minutes later, Celtic found themselves desperately defending the narrowest of advantages. But with virtually the final kick of the game the 'Eagles' swooped again to equalise through Diamantino and force the tie into extra time.

The additional thirty minutes failed to produce another goal, and with both teams having scored three times at home, Celtic's fate rested on the toss of a coin. Happily, Billy McNeill guessed correctly.

Celtic's quarter-final opponents were Fiorentina. They came to

Celtic Park on 4 March boasting a proud tradition of European success, but the Italians' reputation took a battering in front of 80,000 fans who witnessed a tactical masterclass by Stein. His decision to recall Bertie Auld after an absence of several weeks provided the key to unlocking a nine-man defence. Auld scored the first of three Celtic goals on the half-hour mark and engineered the other two, an own goal by Carpenetti shortly after the restart, and a strike by Wallace.

Celtic came under heavy pressure in the second leg and were perhaps a shade fortunate to escape with a 1–0 defeat after Chiarugi, Fiorentina's best player, scored in thirty-six minutes. In an intriguing tactical move, Jinky was given a free role in Florence and instructed to keep possession as much as possible in an effort to frustrate the opposition. It happened as Stein had planned.

With Leeds added to their list of vanquished opponents, Celtic and their fans looked forward to a second European triumph, in the belief that the outcome was little short of a foregone conclusion. But football punctures pride. For once in his life, Jock Stein was guilty of seriously underestimating the opposition. Normally so fastidious in his preparations, he became almost slipshod in the build-up to the final, declining to even visit the San Siro Stadium to inspect the playing surface on the eve of the match, a decision completely out of character.

The fact that Stein had watched Feyenoord only once – in a 3–3 draw with their great rivals Ajax – also suggested that he did not really rate the opposition. Although he was at pains to warn his players not to underestimate Feyenoord, Stein's show of confidence was bound to have some impact on the players, lulling them into a false sense of security.

The fact that Celtic played only one competitive fixture after beating Leeds on 15 April – against St Mirren three days later when they won 3–2 in their final league game of the season – was also prejudicial, given that Feyenoord were still involved in playing meaningful matches.

Another distracting factor was the club's choice of pre-match base at Varese, thirty miles outside Milan, for the players felt detached from the build-up. One reporter went as far as to suggest that the team's hilltop hideaway had taken on the appearance of a rest home rather than a training camp.

But the most damning indictment of Stein's laid-back handling of the build-up was his decision to allow a business manager he had appointed to oversee the players' commercial interests to take up residence at the squad's hotel with his blessing. Glasgow journalist Ian Peebles had been introduced to maximise the players' earning potential from commercial deals. But when these deals failed to materialise the players were accused by some critics of being distracted by extraneous activities, taking their eye off the ball. It was also suggested that they had formed a syndicate in an effort to cash in, and that this had led to quarrels about the division of the spoils.

But for all these alarms and excursions, Celtic were firm favourites when they stepped on to the pitch on the evening of 6 May 1970 in front of a crowd of 53,187. Seven survivors from Lisbon lined up as follows: Celtic: Williams; Hay, Gemmell; Murdoch, McNeill, Brogan; Johnstone, Lennox, Wallace, Auld and Hughes. Feyenoord: Graafland; Romeyn, Laseroms; Israel, Van Duivenbode, Hasil; Jansen, Van Hanegem, Wery, Kindvall and Mouljin. The referee was Concetto Lo Bello of Italy.

The fluency and sweet passing movements that Jinky had inspired in the two games against Leeds were not in evidence when the match kicked off. Celtic had lost their edge in the three weeks between the semi-final and the final itself. Their movement was sluggish, and it was clear from the start that Feyenoord were not intimidated by their rivals' reputation.

Yet it was Celtic who scored first after half an hour. Murdoch sent a short free kick to Gemmell, and the defender, who had scored the equaliser in Lisbon three years earlier, drove the ball powerfully past Graafland. But the lead was short-lived. Within three minutes of Gemmell's goal, Celtic's defence was caught out when Rinus Israel's looping header found the target. From then on it was virtually one-way traffic as Feyenoord piled on the pressure. Only a combination of superb goalkeeping by Evan Williams, Dutch profligacy and friendly woodwork gave Celtic the chance of extra time.

Ernst Happel, the Feyenoord coach, who had expressed deep concern about his team's ability to live with Celtic after watching the games against Leeds, had also been astute enough to spot certain weaknesses in the opposition. Having compiled an extensive dossier on the other side's strengths and weaknesses, the instructions he gave to his players to nullify the obvious threat posed by Murdoch and Auld in midfield proved key to Feyenoord's success. With their link men starved of possession, Celtic were largely ineffectual.

Stein tried to alter the flow by sending on George Connelly in place of Auld after seventy-five minutes, but the switch came too late to decide the final outcome. Another key factor was that Happel had identified the potential threat posed by Jinky and had found a means to counter it. Perceiving that Jinky was bound to cause havoc if left to his own devices, he assigned two players to track the wee man all over the pitch. Shadowed by two defenders, Jinky never managed to impose his personality on the final. Later he described one of his escorts, Laseroms, who inflicted an early ankle injury, as the hardest player he had encountered in his entire career.

Lucky to make it into extra time, Celtic very nearly stole the lead afresh thirty seconds into the additional thirty minutes when Hughes's powerful solo run forced the goalkeeper to make a save. But it would have been a travesty had Celtic won and Ove Kindvall's winner in the 117th minute, after he had swept round McNeill, who had handled a high cross deep into the penalty box, and lobbed the ball into the net, was no more than Feyenoord deserved.

All in all, Feyenoord were tactically superior, physically stronger and mentally tougher. Happel, who had been concerned about what effect conceding the first goal might have on his players, out-foxed the fox, and Stein was charged with complacency and badly misjudging the class of the opposition.

Ironically, it was Wim Van Hanegem, whom Stein had dismissed as little more than a poor man's Jim Baxter, who dominated the play. His powerful challenges in the middle of the park and intelligent use of the ball won Feyenoord early control.

The fallout from Celtic's defeat was predictably toxic and

recriminations raged. Stein, who had a habit of taking a bow for his tactics when the team played well and turning his back on his charges when their performance fell below par, pointed a finger at the players. Feyenoord, he said, had played exceptionally well. Celtic had performed poorly. They had lacked their normal drive and cutting edge.

Stein claimed to know exactly why Celtic had lost, but stressed that he would never criticise his players in public. At the same time he denied that his players' apparent preoccupation with financial interests had cost Celtic the chance to join Real Madrid, Benfica and Inter Milan as multiple winners of the European Cup. Not surprisingly, a number of players took offence at their manager's remarks and apparent refusal to accept any responsibility for what was a crossroads for the club. But, unquestionably, Stein's reputation did suffer.

The players' mood was not improved by having to undertake a close-season tour to Canada, the USA and Bermuda in the wake of their bitter disappointment. The club's directors insisted that they had agreed to participate in the Toronto Cup tournament because of the prestige involved in playing against the likes of Manchester United and Bari of Italy, but the true lure was financial.

The squad's morale, already at an all-time low, was not helped either by Stein's decision to allow Jinky to remain at home. He mentioned the player's fear of flying and the injury he had suffered against Feyenoord as the reasons behind his decision, but there was a current of resentment among Jinky's team-mates. However, Jinky was almost certainly excluded from the travelling party because he had tabled a transfer request fifteen days after the final in Milan, on 21 May.

Jinky was only one-third of the way through a six-year deal when he demanded a substantial increase in his earnings. He was almost certainly motivated by his own sense of increasing worth and the fact that both Spurs and Manchester United had been linked with him. Gemmell too had asked for a move, and the players were told that they would be allowed to leave if realistic offers were made for their services.

A tour that had been fraught with difficulties and resentment from the outset disintegrated into farce when Stein suddenly upped and left. He made his exit fifteen minutes from the end of the match against Bari, taking both his assistant Sean Fallon and his players by complete surprise. At the end of the 2–2 draw the Celtic players were reduced to quizzing journalists accompanying the team as to the whereabouts of their boss.

Eventually, Stein released a statement to the effect that he had returned home to attend to a backlog of paper work and endeavour to resolve Jinky's contractual dispute. He added that he also required treatment for the recurring ankle problem he had suffered with since being forced to quit playing because of injury.

One key development was that Manchester United had appeared on the scene, and Sir Matt Busby was keen to persuade Stein to succeed him as manager at Old Trafford. There was even talk that Stein had been involved in lengthy telephone discussions with officials while still in Canada. The SFA, it was said, were also keen to secure Stein's services. But, for the time being at least, the manager stayed in place.

In the interim, Fallon had been placed in charge of the squad on their North American tour and had the unpleasant task of sending Gemmell and Auld home following a breach of club discipline. It was, in every sense, the unhappiest period in Stein's five-year reign up to that point.

Some critics offered the view that Stein had been asking for trouble because he had failed to investigate the other side's strengths and weaknesses, or to make the same meticulous preparations that his team had carried out before the 1967 final in Lisbon. Sean Fallon offered a simpler explanation for what had happened – the players had nothing more to give after two gruelling games against Leeds United, and were a spent force when they stepped on to the pitch at the San Siro.

Fallon said: 'Leeds had a great side and they were in the running for everything that season. They were two memorable nights, two great games, but we killed each other for the final. I honestly believe that we beat each other that night for the ultimate glory. We failed against Feyenoord in the final and if Leeds had gone through they would have done the same because I think both teams gave everything in the two semi-final matches. That was the mistake that maybe both of us made.'

But Fallon also accused the players of allowing themselves to be sidetracked by outside influences. 'The players set up a pool for off-field deals and were having meetings with the agent before the game,' he complained. 'He was wanting various deals set up – but all this was happening before the game. I can remember the dressing room at the San Siro Stadium after we had been beaten in extra time. The chairman was sitting there, and he was so disappointed. But even then Sir Robert was more upset at the way the team had played. I can still remember him saying: "I don't mind losing, but not the way we lost. That was wrong for this club and it supporters. The attitude was wrong."

'But by the time that Jock and I realised that, it was too late. The players were wanting to charge photographers money for pictures before we even went on to the field.'

Celtic's captain, Billy McNeill, a fiercely proud and honourable man, strongly denied this claim in his autobiography, *Hail Cesar*. According to McNeill: 'In the wake of our defeat I heard ridiculous stories about how we had only been interested in the financial rewards to be gained from reaching the final and that our attitude had contributed to our downfall. According to the rumour-mongers, the Celtic players had not been able to agree a share-out of the cash and we had allegedly squabbled among ourselves right up to the kick-off. The only flaw in that particular theory was that there had been no cash to share-out!'

McNeill felt that the explanation was much more straightforward – Feyenoord was a game too far. Following their semi-final against Leeds United the previous month, the Celtic players were forced to twiddle their thumbs for the best part of three weeks. The league finished on 18 April and the Scottish Cup final was played on 11 April. And the mood of the players was not helped by losing 3–1 to Aberdeen at Hampden.

Celtic's preparations for the European Cup final included games against Stenhousemuir, Fraserburgh and Gateshead, while Feyenoord were still in competitive action. Jock Stein and his assistant Sean Fallon also appear to have conveyed the message to the players that Feyenoord 'weren't anything special'.

It later emerged that Celtic's defeat had cost the players in the region of £10,000 in endorsements, syndication fees and bonuses. It was a high price to pay for the sin of complacency.

Jinky, for his part, contended that Celtic's defeat was down to one thing and one thing only: overconfidence on the part of the players.

He pointed out that seven of the team – Gemmell, Murdoch, McNeill, Wallace, Auld, Lennox and himself – were survivors from Lisbon and were still household names around the world. Holland on the other hand still hadn't rated as a strong football nation, despite the appearance of Ajax in the 1969 final. In his opinion, Celtic saw themselves as the stars and Feyenoord as the supporting cast. It was a straight reversal of Lisbon, where Inter Milan were the established force in the eyes of the world and Celtic could only be classed as underdogs.

But he was adamant that money never came into it. While it was true that the players had wanted to make as much cash as possible the second time around, they were completely satisfied with what was on offer. There was no question of their having let commercial interests distract them.

'Quite simply, we had written Feyenoord off,' he said. 'All we had to do was go out on the San Siro pitch and pick up the Cup. The hard work had been done when Leeds were beaten at Hampden Park. We wanted to win for the 20,000 fans who had followed us to Italy and we assumed the script would not fail.

'Feyenoord, unwittingly, fuelled our arrogance. As we walked to the dressing rooms before the game their players stared at us and you could almost feel their admiration. They recognised each and every one of us. It was like Lisbon all over again, except this time we were being treated like gods.'

The match was one long nightmare for Celtic and their fans. No player rose above the mediocre, while their rivals' football surpassed even their highest expectations. Feyenoord competed for every ball while the Celtic players chased shadows. Van Hanegem and Hasil controlled the middle of the park and the Celtic defence was always under pressure. The general consensus was that Celtic had been extremely fortunate to take the match into extra time and might easily have been beaten by a much greater margin.

By the time the new season kicked off, in August, Jinky had withdrawn his transfer request. Having partially recovered from his initial disappointment and reflected on the fact that his heart lay at Celtic Park, Jinky realised he would not be happy playing his football elsewhere. But things were never quite the same again. Jinky's decision to give away his runners-up medal to a young friend coincided with Celtic's steady decline as a force in Europe.

Milan also signalled the beginning of the end of the Lisbon Lions era, although some, such as McNeill, wondered if Stein was a shade premature in breaking up the team that had taken Celtic to the pinnacle of European football.

Although he did not realise it at the time, Jinky would not have another opportunity to play in a European Cup final. Although, had the fates been kinder to Celtic four years later, he might have been able to exorcise the ghosts of the San Siro, which continued to haunt him for a long time.

14

Changing Times

Midway through the 1970–71 season Jinky's form had dipped to the point where he asked to be dropped from the team. Although he had withdrawn his transfer request some time since, he was still suffering from a crisis of confidence in the wake of the Feyenoord defeat. Inevitably his relationship with Jock Stein, always volatile, was put back under strain once again. Stein was critical of the winger's indifferent form and general attitude. This fuelled persistent rumours that Manchester United and Spurs could expect greater encouragement if they renewed their interest in Jinky.

Things came to a head at the end of November, when Jinky indicated to Stein that he was not keen to play against St Mirren because he did not feel mentally prepared for the match. Agnes was pregnant with the third of the couple's children, and Jinky, the born worrier, felt so concerned about his wife's well-being that his worries affected his state of mind.

Indeed, Jinky's increasing habit of seeking the company of pals for a drinks session whenever there was a perceived crisis in his life led Agnes to admit there were times when she threatened to leave him. However, she was persuaded not to carry out her threat by Celtic director Jimmy Farrell, a close friend of the couple. Jinky's generosity and his ability to appear contrite were also endearing qualities. Agnes found it difficult to resist him.

In the event, Stein granted Jinky his wish and his place was taken by Victor Davidson. Celtic beat St Mirren 3–0 at Celtic Park, with two goals for Davidson. But Jinky was recalled the following week, against Dundee United at Tannadice, where Celtic won 2–1.

It might have appeared that the latest rift had been healed when Jinky played in the next two games, a 1–0 home defeat by Aberdeen and a 2–1 win away to Ayr United. But Stein was far from happy with Jinky's performance, and he dropped both him and Billy McNeill for the trip to Cappielow to face Morton on Boxing Day. 'They have not been playing well recently and this may give them the necessary jolt,' Stein explained.

Significantly, when Jinky was recalled for Celtic's next match, against Rangers at Ibrox a week later, 2 January 1971, he performed with much greater urgency and scored in a 1–1 draw. But the result lost all importance in the shadow of the tragedy that took the lives of sixty-six fans and cast a pall over Scottish football.

But football went on. Jinky scored twice in an 8–1 win over Dundee at Dens Park on 16 January. Four days later his son James was born, and a weight of fear was lifted from his shoulders.

Yet the team's form was erratic. Wins over Dunfermline in the league and in a Scottish Cup fourth-round replay, and a win at home against Airdrie, were offset by a surprise 3–2 defeat by St Johnstone at Muirton Park and a draw at Tynecastle, where they were outplayed by Hearts. Celtic were sloppy in these two games, both in defence and attack. Consequently they remained one point adrift of league leaders Aberdeen when they prepared to face Cowdenbeath at Central Park on 13 March, one week after crushing Fife neighbours Raith Rovers 7–1 in the Scottish Cup.

But the breach persisted. Jinky once again risked the wrath of his manager by asking to be left out of the team. Stein agreed to the request, explaining to the media that 'He [Jinky] is not ready for the match.' Jinky had not played well in the European Cup tie against Ajax in Amsterdam the previous midweek, when Celtic lost 3–0 in the quarter-final first leg. This was almost certainly the reason for Jinky asking to be rested. But fresh rumours started at once claiming that Jinky was unhappy with his treatment by Stein, and with the manager's habit of picking on him when results did not go to plan. It was also suggested that Jinky's fear of flying had worsened on the flight to and from Amsterdam.

The emergence of Davidson may also have influenced Jinky's frame of mind. Stein had declared himself a fan of his, and when Davidson played against Cowdenbeath he stood out in a 5–1 win. He kept his place for the next game and scored in a 4–1 victory away to Kilmarnock. Jinky also featured at Rugby Park following a 'clear the air' meeting with Stein.

Jinky's display against Ajax in the European Cup return four days later suggested that he had settled his differences with Stein. In excess of 83,000 fans turned up at Hampden more in hope than expectation that Celtic could overturn a three-goal deficit. But for all that they played to the best of their ability, Celtic found the task beyond them. Jinky, however, recaptured something approaching his best form and scored after twenty-eight minutes.

Barely four years on from their Lisbon triumph, Celtic's starting line-up included only five of the European Cup-winning side: Jinky, Tommy Gemmell, Billy McNeill, Willie Wallace and Bertie Auld. Bobby Lennox, brought on as a substitute for Auld in the home win over Ajax, shared the view that Jinky's disenchantment had its roots in the defeat by Feyenoord the previous season.

'Losing the European Cup final had a fairly traumatic affect on all of us,' said Lennox. 'I don't think people realised just how low we all were for quite a while afterwards. But Jimmy, being a worrier, probably took it worst of all. I can just picture him fretting over what to do next. It wasn't as if he had fallen out of love with Celtic. He was just on a terrible downer.'

But such was the paradox of a player with the heart of a lion on the football pitch that he could be unnerved by the slightest thing when exposed to life's realities. His wife Agnes remembered how the couple owned a large Alsatian dog yet Jinky still insisted on every door of their home having several locks.

On one occasion the two of them visited a cinema in Glasgow, when the patrons were instructed to leave the building because of a bomb scare. When Agnes kidded Jinky that someone had probably spotted him going into the place and placed a bomb under his seat, he refused point blank to return.

Whereas in the previous five season Rangers had been the principal challengers to Celtic, Aberdeen emerged as their closest rivals in the title race. Indeed, it was not until the sides met at Pittodrie on 17 April in a match labelled a 'title decider' that the pendulum swung towards Celtic.

Five days before heading north, Celtic had kept their championship aspirations alive, by means of a 3–0 victory over Motherwell at Fir Park. Jinky played a significant part in the success when he scored the second goal that took the pressure off. But Celtic's preparations for the crucial match against Aberdeen were overshadowed by a fresh approach by Manchester United to try to tempt Stein to succeed Sir Matt Busby as manager.

It is no secret that Stein and Busby met at a motorway service station near Haydock to discuss a possible move. But a combination of doubts about his full control over team matters with Busby peeping over his shoulder, and the knowledge that his wife Jean would not fancy moving house to England persuaded Stein to stay put. In the end he rejected United's overtures, explaining that he 'liked being Celtic's manager'.

A 1–1 draw left Aberdeen one point ahead of their rivals, but Celtic had a game in hand. They also had a vastly superior goal average, and that was just as well, because a 2–2 draw with St Mirren at Love Street on 27 April might have scuppered their chances had not Aberdeen also slipped up three days earlier, losing 1–0 to Falkirk at Brockville. That defeat left Celtic requiring three points from their remaining three games to clinch a sixth successive league championship.

Having picked up one of those points at Love Street, Celtic completed the task just two days later, but fate once again conspired against them winning the championship in their own backyard. Renovation work to the main stand at Celtic Park caused the match with Ayr United to be switched Hampden. A crowd of 25,000 – dwarfed in the vastness of the national stadium – watched as goals from Bobby Lennox in the first half and Willie Wallace in the second sealed a 2-0 win and the title.

In the final league game of the season, played against Clyde at Celtic Park two days after the championship had been secured, Stein created a piece of pure theatre by fielding the Lisbon Lions for the last time. Under normal circumstances the match would have been meaningless, but 35,000 fans came to witness history in the making as the greatest team in the club's history emerged from the partially demolished main stand to take their final bow.

Goalkeeper Ronnie Simpson had retired the previous year, but 'Faither', as Simpson was known to his team-mates, took part in the pre-match warm-up before handing over to Evan Williams, who lined up alongside: Craig, Gemmell; Murdoch, McNeill, Clark; Johnstone, Wallace, Chalmers, Auld and Lennox. Within days Auld left to join Hibs and Clark became a Morton player.

The Lions hallmarked the occasion by demolishing Clyde, 6-1. Jinky was at his best, and when Jinky was at his best, no one could hold him. He revelled in the nostalgic atmosphere, setting up chances for Lennox to score a hat-trick and Wallace, with two goals, and Chalmers to complete the rout.

For all that he was clearly unsettled for much of the season, Jinky figured in fifty-one of Celtic's fifty-eight league and cup matches. He also scored nineteen goals – his highest tally in a single season.

By the start of the following season, he had perked up enough to play well in all six of Celtic's League Cup section matches, the first of them against Rangers on 14 August 1971 at Ibrox. He was, in fact, outstanding in the opening fixture, scoring the first of Celtic's two goals in the 2–0 victory after providing the springboard for much of the team's swift and incisive attacking play. This was the game in which Kenny Dalglish made his Old Firm debut.

Celtic went on to reach the final, where they met Partick Thistle at Hampden on 23 October 1971. The date stands out in the history of Scottish football because it marks Celtic's most humiliating defeat in a national cup final.

The teams that day were: Celtic: Williams; Hay, Gemmell;

Murdoch, Connelly, Brogan; Johnstone, Dalglish, Hood, Callaghan and Macari. Partick Thistle: Rough; Hansen, Forsyth; Glavin, Campbell, Strachan; McQuade, Coulston, Bone, Rae and Lawrie.

Thistle were given little chance of living with a Celtic side that boasted eight Scotland internationals. Celtic were missing their inspirational captain and centre half Billy McNeill due to injury, but that was viewed as little more than a minor nuisance. However, Thistle, the rank outsiders, refused to give an inch to reputation and proceeded to pull Celtic's defence so far apart that after just thirty-seven minutes they led 4–0. Celtic scored a consolation goal through Kenny Dalglish in the seventieth minute, but the full-time score of 4–1 was greeted with disbelief throughout the country.

Jinky played for only twenty minutes of the final. He sustained a nasty gash in his knee which required six stitches following an accidental clash with Ronnie Glavin, who was later to become a team-mate, and was replaced by Jim Craig. His enforced substitution disrupted Celtic's game plan, but it is worth pointing out that Thistle were already two goals up when Jinky limped off.

The defeat was a shock to the system for a team used to dominating and winning cup finals, but Celtic suffered no long-term damage. They followed up with league wins over Dunfermline and Ayr United, although Jinky missed both games because of the injury that took him off at Hampden.

It was one of the rare occasions when injury forced Jinky on to the sidelines. Amazingly, given the hammering he often came in for from unscrupulous defenders, Jinky never suffered a serious long-term injury. His only other injury of note came when he had to have stitches put in an ankle wound following a tackle by the Hibs player Jimmy O'Rourke.

Celtic, who had begun their title defence with a breathtaking 9–1 win at home to Clyde, had in fact been in rampant form in the run-up to the League Cup final. Following their two League Cup section wins over Rangers they inflicted the third defeat on their Old Firm rivals on 11 September 1971, by 3–2, when Jinky rose above the defence to head the winner in the last minute.

But despite losing only once in the league – to St Johnstone on 2 October – Celtic still trailed Aberdeen by a single point when they visited Pittodrie on 6 November. A 1–1 draw maintained the status quo, but by the turn of the year the teams had swapped positions.

A succession of 5–1 victories – over Dundee United, Partick Thistle and Motherwell when Jinky scored in each of the latter matches – was followed by another heavy beating for Clyde, this time by 7–0. Jinky also maintained his remarkable scoring run against Rangers when he grabbed the first goal in the 2–1 win at Celtic Park on 3 January 1972. From that point on Aberdeen were left playing catch-up and the championship was eventually won by a margin of ten points.

Celtic also reached the semi-final stage of the European Cup for the fourth time in seven years. After an uncertain start against BK 1903 Copenhagen, when a 2–1 away defeat was followed by a 3–0 home win, Celtic cruised past Maltese side Sliema Wanderers on a 7–1 aggregate to claim a quarter-final tie with Ujpest Dozsa of Hungary, who included several internationals in their line-up, among them the respected striker Ferenc Bene.

Celtic were without Jinky for the first leg in Budapest after he had been diagnosed with chickenpox. Celtic won 2–1, and Jinky was declared fit enough to take his place on the substitutes' bench for the return on 22 March. It was as well that Stein had Jinky in reserve, for Ujpest scored first at Celtic Park to level the tie on aggregate and threatened for a time to overwhelm their rivals. But the introduction of Jinky in place of Jim Brogan in the second half transformed Celtic's play.

A press report of the match hailed Jinky's performance. 'Jimmy Johnstone calmed Celtic's nerves. The player the Hungarian's feared most unsettled their defence with his willingness to take defenders on in his inimitable style, and he disrupted their self-assurance sufficiently for Maurer's nervous back-header to be intercepted by the live-wire Macari to score the equaliser. On this form few, if any, defences could have lived with Johnstone.'

Dreams of a third European Cup final appearance were

shattered by Inter Milan. The Italians took revenge of sorts for their loss in the final five years earlier by winning a penalty shoot-out after the sides had failed to score a single goal in 210 minutes of action.

In the first leg, at the San Siro, Celtic displayed remarkable concentration and discipline and the closest Inter came to scoring was when George Connelly headed off the goal-line in the second half. The result augured well for the return, but Jinky explained: 'Inter, just as they had done in Lisbon, packed their defence and we could not break them down.'

John 'Dixie' Deans, signed from Motherwell for £17,500 immediately following the League Cup final defeat, volunteered to take the first of Celtic's five penalties and promptly ballooned the ball over the crossbar. Jinky kept his nerve to slot home the third, and Jim Craig, Pat McCluskey and Bobby Murdoch scored theirs. But Deans's miss proved fatal when Inter converted all five.

Celtic partially atoned for the disappointment of failing to go all the way in Europe by completing yet another league and cup double. Jinky did not play in the Scottish Cup wins over Albion Rovers, Dundee and Hearts – in a replay – because of a combination of a dip in form and illness, but when he returned to the side for the semi-final with Kilmarnock he rediscovered the form that made him the world-class player he was.

Kilmarnock's full-backs simply could not contain Jinky. Once again handed a free role by Stein, Jinky utilised the width of the Hampden pitch to show his paces. But it was showboating with a purpose. Jinky persisted with his sometimes infuriating habit of attempting to beat the same player twice in the one movement, but did so to great effect. He played a prominent part in all three Celtic goals, scored by Deans and Macari as the holders secured their place in the final.

When Celtic lined up against Hibs at Hampden on 6 May 1972 only four of the starting XI – Craig, Murdoch, McNeill and Jinky – had played in Lisbon five years previously. Stevie Chalmers had been let go to Morton, Gemmell to Nottingham Forest and Wallace to Crystal Palace. Bobby Lennox was named as substitute. Their places in the pecking order had been taken by a new, much younger generation of likely lads such as Davie Hay, Danny McGrain, Kenny Dalglish and Lou Macari. But while the personnel showed considerable change, Celtic's power to thrill their audience had not.

The 106,000 who turned up at Hampden expecting a closely contested final were not disappointed, for forty-five minutes at least. Billy McNeill opened the scoring after only two minutes. Alan Gordon equalised ten minutes later and although Deans restored Celtic's lead midway through the first half, the match was fairly evenly contested. But when the floodgates opened early in the second half Celtic were simply unstoppable. They gave a masterclass in the art of finishing.

Jinky's darting runs, when he would go up to the full-back and show him the ball before cutting inside his man, were instrumental in weakening Hibs' resolve and gifting openings to his team-mates. Deans benefited most from Jinky's constructive play, eventually claiming a hat-trick. The second of his goal's was a wonderful solo effort when he cut in from the left, rounded goalkeeper Jim Herriot, sidestepped defender John Brownlie and advancing along the byline before again beating the keeper. Lou Macari's two late goals scored in the final seven minutes were the icing on the cake.

It was the perfect ending to a season that saw Jinky play thirty-nine times, including one substitute appearance. Nine of his ten goals were scored in league games.

Celtic had to once again resist a powerful challenge from Rangers to win their eighth successive league title. Their success was built on a remarkable home record. They were undefeated in twenty-six league and cup games at Celtic Park. Celtic, in fact, suffered only six defeats all season.

Jinky played in thirty-nine of Celtic fifty-eight matches in season 1972–73, including two substitute appearances, and scored ten goals. The first of them, the game on 16 September, was highly significant. The rebuilding work at Celtic Park meant Hampden provided the perfect setting for a vintage performance by the winger.

Celtic's early-season displays in the League Cup had been unimpressive and coincided with Jinky suffering a sudden dip in form, for no obvious reason. After playing in a 3–0 win away to Stirling Albion on the opening day and a 1–1 home draw with East Fife, he was dropped for the remaining four qualifying matches. He also missed the first two league fixtures – when Celtic reasserted themselves with the impressive 6–2 win against Kilmarnock and followed up by beating Morton, 2–0 away – as well as the opening European Cup tie against Rosenborg of Norway at Celtic Park, a match Celtic totally dominated but which yielded only a 2–1 win.

But Stein, mindful of Jinky's habit of turning it on in the big games, recalled the winger against Rangers. Jinky gave right back Sandy Jardine a chasing. When Lou Macari scored their third Celtic were uncatchable, eventually winning 3–1 after John Greig notched a consolation goal in the final seconds.

Jinky, who had been substituted in the second half of the Old Firm game after picking up a minor knock, missed the League Cup second-round tie the following Wednesday when Celtic struggled to win 2–1 at lowly Stranraer. But he played in Celtic's next two league matches, a 2–0 defeat at Dundee and a 1–0 home win over Ayr United.

The European Cup second leg against Rosenborg was sandwiched between these games, and Jinky chose the occasion to display his trickery by carrying the ball almost the entire length of the pitch before delivering a superb pass to Dalglish, whose eighty-ninth minute goal wrapped up a 5–2 aggregate victory.

Jinky also featured in the League Cup return match with Stranraer, which Celtic won 5–2, though he was replaced in the second half by Brian McLaughlin. Jinky's form continued to fluctuate and he was dropped from the team for the rest of October, missing a total of five games, including the League Cup quarter-final first leg at Dens Park that brought Celtic their second defeat on Tayside in the space of three weeks, this time by 1–0.

Stein hoped that by relegating Jinky to the reserves it would act as a wake-up call and help him rediscover his touch. The manager, concerned by reports that Jinky was spending a little too much time socialising, at the expense of his family, and angered by his failure to turn up for training on several occasions, had no compunction about wielding the big stick. The strategy had the desired affect. When Jinky returned to the side on 1 November, in the second leg against Dundee, he had rediscovered his old spark, but he could not tilt the outcome of the match, which finished 3–2 in favour of Celtic after extra time, necessitating a play-off.

When Celtic entertained Dundee's city neighbours, United, three days later, Jinky shone in a 3–1 win, scoring the opening goal after thirty-nine minutes and dictating much of the play.

Following impressive wins over Motherwell and Hearts, when Jinky scored the third goal in a 4–2 success, Celtic returned to Hampden on 20 November for the League Cup decider against Dundee. This time they made no mistakes and won, comfortably, 4–1 to clinch a semi-final tie against Aberdeen.

However, Celtic had crashed out of Europe in the intervening period. Ujpest Dozsa, whom they had beaten at the quarter-final stage the previous season, took revenge in the second round. In the first leg at Celtic Park on 25 October, the Hungarians, recalling how hugely influential Jinky had been in steering Celtic to a 1–1 home draw seven months earlier, marked him out of the game. He was replaced by Bobby Lennox a quarter of an hour before the end as Celtic struggled to a 2–1 win.

The return a fortnight later was utterly one-sided. Ujpest, three goals to the good after just twenty-two minutes, won with ease. The defeat prompted Stein to continue to make changes week by week in an effort to rekindle the habitual fluency and consistency of not so long ago. But changes in personnel and the suspicion that the old guard was no longer able to cover for the younger element when they had an off-day left Stein with a dilemma.

After once again being 'rested', this time for a match against Falkirk at Brockville, which Celtic won unconvincingly 3–2, Jinky played in the League Cup semi-final on 27 November. Celtic were pushed all the way by Aberdeen, who led twice, but Jinky struck in the seventy-fifth minute with the Dons 2–1 in front to equalise with a shot from close range and inspire greater urgency. Tom

Callaghan netted what proved to be the match-winner five minutes later.

Celtic's opponents in the final twelve days later were Hibs. Just seven months earlier the Easter Road side had been thrashed 6–1 by Celtic in the Scottish Cup final, leading most critics to conclude that they would be psychologically damaged. The teams lined up: Hibs: Herriot; Brownlie, Schaedler; Stanton, Black, Blackley; Edwards, O'Rourke, Gordon, Cropley and Duncan. Celtic: Williams; McGrain, Brogan; McClukey, McNeill, Hay; Johnstone, Connelly, Dalglish, Hood and Macari.

In all, Celtic showed four changes from the previous cup final meeting between the sides, Hibs just one. But the outcome was very different. Hibs had learned painful lessons from their Hampden humiliation, and with Deans, the scorer of a hat-trick in the 6–1 win, absent from the Celtic line-up, and Bobby Murdoch's influence in midfield no longer a factor, Celtic posed much less of a threat. Hibs won the midfield battle, Pat Stanton and Jimmy O'Rourke scored in the space of six minutes in the second half, and Dalglish's goal in the seventy-seventh minute proved irrelevant. Hibs collected their first trophy for twenty years

The final was a personal disappointment for Jinky. Erich Schaedler, the left back he hated playing against, policed and sub-dued him from the outset. Eventually Stein, hoping to put greater pressure on Schaedler and get in behind the solid Hibs defence in the closing stages, sent on Tom Callaghan in place of Jinky. But the switch didn't work, and Hibs deserved their win.

Jinky, who had substituted for Deans and scored in a 6–1 win at Dumbarton a week earlier, enjoyed an unbroken run of eleven games following the final, scoring in two of them, against Dundee and Kilmarnock, as the championship gradually developed into a two-horse race. But with Stein still in quest of another 'perfect' blend, he sacrificed Jinky, fielding him only twice in six matches between 6 March and 3 April 1973.

Jinky had also suffered the misfortune to be sent off for the fifth time in his career on 17 March. Referee Bobby Davidson judged that Jinky had deliberately kicked the Aberdeen full-back Jim

Hermiston during a drawn Scottish Cup quarter-final at Celtic Park. Davidson, who also disallowed a goal by Jinky in the opening minute on the testimony of a linesman, required a police escort from the ground.

But, for once, Jinky was the victim of a miscarriage of justice. With the backing of his club, he protested his innocence to the SFA the following month and was duly exonerated. Celtic, meantime, beat Aberdeen 1–0 at Pittodrie in a replay in which Jinky, troubled by the events of the previous weekend, was forced to make way for Victor Davidson.

After missing several crucial games in the run-in to the championship, Jinky was spoiling for action by the time he was recalled against Dundee in a Scottish Cup semi-final replay at Hampden on 11 April, four days after replacing Deans in a drab goalless draw. The second match also failed to spark, and a penalty shoot-out was looming until Jinky took a hand in extra time. He pounced in the 101st minute to gather a long ball out of defence, which had been headed on by Dalglish, and shot wide of goalkeeper Thomson Allan. When Dalglish struck again a minute later, Celtic were assured of a place in the final. But Jinky, clearly keen to impress Stein, pinned back his ears in the 110th minute after collecting a pass from Danny McGrain and carried the ball deep into the heart of the Dundee defence before hitting a fierce drive from an acute angle past Allan.

Boosted by his spectacular return to form, Jinky took any lingering frustrations out on St Johnstone the following Saturday. He was back to his scintillating best at Muirton Park, as John Lambie attested. Lambie, who normally played right back for Saints, recalled how he was forced to switch to the left to face Jinky because of an injury crisis. It was the one and only occasion when he was in direct opposition to Jinky and he confessed: 'He ran rings round me. With every twist and turn, every little trick, he left me tangled up. He was virtually unmarkable. I couldn't even get close to him.'

Jinky scored Celtic's second goal in a 3–1 win and the value of the result was highlighted when news filtered through that

Rangers, despite being outplayed by Dundee United, had won 2–1 at Ibrox. Celtic, with a game in hand over their rivals, matched Rangers' points tally in their next match, a five-goal victory at Dumbarton. But, with just two games remaining, Celtic had the advantage of a superior goal average.

Jinky did not feature in the penultimate league fixture, a nervy 4–0 home win against Arbroath on the day that Rangers were held to a 2–2 draw by Aberdeen at Pittodrie, but he was included in the side to face Hibs at Easter Road on 28 April when Celtic needed only a draw to be crowned champions.

It was the sort of occasion Jinky enjoyed, even though he was once again up against Schaedler. But this time the roles were reversed, and the Hibs defender failed to shackle Jinky as he had in the League Cup final. The winger soon put Celtic in the driving seat. Hibs threatened briefly at the start of the second half, but with Jinky supplying the ammunition and Deans and Dalglish the goals, Celtic powered their way to a 3–1 victory – and the title.

The Scottish Cup final a week later, 5 May 1972, offered Celtic the chance to clinch a third successive league and cup double, but while Celtic looked more stylish, their rivals showed more passion and commitment. The 3–2 defeat – Celtic's sixth in nine finals – convinced Jock Stein that he needed new blood in his squad. By the following September, in the wake of Stein's decision to allow Bobby Murdoch to join Middlesbrough on a free transfer, only three of the Lisbon Lions – Billy McNeill, Bobby Lennox and Jinky – remained at Celtic Park. It was soon to be more and more evident that Jinky no longer held the key to the manager's plans.

15

New Kids on the Block

The emergence of a new generation of young stars at Celtic Park could easily have anatgonised the old guard. But for all that the established stars found their places under threat from the likes of George Connelly, Danny McGrain, Kenny Dalglish, Davie Hay and Lou Macari in the seasons following Celtic's European Cup triumph, there was no current of resentment. Jinky embraced the arrival of these young players, and actively encouraged them in the same way that he had been nursed along by an earlier generation a decade before.

Lou Macari, who was sold by Stein to Manchester United in January 1973 for the princely sum of £200,000 after daring to argue that his talents were worth a whole lot more than the wages that Celtic were prepared to pay him, was one of those who benefited from Jinky's tutelage.

Macari, a handful for any defence and a prolific goalscorer during his five seasons at Celtic Park, offered an intriguing insight into Jinky the footballer and the person. He felt that Jinky was misunderstood by many. He also stressed that stories of Jinky's drinking exploits were largely a misconception based on myth and mischief, insisting that alcohol was not the huge factor in his Celtic career that some would have the football world believe.

'I only ever picked up good habits from Jimmy watching the way he trained and prepared himself for a game,' said Macari. 'Often, when we were down at Seamill prior to a big game, we would see Jimmy and Bobby Lennox out doing a little bit extra training in the afternoon.

'People probably tended to think that because Jimmy was such a great player it all just happened naturally for him. But, along with the rest of the Lions, he was an incredibly hard worker. He never took the view that he had it all and therefore did not have to work overtime to improve his skills. For someone with so much talent to want to keep reaching for the next level was fantastic for me and the other young players.

'It was very important for us to witness that dedication from a young age; to look and learn from players like Jimmy, who had done it all; to observe their behaviour and know that they had been successful in the way that we wanted to become.

'Jimmy guided me and others down the right path. We picked up good habits and learned what was required to successfully follow in the footsteps of a player whose preparations were flawless.

'I realise how fortunate I was to play alongside a player like Jimmy. We've all heard the stories about his drinking but I have always believed that there was a large degree of embellishment. With Jock Stein's beady eye watching your every movement the players considered it an achievement if they could manage a half-pint of shandy without the manager knowing about it although, obviously, I can't comment on what happened after I left Celtic.'

While the notorious Largs boating incident, when Jinky put his international career in jeopardy, was fuelled by alcohol, Macari expressed the view that it was blown out of all proportion. It was just Jimmy being the guy he was: a character, and he had to be to reach the level he did.

Macari also questioned whether Jinky really was as much of a headache to Stein as has been claimed. 'I believe that Jimmy's overall attitude and approach to the game actually made life easy for the manager. People say that Jimmy was difficult and that he gave Jock Stein all sorts of problems, but I hold the view that he was in actual fact a manager's dream, the way he worked at the game and the things he could do to win matches.'

Macari felt grateful for the way that Jinky would take the younger players in the squad aside and offer them words of encouragement and advice – sensing, perhaps, that they were in awe of the established stars. Jinky's lack of self-importance made him popular with his young team-mates. 'Jimmy would go out and beat half a dozen men, as was his wont, and deliver the ball to you on a plate so you could stick it in the back of the net and then he would be the first to offer congratulations, telling you how brilliant you were,' Macari recalled.

'Jimmy had the knack of making you feel ten feet tall after he had done the hard work. He was unstinting in his praise and never at any time did you form the impression that he wanted to be the star of the show, hogging the limelight. He didn't want people patting him on the back. We felt comfortable in Jimmy's company because he put you at your ease and made you feel that you had every right to feel part of what was happening.

'Had Jimmy and the other Lions resented us that reaction would have been understandable. Don't forget, we were a new generation come to take their places in the team, so they could easily have felt threatened and not made us welcome. But that was never the case.'

Macari said that he had few opportunities to socialise with Jinky, pointing out that the pairing of Jinky and Bobby Lennox was inseparable, one rarely seen without the other. But he added: 'When you were in the squad, as far as Jimmy was concerned you were one of the boys. There wasn't the least hint of superstar about Jimmy. He was brilliant as a player and a person.'

Bobby Lennox endorsed Macari's comments. 'Those who were introduced by Jock Stein – guys like Davie Hay, George Connelly, Kenny Dalglish and Danny McGrain – were outstanding players who were brought through gradually and Jimmy adapted to the changes,' he said. 'Those players also benefited from having Jimmy as a team-mate. They must always have felt that they had a chance of winning if he was playing.'

16

Troubled Waters

Perhaps no one incident illustrated more clearly Jimmy Johnstone's amazing ability to land himself in hot water than the infamous Largs boating affair in 1974 when Jinky literally found himself up a creek without a paddle.

The national press hung Jinky out to dry for what some hacks chose to perceive as an outrageous display of indiscipline rather than a bout of high jinks that went wrong. In the troubled story of Jinky's international career, this was another nail in the coffin. What had begun as horse play quickly blew up into a full-blown farce that saw the Clyde Coastguard mounting a rescue mission to pluck Jinky from the waters of Scotland's most famous river just hours after Scotland had beaten Wales 2–0 at Hampden Park. Only Jinky could have managed that.

Jinky had been left out of the team which had lost to Northern Ireland by the narrowest of margins the previous Saturday, 11 May 1974. But he was reinstated three days later by manager Willie Ormond to face the Welsh on Tuesday the 14th.

The win set up a Home International Championship decider against England, also scheduled to be played in Glasgow, that coming Saturday, and Ormond had been pleased enough with the performance to reward his players with a night off to celebrate their success on their return to their base, the Queens

Hotel in Largs, on the Ayrshire coast, at around 11.30 in the evening.

In those days pubs closed at 10 p.m., but some of the players were friendly with a local hotelier, Ross Bowie, and persuaded him to open up a private bar and serve drinks long into the night. Dawn had broken by the time Jinky and his team-mates emerged from their celebrations, a little the worse for wear. A combination of the crisp morning air mixed with effects of the alcohol they had consumed and the general party mood almost inevitably led to further antics.

Most of the players had enjoyed a few drinks and were merry when they emerged from the hotel at around five o'clock in the morning. Inevitably, they started to lark around. But according to Jinky it was goalkeeper David Harvey, of Leeds United, who kicked off the fun when he jumped on the roof of a small hut near the shingle beach that runs along the seafront and began to pelt the other players with stones, forcing them to scatter in various directions.

Jinky, along with Rangers full-back Sandy Jardine, who had netted Scotland's second goal from the penalty spot just hours earlier, ran along the beach to escape being stoned and spied a collection of rowing boats. Within seconds Jinky jumped into one of them and invited Jardine to join him for an impromptu early morning sail that was to bring near disastrous consequences.

But instead of jumping into the boat, Jardine gave it an almighty kick that sent it drifting into the Firth of Clyde. Jardine reacted by collapsing on to the beach in fits of laughter. But there were two things neither Jinky nor he had noticed: the tide was going out, and the boat was missing the rowlocks necessary to support the oars. By now Jinky was so far out to sea that Jardine was unable to jump in beside him.

In an effort to rescue Jinky, Davie Hay, his Celtic team-mate, and Erich Schaedler commandeered one of the other boats and set off in pursuit, but the pair of them had hardly gone ten yards before they realised that they too were in trouble. There was a hole in the bottom of the second boat and it was shipping water at an alarming rate. They both made it back to dry land, but by that time Jinky was in grave danger of becoming a dot on the horizon.

There was no option but to alert the local coastguard, who launched a rescue operation by lifeboat. But, unbeknown to the rest of the players, by the time Jinky had been plucked to safety, chalk-white and shivering, someone had tipped off the press.

They headed for bed thinking the incident would soon blow over, but the press pack were assembling, ready to swoop on Largs in search of a story. What had begun as an innocent bit of fun was about to become front-page news.

As the squad were not due to train until the afternoon, most had a lie-in until 11 o'clock. When they eventually surfaced they were greeted by the sight of dozens of reporters and TV crews hovering in the hotel foyer wanting to know exactly what had been going on.

Willie Ormond, who had been woken by an SFA official, was naturally none too pleased, and told Jinky that he would need to give a press conference to account for what had happened. But Jinky was worried sick about Jock Stein's likely reaction. Nor did he fancy confronting the press on his own, and he tried his best to persuade some of his team-mates to sit in with him.

Denis Law was one who agreed to support Jinky in his hour of need, assuming that Jinky did not drop him in it. Some chance. As soon as the press conference was under way, Jinky turned to Law and invited him to explain exactly what had happened after opening up with the line that he and Denis had decided to go fishing.

The press showed no mercy whatsoever. They were highly critical of Jinky and the rest of the squad, proclaiming that it was nothing short of a national disgrace that they had behaved so badly while representing their country.

Scotland answered their critics in the best way possible three days later, beating England, 2–0 in front of 100,000 at Hampden. It was the team's final home game before going to the World Cup in West Germany, and it was decided to do a lap of honour at the end.

But as the players took their bow, Jinky pleaded with the others to stick two fingers up at the press box, which towered above the old south stand, because of the flak he had taken as a consequence of the Largs incident. Jinky went ahead and made the gesture on his own. Predictably, his V-sign earned him fresh condemnation and another ear-bashing from Jock Stein for making matters worse.

Law, who lined up alongside Jinky eight times in a Scotland jersey over a period of ten years from the mid-1960s, remembered Jinky sitting singing away to himself as he drifted further out to sea by the second, while the others shouted to him to come back. But this was no joke, said Law.

'Jimmy was wearing a thin top and none of us had realised just how dangerous the tides are in that part of the world. It was all very laughable at the time, but in reality it was a very dangerous situation and Jimmy was lucky to escape unscathed.

'The Celtic fans would not have been amused either, for Jimmy had turned a shade of Rangers blue by the time he was back on terra firma.'

Jinky survived to retain his place in the squad selected for the World Cup finals, winning his twentieth cap a fortnight later, on 1 June, in the warm-up match against Belgium, when he scored in a 2–1 defeat in Bruges. But by then a lot of damage had been done. Several SFA officials wanted him axed by Ormond, but the manager refused to succumb to the pressure from upstairs.

Five days after the defeat in Belgium, Jinky was again included in the team to face Norway in Oslo in the final friendly prior to the Finals. Scotland won 2–1 with goals from Joe Jordan and substitute Kenny Dalglish, who had replaced his Celtic team-mate

But the storm which had been brewing over Jinky gathered in strength on the flight from Belgium to Oslo when he and captain Billy Bremner, another fiery redhead with a gift for attracting adverse publicity, indulged in the free drinks on offer. By the time they touched down in the Oslo they were 'flying' themselves.

The scowls on the faces of certain SFA officials did not bode well for the errant pair, but worse was to follow when Jinky and Bremner, unhappy at the standard of the squad's accommodation, headed for the nearest bar and proceeded to hit the sauce once again.

'Billy and I hit it off straight away, probably because we both loved a drink,' Jinky recalled in a newspaper interview in 1997. 'But the SFA tried to keep the squad off the drink and none of our hotels had a bar.

'In Oslo, they booked us into a youth hostel, thinking it wouldn't have a bar, but they were wrong. As soon as Billy and I walked in we clocked the boozer and couldn't believe our luck. We couldn't put stuff in the room quickly enough before going back down for a drink. None of the others came down, so Billy and I thought it was our duty to have one for everyone!'

The pair were eventually persuaded by a couple of SFA officials to leave the bar and return to their rooms, but they then made the cardinal mistake of heading for the manager's room instead. They roused Willie Ormond to inform him that they were unhappy with their surroundings and to offer advice on how he should set his team out for the forthcoming World Cup matches against Zaire, Brazil and Yugoslavia.

Neither man was exactly whispering, and their advice was over-heard by SFA officials in adjoining rooms. The upshot was that Jinky and Bremner were threatened with disciplinary action, a prospect they didn't take kindly to. They informed the stunned officials that they no longer wished to be part of the action.

Having packed their bags and ordered a taxi to take them to the airport, in spite of Ormond's pleas that they should stay, the pair at last saw sense. But they awoke next morning with giant-sized hangovers and the realisation that their international careers hung by a thread.

Ormond resisted the cries to send the players home in disgrace. Refusing to disrupt his team's build-up, the manager closed ranks rather than cause further disharmony. However Jinky and Bremner were given a severe dressing down by the manager on the eve of Scotland's first appearance in the World Cup finals for sixteen years.

Publicly, Jinky was forgiven. Privately, he was to be made to pay the price for stepping out of line once too often. While Bremner, as captain, kept his place, Jinky was denied his final opportunity to appear on the world stage. It should have been one of the crowning moments of his distinguished career. Instead, he had to sit on the bench, and a worldwide TV audience of millions were denied the sight of a truly world-class player strutting his stuff.

In the event, the team surpassed all expectations by beating Zaire and drawing with both Brazil and Yugoslavia. But it wasn't quite enough to win Scotland a place in the latter stages of the tournament. Perhaps if Jinky had played his brilliance might have o made the difference. We shall never know.

Years later, Bremner, who sadly died in 1997 following a heart attack just two days short of his fifty-fifth birthday, revealed that he had pleaded with Ormond to send Jinky on as a substitute against Yugoslavia with twenty minutes remaining, in the belief that that he had it in him to produce a flash of match-winning brilliance. The plea went unheeded.

Billy McNeill always lamented what happened, and regretted that Jinky never had the chance to parade his talents on the world stage. He insisted that his former team-mate would not have been out of place in any football company.

McNeill said: 'It's a pity that Jinky never had the chance to headline his talents on the World Cup stage. He would have loved to have had the opportunity of taking the ball up to an Italian or Brazilian full-back and mesmerising his opponent with his trickery. The rest of the world would have enjoyed the sight, too.'

But Jinky was not bitter. 'I paid a terrible price for stepping out of line once too often,' he conceded. 'But Willie Ormond was one of the fairest men I ever met in the game and I was grateful for his loyalty. He could easily have sent me home from Oslo, and I would have had to face an inquisition as if I had committed a murder, and anything was preferable to that – even sitting on the bench.'

Jinky wore the dark blue of Scotland only twice more following his escapades in Largs and Oslo, first against East Germany at Hampden the following October, and then against Spain in another home game three weeks later on 20 November 1974. Scotland won the first of these games 3–0 and lost the second 2–1. It was an inglorious ending to a largely unfulfilled international career that should have left a scrapbook-full of memories.

But Jinky seldom enjoyed the experience of playing for his country. Like others before him and since, he was rarely able to replicate the artistry that hallmarked his play in a Celtic jersey when he swapped it for the dark blue of Scotland. By his own admission, Jinky was relieved when it ended that night at Hampden on 20 November 1974, for he told the author some years ago: 'I was never all that bothered about playing for the national side. I want to be remembered as a Celtic player.'

17

Nine in a Row

Celtic's remarkable achievement in winning nine successive league championship titles encompassed a total of 306 games. Jinky played in 230 of them and made five other appearances as a substitute. Only the captain, Billy McNeill, featured in more.

But in the season 1973–74, when Celtic equalled the world record held jointly by MTK Budapest of Hungary and CDNA Sofia of Bulgaria, Jinky started in just thirteen of the thirty-four First Division fixtures, coming on as a substitute in two others. His goals tally amounted to only eight. Yet Jinky made a vital contribution to the team's success in winning both the championship and the Scottish Cup.

What was a very good season very nearly became a great one. But for the disgraceful behaviour of Atletico Madrid, Celtic might well have gone on to win the European Cup for a second time, while in the League Cup final against Dundee they paid a heavy price for failing to treat their opponents with due respect.

The first of Jinky's five domestic goals proved crucial in beating Rangers in the third Old Firm meeting of the season. Twice in August the sides had clashed in the League Cup. It was in the second of these games that Jinky saw red for the sixth time in his career, thanks to his scrap with Alex MacDonald. Jinky's fourteen-day ban meant he missed Celtic's final League Cup qualifying tie, a 3–1 win at Arbroath and the opening league fixture, on 1 September, away to Dunfermline, who were beaten 3–2. Jock Stein, furious that Jinky had once again overstepped the mark, also issued a public rebuke and a warning that such sudden outbursts of temper would not go unpunished. Jinky faced the prospect of being disciplined by his employers if he continued to flaunt the rules.

Jinky gave the distinct impression that he had lost his appetite for the game. He struggled to reproduce the standard of play the fans were accustomed to seeing. The upshot was that he was left out of the team for games against Dundee and Hibs in mid-October and Ayr United, Partick Thistle and Dumbarton in November (although he did feature in the latter encounter as a substitute).

Just what it was that led to Jinky's sudden decline is unclear, but he remained under a cloud for some time, and his demotion to the reserve team for a large part of the season did nothing to ease the growing tension that had built up between him and his manager. Jock Stein was unhappy with Jinky's attitude, and increasingly concerned by rumours that the player was misbehaving. He reacted as he usually did when his authority was challenged by imposing the ultimate sanction – banishment from the first team.

Stein, who had grown accustomed to contending with his way-ward star's erratic mood swings, had remarked the previous season that Jinky was playing better in the early 1970s than he had done for several years. Now Stein was so exasperated that at one point he demanded publicly that Jinky show greater dedication. In the latter part of the season, when the penny dropped and Jinky began to play with some of his old magic, Stein was moved to comment: 'He suddenly takes a tumble to himself and there's the old artistry and ball skills in full flower.'

In Jinky's defence, Stein had grown less and less tolerant over-all. He no longer held the same sway over the new breed of Celtic stars that he had enjoyed when the Lisbon Lions were at their peak. The next generation were not willing to accept a low basic wage topped up by lucrative bonuses, as the Lions had been. They demanded the going rate for the job, and in some cases at least, their loyalty was to themselves and their families rather than to Celtic, as was witnessed by Lou Macari's departure to Manchester United, Kenny Dalglish's to Liverpool and Davie Hay's to Chelsea.

It may well be that part of Jinky's disillusionment stemmed from the knowledge that his earnings potential would have been far greater had he sought a move to one of the top English or European clubs. Instead, he remained fiercely loyal to Celtic. But even by the standards of the time, a basic wage of £125 a week did not represent a fortune. Had Jinky chosen to tread the path taken by others he could probably have earned twice as much. But Celtic played on his loyalty, and Stein was not noted for fighting his players' corner when it came to pressurising the Celtic directors to strengthen his hand in wage negotiations.

But even when Jinky was struggling to rediscover his zest for the game he still produced the odd flash of brilliance and it was his goal that earned Celtic last-gasp victory over Motherwell in a play-off for a League Cup quarter-final place after the sides had drawn 2–2 on aggregate. But despite the significance of his contribution, there was no place for Jinky in Celtic's starting X1 when they faced Aberdeen just two days later on 31 October 1973.

Jinky featured briefly as a substitute in the return at Pittodrie three weeks later as Celtic ground out a nil–nil draw to set up a semi-final meeting with Rangers. Jinky had to watch most of the match from the bench as Celtic won, 3–1, by dint of a Harry Hood hat-trick.

The final itself, played at Hampden on 15 December 1973, was a strange affair. Due to the State of Emergency that the government had declared to combat the effects of the miners' strike, the match had a surreal atmosphere. Only 27,974 were present when play kicked off at 1.30 on a bone-hard pitch.

Dundee coped better with the treacherous underfoot conditions, and a goal by Gordon Wallace fifteen minutes from time consigned Celtic to their fourth successive final defeat. Celtic made strong claims for a penalty in the dying minutes when Jinky was bundled off the ball by centre half George Stewart, but referee Bobby Davidson dismissed their frantic appeals.

Apart from playing in the final, Jinky made only one other appearance in December, at Arbroath, where Celtic struggled to a 2–1 win. He remained a reluctant spectator until March 1974, when Stein recalled him for a league game against Ayr United on the 16th. Jinky repaid his manager with two goals, both from the penalty spot, in a 4–0 win and was rewarded with a run of three games.

It was obvious that Stein no longer considered Jinky a key player, seeing that he was in and out of the side until the end of the season, missing four of Celtic's last seven league games and being substituted in two others. But in at least one of these games, a 2–0 win over Dundee United at Tannadice on 13 April, Jinky was missing because of injury after being kicked upside down by the cloggers of Madrid, as described in the following chapter. Jinky's involvement in the European Cup ties against Basle and Atletico Madrid, when he was the victim of appalling treatment by the cynical Spaniards, was a signal of Stein's belief that his off-form winger still had it in him to 'turn it on' on the big stage.

Having missed Celtic's first three Scottish Cup ties – against Clydebank, Stirling Albion and Motherwell – Jinky was recalled for the semi-final against a Dundee team looking to do the double over the beaten League Cup finalists. Stein, a master of psychology, was no doubt partly influenced in his decision by a comment made by Tommy Gemmell, who had left Celtic three years earlier to ply his trade with Nottingham Forest.

Jinky's former Lisbon Lions team-mate, now with Dundee, made the mistake of questioning the winger's current value to Celtic. But Gemmell's intended 'wind-up' rebounded spectacularly. Fired up by the taunt, Jinky displayed something like his old form at Hampden on 3 April, volleying home a head flick from Billy McNeill from Harry Hood's corner in the forty-third minute to claim the only goal and book Celtic's ninth Scottish Cup final appearance in ten years.

Celtic's opponents on 4 May 1974 were the other half of the

Dundee duo, United. Perhaps sensing that there would not be many more opportunities for him to shine on the Hampden stage, Jinky seized the occasion to display his repertoire of skills, setting up Stevie Murray for Celtic's second goal in a comfortable 3–0 win.

Celtic had clinched the league title the previous week. A 1–1 draw at Falkirk was enough to kill off Hibs' challenge in second place. But three successive draws, with Aberdeen and twice with Morton, in their last three games, played in the space of just eight days to clear the way for the Home International Championship matches and Scotland's participation in the World Cup finals in West Germany, reduced the winning margin to four points.

After the highs and lows of the previous nine months, Jinky departed Celtic Park for international duty in better heart than he had been for some time. But fresh problems lay around the corner. His rash impromptu boat trip at Largs left him floundering in even deeper waters with his manager. When reports of the incident reached Stein's ears he reacted with fury, once again questioning his problem child's professionalism.

Jinky wasn't back-page news on that occasion. His escapade made front-page headlines, the sort Stein that abhorred. In Stein's opinion Jinky had once again let himself and Celtic down. Jinky was out of range of his manager's tongue, but Stein's patience had worn dangerously thin, and the events of the next few weeks, when Jinky's World Cup adventure turned sour, moved him a step closer to the exit door at Celtic Park.

18

Madrid Revisited

Jinky was fast asleep in the room he was sharing with his close pal Bobby Lennox in a hotel on the outskirts of Madrid when the shrill ring tone of the bedside telephone woke him up in the small hours of the morning. Still half asleep, he reached across to answer it and was jolted wide awake by what he heard.

'Johnstone, you are dead.' The Spanish voice sent a shiver down his spine.

It seemed that the Madrid nightmare would never end. Seven years previously Jinky had visited Madrid and been given a standing ovation by 120,000 Real Madrid fans on the evening when he upstaged the great Alfredo di Stefano at the Bernabeu Stadium. This time Jinky and his Celtic team-mates were hate figures.

A campaign of intimidation stirred up by the local media, who had been unstinting in their praise of Jinky and Celtic on the occasion of di Stefano's testimonial in June 1967, reached fever pitch when Jock Stein's men arrived in the Spanish capital two days ahead of their European Cup semi-final second leg against Atletico Madrid on 24 April 1974. As one prominent Scottish journalist put it, Celtic flew into a war zone!

Spurious reports put about by the leading newspapers, alleging that the Atletico players had been assaulted by Glasgow police officers, had stirred up the Atletico fans to threaten acts of extreme violence. But no threat was more direct or chilling than the one issued to Jinky on the eve of the return leg. Jinky went to pieces when he heard it – and who could blame him?

The madness and the badness had set in at Celtic Park a fortnight earlier, when the Atletico players disfigured the 'beautiful game' with the open encouragement and blessing of their Argentine coach. Juan Carlos Lorenzo had been in charge of his country's national side at the 1966 World Cup finals when Sir Alf Ramsey branded England's quarter-final opponents 'animals'. And Lorenzo had another claim to fame. Some seasons before, while he was coach of the Italian side Lazio, his players had disgraced themselves and their club by being banned from European competition for violent conduct.

The presence of Ruben Diaz in the Atletico squad was a painful reminder for the Celtic players of their nightmare three games in the World Club Championship against Racing Club of Argentina seven years before. Diaz was one of several Argentines who were playing for Atletico at that time.

But no one had foreseen the violence that broke out when the first leg kicked off in front of 70,000 spectators at Celtic Park on 10 April 1974. Celtic, just one step away from a third European Cup final appearance in the space of eight seasons, were quite literally kicked out of the competition by a bunch of thugs dressed up as football players.

Celtic had come through to the last four of Europe's premier tournament, thanks to wins over TPS Turku of Finland, Vejle of Denmark and the Swiss side Basle. But it hadn't been a stroll in the park.

Celtic overran Turku in the first round, by an aggregate score of 9–1, with Jinky claiming three of his team's goals over the two legs. But their early flair deserted Celtic when they faced Vejle at Celtic Park the following month. Jinky, who captained the side for the night in the absence of the injured Billy McNeill, was unable to provide the spark of inspiration needed to improve on a goalless draw. But the ultra-defensive Danes, at a loss for attacking ideas, were unable to build on their work when they played at home. A

Bobby Lennox goal, scored in the first half, gave Celtic a 1–0 aggregate victory.

A 3–2 first leg defeat in Switzerland placed the quarter-final on a knife edge when Basle came from two goals behind at Celtic Park to put themselves back in the lead. But Jinky's fifty-seventh-minute corner kick enabled Tom Callaghan to score and force the tie into extra time. Celtic eventually squeezed through, 6–5 on aggregate, when Steve Murray headed the decisive goal in the ninety-eighth minute.

For the semi-final first leg at home Celtic lined up as follows: Connaghan; Hay, Brogan; Murray, McNeill, McCluskey; Johnstone, Hood, Deans, Callaghan and Dalglish. Atletico: Reina; Melo, Diaz; Benegas, Overjero, Eusebio; Ayala, Adelardo, Garate, Irureta and Heredia.

After ninety minutes of mayhem Celtic still had their full compeiment of players. Atletico had lost three of theirs, ordered off by the overwhelmed Turkish referee, Dogan Babacan. Seven received cautions. Given their rivals' level of intimidation and the fact that several of the their players were noted 'hard men', in particular Davie Hay, Jim Brogan and Pat McCluskey, Celtic maintained a remarkable level of discipline. Only two of their number were cautioned.

Predictably, Jinky was the principal target. The game was only seven minutes old when the referee issued the first caution, for a vicious assault on Jinky. Soon after that Diaz, hot to renew his acquaintance with Jinky after kicking lumps out of him at Hampden in 1967, was similarly dealt with. The crowd, already seething at the sight of Jinky being constantly body-checked and scythed down, were further incensed when Celtic had a goal disallowed.

But the hacking persisted, the spitting continued, the kicking went on unabated. Jinky was used as a punchbag. The next day's newspaper pictures showed him covered in bruises. He was even kicked in the stomach as he made his way up the tunnel at full time! This sparked a full-scale brawl, and police had to intervene to separate feuding players.

Midfielder Tom Callaghan recalled: 'That game turned into one of the most shameful episodes in European history. Atletico came for the first leg and simply booted us off the park, or, to be more precise, booted one man off the park. They went after wee Jimmy Johnstone from the start. We stood and cringed every time Jinky got another smack.

'The Atletico left back, Diaz, was an absolute bear and went at the wee man. It was terrible provocation and the hardest thing for the rest of us was not getting involved and ending up in trouble ourselves, though at full time there were a few scuffles.'

Billy McNeill said: 'The dreadful Juan Carlos Lorenzo clearly remembered Jimmy from seven years previously. How else do you explain the outrageous treatment Jinky was subjected to over the course of 180 minutes of football?'

Incredibly, in spite of the shameful scenes that had been witnessed on TV sets all over Europe, UEFA lost its nerve. It failed to take the step of expelling Atletico from the competition. Instead, European soccer bosses hit the Spanish club with an almost laughable £14,000 fine and banned six of their players from the second leg when UEFA's disciplinary committee convened in emergency session. It also emerged that the referee had not noted a single name of those he had ordered off and cautioned, although had Atletico been reduced to seven players he would have had no option but to abandon the match.

Lorenzo's motives for instructing his players to behave in such an appalling manner were never fully explained, but one theory was that the coach had hoped that the Celtic fans would react to the provocation by rioting and invading the pitch. Had they not followed the example of the players and displayed remarkable restraint, such an invasion would almost certainly have resulted in Atletico being awarded the tie and led to Celtic's expulsion from European competition for a season at least.

Atletico officials must have felt that the fine imposed on the club was worth every penny. For all their pressure, Celtic, continually frustrated by lengthy stoppages in play, were unable to turn their attacking play and superior numbers into goals.

But perhaps Jock Stein had seen it coming. When Stein learned that Atletico would be Celtic's semi-final opponents he told journalists: 'They've got half a dozen Argentinians in their squad and the manager's one – so that means a riot for a start.' It turned out to be a chilling prophecy.

Celtic were subjected to suffocating security on their arrival in Madrid. The players were confined to the grounds of their hotel, where they were surrounded by armed police. The squad was also denied proper training facilities, and when the players did go training under escort their coach was followed by dozens of hostile fans shouting abuse.

The Spanish daily newspaper *Marca* attempted to fuel the situation by carrying a headline billing the return as 'Atletico versus Celtic and UEFA' in a direct reference to the club's punishment. Even high-ranking government officials attempted to turn up the heat, with one declaring: 'There could very well be a death if somebody is crazy.' That was the last thing Jinky needed to hear.

Having spent what remained of a disrupted night mulling over the telephone death threat, Jinky was further alarmed on the morning of the game when rumours spread that a sniper was planning to shoot him and Stein, who had also received a telephone threat against his life.

Stein attempted to buck up Jinky by telling him that he had less to fear because once he began jinking about the park no bullet would be able to hit him. Stein, on the other hand, would be a sitting target in the dugout. Jinky was not reassured by his manager's attempts to play down the situation. Stein was also clearly concerned, for he gave Jinky the chance to withdraw from the team, an offer he refused on the grounds that he felt safer out in the open.

But the threats were successful. Jinky was a shadow of the great player capable of destroying even the most organised defence on his day. Once again the target for Atletico's hatchet men, he finished the match covered in fresh bruises and sporting two black eyes.

Celtic, who had replaced Tom Callaghan and Dixie Deans with Danny McGrain and Bobby Lennox in a tactical reshuffle, were beaten by two late goals, scored by Garate and Adelardo in the last thirteen minutes of the match. Instructively, it emerged that the cynical Lorenzo had left most of his first-choice players out of the Glasgow leg with the express intention of sacrificing certain players for the sake of achieving a result by any means possible. The exception was the gifted and dangerous winger Ayala, one of the six suspended players.

The highly respected sports journalist Bryan Cooney, Scottish football correspondent for the *Sun* at the time, remembered in detail the build-up to the second leg and the threats that may have cost Celtic the chance to contest a third European Cup final. He believes that Stein's indiscretion was a factor in unsettling Jinky.

On the team's arrival in the Spanish capital, Cooney had been approached by a freelance news reporter called Tim Brown, who was the *Sun*'s man in Madrid. Brown told him he had this fantastic story connected to threats to wipe out the Celtic team and Jinky in particular.

Cooney now headed back to the team's hotel, where the press corps was also billeted. He had fallen foul of Stein in the past, and was effectively on a final warning from him, so when he got to thinking about what he had been told and analysed the story and its value to his newspaper, he reached the conclusion that if the *Sun* published claims of death threats he would be accused of scaremongering and probably of losing Celtic the match.

Cooney decided to sit on what was potentially a headline story, but he also saw it as an opportunity to inform Stein of the facts and remind him that by suppressing what he knew he was doing him a huge favour. But when he explained to Stein that he had decided to kill the story because of the harm it could do to his team's performance, the manager just nodded. Stein's response was so utterly non-committal that Cooney is not even sure if he received any thanks.

The following day Cooney discovered that Stein had spilled the contents of their 'private' conversation to another journalist, whose paper was leading its front page with the story. By then it was too late for the *Sun* to do anything about it. Cooney naturally feared for his job because a rival newspaper had his story, so when the team returned from training, he sought out Dixie Deans, who was a close confidant, and told him that the players would probably be approached about a story that they were the subject of death threats. He also informed Deans that he had had the story first but had decided not to use it because it would be seen as hysterical nonsense and might affect the team's performance.

Deans reacted by passing on the new to the other players, and when Jinky heard reports of a sniper lying in wait he took fright and confronted Stein.

Stein confronted Cooney next day and a very public row broke out aboard the press coach taking journalists to the match. Stein accused Cooney of demoralising Jinky by putting him in fear of his life. But the journalist refused to simply sit back and be abused by his accuser. He told Stein that he had got what he deserved after failing to respect a confidence.

Cooney was subsequently given a year's ban by Celtic and warned off by Stein against talking to any of his players, but the journalist insisted that he had the support of several members of the side, who shared his view that Stein had inflamed the situation by his actions.

Celtic clinched a ninth successive league title just three days later, but the achievement was overshadowed by the team's failure to beat Atletico. Indeed, Jinky described missing out on his last chance to play in another European Cup final after the disappointment of losing to Feyenoord as the biggest letdown of his life.

But a crumb of comfort fell to Jinky and his team-mates when justice was seen to be done the following month. Atletico were just one minute away from being crowned champions of Europe when Bayern Munich equalised to force a replay, which they went on to win 4–0.

19

Heartache

Desmond White's words came as a dagger to the heart. 'We are giving you a free transfer,' the Celtic chairman told Jinky on 10 June 1975. White might as well have placed a black cap on his head and pronounced the death sentence.

Jinky had sensed nothing amiss when he learned from Jock Stein that the board of directors wished to see him. He was no stranger to them and assumed that he was simply to be reprimanded for a minor breach of club discipline. Recalling the moment when he learned that his fourteen years at Celtic Park had been brought to an abrupt end, he confessed: 'I was speechless. Tears welled up in my eyes as I virtually keeled over with shock.'

The club's offer of a joint testimonial with Bobby Lennox the following season meant nothing. Jinky, in a complete daze, had to be driven home by director Jimmy Farrell, who broke the news to his wife, Agnes.

'Playing for Celtic was much more than a job to me,' he said. 'It was a pleasure and an honour and I could not fathom what to do without it. Celtic gave me very little by way of an explanation for their decision and for days I lay about in a deep depression.'

Several days later Jinky returned to Celtic Park to collect his boots and other personal belongings. He described it as a horrible ordeal and an all-time low in his life. The deafening silence of an empty dressing room screamed at him.

Billy McNeill was one of the first to learn of Celtic's decision to release Jinky and he admitted: 'I was surprised to learn the news. I was aware that Jimmy had been misbehaving a wee bit but that was nothing new. It was no secret that he took a drink, but it was more for the company than anything because he enjoyed a laugh and a joke. I honestly don't believe Jimmy was a massive drinker then.

'He called me and what came across was his feeling of rejection. It was too much for Jimmy to bear. I tried my best to sound positive by telling him he now had a chance to go elsewhere and express himself but I don't think my words meant anything because he was so down.'

Bobby Lennox recalled a similar conversation. 'Jimmy was really upset because he loved Celtic, and when you are part of something that is so special you think it's going to last for ever.

'Personally, I think the Lisbon Lions could have gone on playing for a bit longer because we knew how to win. Jimmy certainly could have. But when Big Jock got something in his mind, that was it, and he believed he had the basis for another very good team.'

After nearly a decade of supremacy, Celtic's reign as league champions had ended two months before Jinky was shown the door. Rangers' achievement in winning the title, by a margin of seven points over Hibs and eleven ahead of Celtic, led to an inevitable overhaul of the club's playing staff by Jock Stein and the club's board.

Billy McNeill's decision to retire immediately following Celtic's Scottish Cup final win over Airdrie in May left only two of the old guard, Jinky and Bobby Lennox, still in place. But while Stein felt that Lennox still had a minor part to play in his short-term plans, these did not include Jinky. At the age of just thirty, he was rated surplus to requirements.

It seemed absurd that a player with such talent and match-winning capabilities should be discarded so relatively young, but Stein's patience with Jinky had worn noticeably thinner in the months before. Reports of Jinky's drinking had reached his ear on more than one occasion, and he was no longer prepared to tolerate the winger's regular lapses.

Jinky had featured in thirty of Celtic's fifty-one league and cup matches, six of them as a substitute. He had also contributed eight goals, five in the league and three in the League Cup. But there had been few occasions when Jinky had recaptured the magic of past seasons. There had been the odd flash of brilliance and the occasional reminder that he still possessed the ability to torment defenders, of course, but it had not happened often enough to persuade Stein that Jinky was any longer worth the bother.

Jinky claimed to have had no hint of Stein's intentions, but perhaps he should have seen it coming. There had been some indication surely that he was no longer central to Stein's thinking in the fact that he only once wore the number seven in his fifteen league starts. Mostly Jinky had been fielded at number nine or at outside left on three occasions. It was as if the manager saw Jinky more as a bit player.

Having played in both legs of the European Cup tie with Olympiakos, when Celtic were beaten 3–1 on aggregate, Jinky deserved better than to be classed simply as a squad player in a season when he produced two outstanding performances at least, one of them truly memorable. There had been a virtuoso display against Dundee at Dens Park on 14 December, culminating in two goals and a 6–0 win, after he had been restored to the side following injury. But it was against Hibs two months earlier that Jinky produced one of his greatest displays in a Celtic jersey.

Jinky did not feature in the League Cup semi-final win over Airdrie, by the narrowest of margins, after appearing in six of Celtic's previous eight matches in the competition, including scoring twice in a 5–2 win against Ayr United. But when it came to the final itself he was immense. Dixie Deans, as was his wont against Hibs, scored a hat-trick in a 6–3 victory. But it was Jinky who ran the show with a display of devastating wing play comparable with anything previously seen in his career.

The teams for the final, played on 26 October 1974 in front of a crowd of 53,848, were: Celtic: Hunter; McGrain, Brogan; Murray,

McNeill, McCluskey; Johnstone, Dalglish, Deans, Hood and Wilson. Hibs: McArthur; Brownlie, Bremner; Stanton, Spalding, Blackley; Edwards, Cropley, Harper, Munro and Duncan.

Jinky was desperate to end a run of four successive defeats in his tenth League Cup final appearance and erase the memories of losses to Rangers, Partick Thistle, Hibs and Dundee. In the event, it took him only six minutes to lay down his marker when he shook off his pursuers and raced clear to pick up a pass from Kenny Dalglish and sweep the ball past Jim McArthur. It was the perfect start for Celtic and the ideal confidence-booster for Jinky.

Jinky, at his impish best, proceeded to mesmerise the Hibs defence with his dribbling skills, sweeping past defenders and cutting the ball back from the byline into the path of Deans and Dalglish. Hibs had no answer to him, and for all that they hauled themselves back into the match when Joe Harper scored shortly before half-time after Deans had added to Jinky's opener, the gulf between the teams stretched too wide.

With Jinky in irrepressible mood, Celtic regained a two-goal advantage three minutes after the restart, through Paul Wilson, and, no sooner had Harper again reduced the leeway, than Deans hit Hibs with a devastating one-two, scoring twice in the space of three minutes. The second of these goals might have been credited to Jinky in other circumstances, for he had unleashed a shot from Harry Hood's corner kick that was headed for the net until Deans launched himself at the ball and guided it past McArthur with his head.

It hardly mattered that Steve Murray claimed a sixth goal for Celtic, or that Harper completed a hat-trick to lay claim to being the first player to do so in a cup final and still end up on the losing side. Celtic, inspired by a vintage Jimmy Johnstone performance, already had the match won.

Jinky did not know when he collected his nineteenth winner's medal that it would also be his last. His goals against Dundee, as it turned out, were also the last of the 130 he scored for Celtic.

By the time Celtic returned to Hampden the following May, for the Scottish Cup Final, Jinky had once again disappeared off the scene. When Celtic beat Airdrie, 3–1, to complete a cup double, Jinky could not even claim a place on the substitute's bench.

Having spent a sizeable chunk of the second part of the season languishing in the reserves, Jinky made his final appearance for Celtic in a league match at Muirton Park on 26 April 1975. When St Johnstone beat Celtic 2–1 and Jinky was replaced by Harry Hood in the second half, it was as if the fates had conspired against a player deserving of a more fitting finale to his outstanding Celtic career.

Jinky got his due on 17 May 1976 when more than 50,000 turned out to pay tribute to him and Bobby Lennox in their joint testimonial against Manchester United. Jinky was by then a Sheffield United player struggling to hold his career together, but it was a measure of his affection for the Celtic fans that he hammered himself in training to ensure that he was in the best possible shape.

'I never felt more nervous before any match than I did the night before the testimonial,' Jinky claimed. Despite all the domestic and European games he had faced, he was almost overcome by a fear of letting the fans down. 'I felt like a young schoolboy turning up for a trial with his favourite team,' Jinky said. 'But the warmth that was generated from the terraces was overpowering.'

When Celtic beat United, 4–0, it was as if the script had been written in Hollywood. Jinky confirmed that he could still hold his own on any stage, while Lennox hallmarked the occasion by scoring to add to Kenny Dalglish's hat-trick.

Afterwards, as he and Lennox set off on a lap of honour, Jinky fought back tears, at one point breaking off to head for the 'Jungle', one of the best-known football terraces in Britain. He threw his boots into the crowd. It was a genuine gesture of affection on the part of the 'Greatest Celt', but Jinky need not have worried – there was never any chance of him walking alone.

20

American Odyssey

Once upon a time in America Pele ran half the length of the pitch to shake hands with Jimmy Johnstone. The gesture from the greatest football player the world has ever seen was confirmation of Jinky's standing in the game.

Johnny Moore, who was responsible for giving American fans the chance to witness Jinky's skills at first hand, recalled: 'I will never forget the time when San Jose Earthquakes and Jimmy came up against the New York Cosmos and Pele. I was warming up next to Jimmy at the time and Pele ran seventy yards to shake his hand. He ran that distance just to come over and say hello to him and welcome him to America. Pele obviously knew who Jimmy was and the wee man proceeded to turn it on. He was magnificent.'

That game turned out to be Jinky's best for San Jose, so brilliant that Pele approached him again early in the second half and patted him on the back before complimenting him on his skills. It was a very special moment for Jinky because afterwards he couldn't stop talking about what Pele had said to him.

Pele was not the only world star to accord Jinky legendary status. On another occasion when Earthquakes played, the players were sitting in the dressing room when there was a knock on the door and Eusebio entered along with his fellow countryman Antonio Simoes. They wanted to shake Jinky's hand!

Circumstances had forced Jinky to look in towards the States for a living in the summer of 1975. For several days he had sat around at home sinking ever deeper into gloom as he tried to come to terms with the grim realisation that his Celtic career was over. But with no trade to fall back on other than football, and a wife and three children to support, Jinky soon awoke to the realities of his situation. The stark choice was football – or the dole queue.

New York Cosmos were the first to express an interest in Jinky, but he turned them down, despite being offered a highly lucrative short-term contract. He wanted the security of a longer-term deal. Jinky was also reluctant to settle in New York, having previously visited the city and found it intimidating.

But at the same time as the Cosmos were endeavouring to persuade Jinky to move to the 'Big Apple', San Jose Earthquakes made him an even more tempting offer to play for them for the duration of the two-month American season. The idea had much greater appeal, and Jinky packed his bags for California, travelling ahead of his family. He probably felt that the Californian sunshine would relax him, and a move to San Jose made a lot more sense in the frame of mind he was in at that time.

Moore, a player with San Jose at the time and also assistant manager, received a telex informing him that Jinky was available. He was aware that Jinky had spoken with Cosmos officials but decided to pursue his interest anyway. Jinky was one of Moore's heroes. He remembered seeing him play in America, against Spurs, the year before Celtic won the European Cup and thought he was magnificent.

'I think Jimmy was persuaded to come to San Jose because there were a few Scottish boys at the club, myself, Davie Kemp and Mike Hewitt, who were both from Dundee,' said Moore. 'When I had a conversation with him on the telephone he was a little more comfortable because he felt there were people he could get to know right away.'

Jinky had been offered £12,000 by the Cosmos for a ten-week season, but he said: 'I had no firm idea of what was to happen when the time was up, so I turned them down and asked for more money. My reasoning was that if they were looking for instant status for their club the terms were not in keeping with the job that had to be done and, although I never did get the money, I think my point was proved to be a valid one when they went for Pele instead and paid him a fortune for going to the States.'

Jinky had also tried to persuade his Celtic team-mate, Billy McNeill to join him on the American venture. McNeill revealed: 'The pair of us were attending Pat McCluskey's wedding when he told me about the offer from San Jose. I had only newly retired from Celtic and I remember him turning to me and saying, "Big Man, could you not come with me?" On reflection, it was probably the last place Jimmy should have gone to. It was just too far from home for him.

'The club Jimmy loved was just along the road from his home and he had all his pals close by. But, suddenly, when he realised what he was leaving behind to go to a country full of strangers, I think he immediately had second thoughts.

'Yet it was a great opportunity for him. He could have become a superstar in America because he had all the ingredients the Americans love. His red hair made him stand out and he possessed the sort of skills they would have drooled over. But Jimmy couldn't handle being separated from familiar surroundings and people he felt comfortable with. I can picture him sitting on his own feeling lonely and vulnerable.'

Almost predictably, when Jinky set out for San Jose things did not go quite as planned. His luggage went missing in transit, and when he eventually touched down in California he had only the clothes he was standing in. It took three days to reunite him with his suitcases. But the welcome he had from the fans and the local press dispelled any initial misgivings about heading across the Atlantic to continue his career.

'Jimmy was held in such high esteem outside Scotland and I don't think a lot of people in Scotland understand the impact he had,' Johnny Moore said. 'At that time in America we had Pele, and eventually we also had the likes of Franz Beckenbauer, Johan Cruyff, Eusebio and George Best. I had the opportunity to play against them all, and for me Jinky was up there with the likes of Pele and Bestie. If I had to pick someone after Pele, Jinky would be my No. 2.'

Jinky, never the best of drivers, ended up crashing three times during his brief stay in the States. He later confessed that driving on the right had confused the hell out of him and led to various scrapes. But for all that he was prepared to risk his life on the American freeways, Jinky's natural shyness prevented him from joining in the razzmatazz that accompanied games. For example, when he was asked to perform his ball-juggling skills in front of a live tiger he instantly declined the offer.

But for a short time at least life was good again. Jinky and his family stayed at a condominium complete with full-size swimming pool and lived a millionaire lifestyle. San Jose trained in the evening to escape the worst of the humidity and their cosmopolitan collection of Scots, Mexicans, Poles, Englishman and Yugoslavs played in front of capacity crowds of 25,000.

Inevitably, Jinky managed to land himself in hot water following a spot of skinny-dipping in a hotel pool during a three-day stopover in Vancouver. The pool, situated in the basement of the hotel the squad was staying at, was off limits to the public, allowing the players to strip off. But when his team-mates decided to hold an initiation ceremony of sorts to welcome the newcomer, Jinky jumped out of the water and made straight for an elevator. He managed to close the doors before the others reached him and pressed the button for the sixteenth floor, where his room was. But when the lift stopped for the first time the doors opened on the ground floor, which was packed with residents. The sight of a little red-headed guy standing naked with his hands strategically placed across his manhood was not what the guests were expecting.

Jinky, by now in a panic, could hear the screams of startled female guests as he urged the lift upwards, desperate at the prospect that details of his latest escapade would reach the ears of Canadian pressmen, and in turn make the sports pages back home. His problems redoubled when the lift suddenly stopped again and the doors opened to reveal a large lady. Jinky feared that her screams as she fled down the corridor would bring security staff running and lead to the police being called.

Close to tears, he eventually reached his floor only to discover that he had no room key. Determined not to risk more attention, he made for the emergency stairs, where he sat shivering for more than an hour before being rescued by laughing team-mates. But by the time they found him Jinky had turned blue with cold after being forced to sit stark naked on concrete steps while the outside temperature plummeted.

The two months Jinky spent in the States were a pleasant interlude at a time of low self-esteem. But for all that he proved popular with the fans, who appreciated his showmanship, he never felt truly at ease in his new surroundings. By his own admission he rarely gave 100 per cent commitment because his heart was still at Celtic Park.

'Jimmy arrived when we were already a little bit into the campaign and he stayed for a season,' said Moore. 'We were very happy to get him but he had a hard time of it because he was heartbroken to leave Celtic. It affected him badly and he admitted that, but when he did turn it on he was absolutely unbelievable. But we felt, as he felt, that he wanted to go back home.

'Jimmy enjoyed his time here because he could walk the streets and no one knew who he was. But he loved the Celtic fans more than anything and that broke his heart. He missed Scotland, but more so Celtic and the fans, because it was such a big thing in his life. He loved California but a big part of his being was Celtic through and through. There was no escaping it for him. When you saw him around Celtic fans you could understand why he had a love for the club.'

When Jinky returned to Scotland in the autumn of 1975 he was once again confronted by the demons that had stalked him for much of his career. But there was no escape through playing for his beloved Hoops. Instead, he was forced to settle for second best for the first time in his career, in the colours of Sheffield United.

21

A Blunted Blade

Drink had been a regular pastime for Jinky throughout his career, but it was fast becoming a major problem by the time he signed for Sheffield United. By now he was using alcohol as a crutch to try to cope with the heartbreak of his split from Celtic. But rather than drowning his sorrows, the booze increased the depth of his despair. Without Celtic, life had lost its relish, and with hours left to kill every day, Jinky spent more and more time at the bar.

Yet it appeared that Jinky had been thrown a lifeline when Jimmy Sirrell, the manager of Sheffield United and a fellow Scot, got in touch in November 1975 with the offer of a two-year contract. Playing in the First Division against the likes of Arsenal, Manchester United and Liverpool should have provided Jinky with the ideal platform on which to display his skills and rekindle his flagging career. Instead, he jumped feet-first into the drinking culture which existed at that time in English football. He lacked his customary enthusiasm for training. The passion was missing. Pulling on the red and white stripes of Sheffield United just wasn't the same as wearing the green and white hoops of Celtic.

Whereas during his Celtic days Jinky had been accustomed to enjoying himself at weekends, he took full advantage of the more relaxed atmosphere of his new surroundings and started to drink on most days. Usually he drank beer with the occasional short thrown in. Others among his new team-mates did the same.

Jinky's wife and children did not arrive until several weeks after his move from Viewpark. In the meantime he stayed in a city-centre hotel. Often he would invite team-mates back for a late-night boozing session as the party atmosphere spread. He also complained that Bramall Lane was full of soccer mercenaries, players who were there just for the money and who felt no loyalty at all towards the club. It was an attitude that was alien to Jinky's way of thinking about the game, but he soon became one of them. On wages of £300 a week he could afford to live the high life. The times grew fewer when he would go on the wagon for a few days before embarking on yet another drinking binge.

But when Jinky began to miss training the penny dropped. By his own admission, he was going to the dogs. The realisation that he was causing his family pain acted as a wake-up call.

Jinky made his debut for United in a 2–1 defeat at Stoke on 22 November 1975. He was substituted but retained his place the following week against Ipswich at Portman Road. United drew 1–1. But following successive home defeats by Tottenham (1–2) and Manchester United (1–4), he was reduced to playing for the reserves.

Part of the problem was that Jinky had been out of action for almost two months following his spell in America. It took him several weeks to achieve match fitness. Then, having done so, he was unlucky to damage knee ligaments in a reserve match against Spurs at White Hart Lane. This sidelined him for a further month and again affected his level of fitness, with the upshot that he struggled to produce anything approaching his best form when he was recalled for an FA Cup-tie against Leicester City at Filbert Street in early January 1976. Leicester won 3–0 and the defeat cost Jinky his place.

Jinky was eventually recalled to the first team on 13 March, scoring his side's only goal in a 4–1 home defeat by Wolves. A week later Ipswich were the visitors and again United lost, 2–1. With the team staring relegation in the face, Jinky was dropped for the remaining fixtures. The inevitable happened and United were relegated.

Playing in front of a few thousand spectators at Carlisle and Hull did not raise Jinky's spirits, but at least he had the satisfaction of assisting United to a 3–0 win at Brunton Park, the only time he was on the winning side in twelve appearances for the Blades. Jinky was substituted in his next two games, a 1–1 draw at Hull and a 1–0 defeat at home to Blackburn towards the end of September.

Jinky expressed a preference for the English style of play. He said that he enjoyed the slower build-up, which left him more time and space to play. It also suited him that the tackle from behind was more heavily punished. But while he had greater freedom to express himself, Jinky's enthusiasm had waned to the point where he was merely going through the motions.

There was one final highlight, however, in what turned out to be his penultimate game for United. It happened on 16 October 1976 when Fulham were the visitors to Bramall Lane. Fulham boasted a trio of legends in their line-up in the shape of George Best, Bobby Moore and Rodney Marsh. Not surprisingly, the match sold out, and a crowd in excess of 40,000 packed into the ground to catch a glimpse of four footballing greats in the twilight of their careers displaying their artistry.

So much did Jinky revel in the big-match atmosphere that he upstaged his stellar rivals in a 1–1 draw and was voted man of the match. It was a fitting tribute on his final appearance on the big stage.

One week later Jinky played his final first-team game for Sheffield United. He scored against Charlton Athletic at The Valley, but his goal was not enough to prevent his side from going down 3–2.

Relations between Jinky and Sirrell had also deteriorated. Reports of Jinky's drinking had reached the ears of the manager and Sirrell, struggling to hold on to his job, felt left down. Jinky, to his credit, held his hand up and confessed to not having given the club the commitment it deserved. Sheffield United succeeded in avoiding relegation for a second successive season, but only just.

There was inevitability about the club's decision to hand Jinky a free transfer. By his own admission, he had fallen well short of the standards he had set at Celtic Park.

Fellow Scot Jim Brown, capped against Romania in 1975, was United's goalkeeper at the time. But Brown, commercial manager at Chesterfield since 1985, did not feel that Jinky was given the chance to shine with the Blades.

'Jimmy had a big reputation when he arrived in Sheffield and it was fully justified,' said Brown. 'He was still a fantastic player; you could see that in training. Surprisingly, he mostly played for the reserves versus the first team in practice matches and he ran the established stars ragged. Yet, for all his brilliance Jimmy never seemed to get a sustained run of first-team games.

'I remember he crashed his car on one occasion and maybe the manager saw things that the rest of us didn't. But I can honestly claim never to have seen Jimmy the worse for wear through the effect of alcohol. If he was hitting the drink in a big way, he hid it well.'

Tony Currie, the mercurial England midfield star, was Sheffield United captain. He recalled Jinky being great company, and felt that he enjoyed not being in the spotlight all the time, as he had been at Celtic. Unknown to many people in England, he was able to go out in Sheffield and not be recognised wherever he went, so the pressure was less. The press weren't hounding him in the way they do the top players nowadays. If a group of players went for a drink they were left pretty much to their own devices. They could even have a drink at the team's hotel on a Friday evening before a match, because that was viewed as a normal way to relax the players. Jinky gave the appearance of being relaxed. But appearances are often deceptive!

However, while guilty of missing training on occasion, it appears that Jinky put in as much effort as any of his team-mates when he did show up. Skill-wise, he had not lost it either. His legs might not have the same spring, but he was still a fabulous football player. That's why most could not understand the manager's apparent reluctance to play him regularly. But Jinky's heart wasn't in it as it once had been. Part of him was still at Celtic. When you have been with the one club for so long and enjoyed so much success it must be very difficult to move elsewhere and play with the same enthusiasm.

But Brown added: 'It was a shame that things turned out the way they did for Jimmy at United, because I think he could have done a great job for the club, had he been given the opportunity.'

Jinky's spell with United turned out to be his last chance to shine at the top level. What followed was a very public decline in the fortunes of a player who had once commanded centre stage in the company of football's biggest names.

22

Dublin via Dundee

Davie MacKinnon's jaw dropped open in sheer disbelief. The sight of Jimmy Johnstone standing just a few feet away from the Dundee defender made MacKinnon wonder for a second if he was seeing things. But this was no Jinky apparition.

Shortly after quitting Sheffield United, Jinky was approached by his former Celtic team-mate Tommy Gemmell. Gemmell was manager of Dundee and he was keen to take Jinky to Dens Park. Out of work, and with no other offers on the table, Jinky jumped at the chance to link up with his old buddy.

Dundee had already begun pre-season training when Jinky arrived, unexpectedly, on Tayside. Not even his new team-mates were aware of the manager's move to sign him.

MacKinnon remembered: 'One day I arrived for training and Jimmy just appeared all of a sudden. I think we all got a shock when we saw him standing there. I am sure my jaw dropped open seeing a guy who was such a legend in our midst. But what an unassuming guy! There was nothing big-time about Jimmy. He was just one of the boys. Well, at least in the sense of how he mixed with the rest of us.'

But there was nothing ordinary about Jinky when he had a ball at his feet. Shortly after he arrived the club held an open day for the fans and most of them had never seen dribbling skills like the bag of tricks Jinky possessed. His close control confirmed everything they had heard about him. One training drill involved passing the ball under a hurdle, jumping over it, and then collecting the ball on the other side. That was no problem for Jinky.

But the road to Dundee was not paved with gold. The move was ill-fated almost from the moment Jinky signed for the Dens Park club. The thought that he would one day have to face Celtic was a frightening prospect. Indeed, he confessed to being in a state of panic. Perhaps it was this that led Jinky to go off the rails.

Gemmell had thought it a good idea to offer Jinky the chance to return to Scottish football's top flight. He was, after all, still one month short of his thirty-third birthday and was the sort of high-profile personality capable of pulling in the crowds. So, after talking it over with his coach, Willie Wallace – another of the Lisbon Lions – Gemmell contacted Jinky to offer a lucrative contract based on performances and results.

Gemmell recalled that he was earning £15,000 a year at the time. Under the terms of Jinky's deal he could potentially earn considerably more than his manager. 'It was possible for Jinky to earn something in the region of £500 a week if he played Saturday–Wednesday–Saturday,' Gemmell said. 'I took a gamble signing Jimmy but I felt it was one worth taking. I knew if he did the business for us he would earn accolades like nobody's business. Fans everywhere still loved and admired him and you could sense the hush of anticipation when he ran onto the park.'

But just three games into his new career, Jinky imploded. Billy Pirie, a striker whose goals made him a big hit with the Dundee fans, found Jinky a quiet guy – until he had taken a drink or two. He also praised his former team-mate for his generosity, adding that Jinky was always quick to stand his round.

Pirie remembered: 'On the day Jimmy had his bust-up with the manager I had been with him and a few of the other lads at a bar in the city centre. By the time I left to catch my train back to Aberdeen we had sunk quite a few. But, regrettably, the session didn't end there.'

Jinky was staying at the Commercial Hotel at Errol, a hamlet situated roughly midway between Dundee and Perth, which was owned at the time by Gemmell. He was staying free of charge, according to Gemmell, who had been careful not to give him a front-door key so that he could monitor Jinky's movements.

The local pub was situated directly opposite the hotel, and Jinky and team-mate Gordon Strachan made for the hostelry to continue their drinks session. But within minutes of their arrival there, Gemmell was made aware of it.

'One or two locals were quick to inform me that Jinky and Strachan were propping up the bar across the road,' he said. 'They had been stupid enough to take a taxi from Dundee and start drinking again right under my nose. Eventually, wee Strachan arrived on my doorstep in tears saying how sorry he was, so I put him in a taxi and sent him back to his digs in the city. But there was no sign of Jinky at that stage.'

Jinky was sharing a room with another player, Iain MacDougall, but when he reached the hotel the place was in darkness and the front door was locked. In an effort to attract the attention of his room-mate, Jinky began throwing pebbles at the bedroom window, which was to the front of the hotel. But MacDougall was fast asleep. Eventually, there was a crash and the window smashed. The lights came on and Gemmell discovered Jinky standing on his doorstep at two o'clock in the morning.

The next day at training Gemmell hammered Jinky and was not surprised when his former team-mate took it without complaint. But Gemmell was under no illusions. 'I knew then that it just wasn't going to work. Jimmy refused to behave himself. But it was a great opportunity for him and it was a shame he didn't grab it with both hands.'

There was a humorous postscript to Jinky's sudden departure. Apparently, when one of the local newspaper reporters went in search of him to find out what had happened, he discovered Jinky propping up the jukebox in the local pub. The song that was play-ing was 'You Picked A Fine Time To Leave Me Lucille'!

Strachan, who renewed his acquaintance with Jinky when he became Celtic manager in 2005, said: 'I don't think many people will know I actually played with Jimmy at Dundee. It was the smallest right side of midfield the club ever had. People will say Jinky lived life to the full on and off the pitch. I lived life to the full with him just one day and my liver is still recovering. It was only one day but it felt like a week, but it was great fun. I would never give that day back.'

The record books show that Jinky wore the dark blue of Dundee just three times. His debut against Airdrie, on 13 August 1977, resulted in a 3–0 home win in front of a crowd of just 5,450, a fraction of the number Jinky was accustomed to entertaining at the peak of his career. The following week Dundee were beaten 2–1 by Hearts at Tynecastle and Jinky suffered the hurt of being substituted. Seven days later, when Dundee faced Stirling Albion at Dens Park, Jinky was reduced to the role of substitute, eventually replacing Strachan, though he was unable to prevent Dundee slipping to a second consecutive defeat, this time by 1–0.

Following his brief sojourn with Dundee, for several months Jinky was forced to eat into his savings. But he was not quite yet the forgotten man. Celtic's strong Irish roots meant that Jinky was remembered with great fondness by some at least in the Emerald Isle.

The offer from the League of Ireland club Shelbourne came out of the blue, but it was tempting all the same. The financial terms were appealing and there was the bonus of the club allowing Jinky to fly to Dublin on the day of home games and return immediately afterwards. But Jinky was not keen to sign the one-year contract being dangled in front of him, for fear that by doing so he might block other avenues of opportunity.

Jinky sought wise counsel in the form of Jock Stein, and was told by his former manager to reject the offer of a twelve-month contract. Stein's advice was to sign on a month-to-month basis instead, sparking the notion in Jinky that there might actually be a way back to Celtic.

'Stein had allowed me to train with the Celtic players, which was a real confidence-booster. But when I approached him about the Shelbourne offer my heart missed a beat,' he recounted. 'He didn't want me tied down for a year. I sniffed something in the air and asked the Big Man outright if there was still a chance of a return to Parkhead. He replied: "Wait and see," but it was enough for me. I was alive again. The thought of a second time round at Parkhead filled me with the sort of expectation a young child feels on Christmas morning.

'At the time Celtic were going through a bad patch. They could not recapture the form of the late 1960s and early 1970s. Jock was under pressure to rekindle the glory days and maybe he saw my possible return as a morale booster for everyone. I had to believe the Big Man wanted me back. Maybe it was his final master stroke, I thought.'

Buoyed by the idea that Stein was giving serious consideration to offering him the chance to rekindle his Celtic career, Jinky threw himself into training with fresh gusto and soon regained the level of fitness necessary to kick-start his career at the age of thirty-three.

After two years of mediocrity, Jinky recaptured the form that had won him international recognition. Playing against Shamrock Rovers, who had former Leeds United and Republic of Ireland star Johnny Giles in their line-up, Jinky made headlines, and it was even rumoured that Celtic assistant manager Sean Fallon was planning a trip to Dublin to assess his form.

But, true to form, Jinky blew it big time. Once again drink was the cause of his downfall after several months on the wagon. His period of abstinence ended on Hogmanay 1977 in a hotel in the quaintly named town of Ballybofey. Shelbourne were due to face Finn Harps in Donegal the following day, but the temptation to celebrate New Year proved too great. According to Jinky, the Hogmanay booze session was nothing out of the ordinary, but when word of his latest indiscretion reached Stein's ears the door to an emotional return to his first love slammed shut in his face.

If Jinky was to be believed, the drinks session involved a bottle of Jameson's Irish Whiskey produced by a team-mate being shared between several of his colleagues.

It wasn't, he claimed, a big bevvy session, but Shelbourne were soon persuaded to call time on Jinky after just nine games and two goals.

23

A Highland Fling

Following his stint in Ireland, Jinky was once again left wondering what the future might hold. With his hopes of a return to Celtic Park shattered and no queue of eager employers lined up outside his front door, he was in despair. But just when it seemed that his playing days had finally run out, a telephone call from an unexpected source revived his hopes.

Tom Gordon, Elgin City's astute chairman, had suggested to the club's committee at a meeting on 19 September 1978 that Jinky might be the man to transform the Highland League club's flagging fortunes. The committee agreed, and manager Ally Shewan, an old adversary of Jinky's during his days as an Aberdeen full-back, was instructed to sound him out.

Gordon had taken the precaution of contacting Billy McNeill, whom he had got to know during his stint as Aberdeen boss before he returned to Celtic as manager that summer, to gauge Jinky's likely response to such an offer. When McNeill indicated that it was likely to be well received Elgin moved fast to try to get their man.

The quartet of Gordon, Shewan, treasurer Alistair Sheach and committee member Bobbie Brown travelled south to Perth on 1 October for a meeting with Jinky. A wage of £80 a week plus travelling expenses was agreed, for an eight-week trial period, subject to Shelbourne terminating Jinky's contract and cancelling his registration with the Football Association of Ireland.

After a spate of media speculation Jinky arrived in Elgin on 14 October for his debut against Brora Rangers. Elgin had been averaging crowds of around 600 up to that point. Jinky's appearance boosted the attendance at Borough Briggs to 854, a rise of more 40 per cent. Such was the level of interest in the area that Grampian Television sent a camera crew to cover the game. City won, 3–1, and Jinky was hailed a success, having dispelled any lingering doubts about his fitness.

When Jinky emerged from the showers and was handed a blue towel he allegedly told the Elgin secretary, Frank Masson, that while he was prepared to dry himself with a towel in the colours of Celtic's arch-rivals on this occasion, he would in future bring his own green one! Jinky also informed chairman Gordon that his clearance from the FAI was on its way.

The following Wednesday, Jinky played in his only midweek game for City, a 1–1 draw with Keith at Borough Briggs. The attendance fell just short of 1,000. But a few days after watching Jinky display his tricky dribbling skills in a 5–3 derby win over Forres Mechanics at Mosset Park, Gordon was forced to inform his committee that he had still not received any evidence of Jinky's release from Shelbourne.

Yet when Elgin lined up against Buckie Thistle, Jinky was clearly enjoying himself. Noticing that Buckie were kitted out in green and white hooped shirts, he quipped to his team-mates: 'I must be playing in the wrong team.' But he was not put off by the reminder of his days at Celtic Park. Indeed, he gave one of his best performances in the black and white stripes of Elgin, running the show in midfield and providing a steady supply of passes to the wingers, Frazie Kellas and Ian Wilson, who was to go on to play for Leicester City and Scotland. Elgin won 2–0.

Wilson, just a teenager at the time, sat enthralled listening to tales of Jinky's career with Celtic and Scotland. 'I was nineteen years old and obviously very impressionable, and, I suppose, overawed in his company,' said Wilson. 'But Jimmy was a great story-teller and I never tired of listening to him. Occasionally, a couple of us would pick him up at Aberdeen railway station and drive him to Elgin. After the match we would head back to Aberdeen and, depending on the time, he would either catch the last train home or stay the night, when we would join him for a few beers. It was a wonderful education for a young player.'

According to Wilson, Jinky was still very much the prankster during his time with Elgin, regularly nailing players' shoes to the floor. He also entertained his team-mates by adopting a rolling gait, mimicking the movement of a train after claiming that British Rail had offered him a job because he spent so much time travelling.

The Elgin committee were sufficiently impressed by their recent signing to offer Jinky a contract to run until 30 April 1980, but the vexed question of FAI clearance continued to trouble the chairman. The club's concerns were justified when, on 14 November 1978, a letter arrived from the SFA stating that Jinky could not be registered as an Elgin player until a fine amounting to just four pounds was paid to the FAI.

Worse was to follow. Having gone top of the league for a brief time, Elgin officials were alarmed to receive a letter from the Highland League informing them that, although Jinky's registration had finally been accepted by the SFA on 17 November, it was very possible that they would be heavily fined and deducted the nine points won during the period when the player had turned out while unregistered.

During the next two months, Highland League football went into virtual hibernation because of a particularly cold spell of weather. This led to the infamous Inverness Thistle–Falkirk Scottish Cup tie being postponed a record of twenty-nine times, in what became known as the winter of discontent. There was discontent, too, at Borough Briggs when Elgin were hit with a £60 fine and severely censured by the SFA for failing to adhere to the Association's registration procedures.

The following month, on 3 March, Elgin were appalled when they were fined an additional £250 by the Highland League. Later the SFA upheld an appeal against the punishment and the fine was quashed, but life never did run quite smooth when Jinky was around.

When the season ended Elgin were in sixth place in the league. But hopes of further improvement were dashed by the unhappy events of the summer of 1979 when Jinky once again imploded in his usual inimitable fashion.

Jinky returned to Borough Briggs at the end of July for a pre-season tournament involving Ayr United and Clyde. He gave the appearance of being fit after several training sessions at Celtic Park and there was a general air of optimism that his second season with Elgin City would turn out to be a success. It didn't happen.

Jinky, along with team-mates Brian Cooper and Eric Martin, was booked into the Southbank Guest House in Elgin. On the Saturday evening, the trio had dinner, then headed out on the town. Following a drinks session they returned to their digs in the early hours of the morning only to find the doors locked. Undeterred, they attempted to gain access via a toilet window. When their efforts proved futile they retired to a neighbouring garden and consumed the contents of their 'carry out'.

It appeared that the incident had blown over when Jinky was selected to play against Deveronvale on 18 August, a match Elgin won, 3–1, before a crowd of 545. But it proved to be his last appearance for Elgin. Immediately after the fixture, Ken Tedcastle, who had replaced Ally Shewan as manager, announced that the trio of Johnstone, Cooper and Martin had been released by the club for a breach of discipline. Tedcastle had the full backing of the club's committee.

Perhaps Jinky would have escaped such terminal punishment for his latest indiscretion had he not had the misfortune to be employed by a club renowned for its discipline. Elgin had sacked five players some years earlier after they were discovered drinking on the eve of a match in 1963.

Jinky's Highland Fling lasted barely eleven months. In that time he played eighteen games for Elgin, scoring twice. Elgin won ten of these games, drew four and lost four. Unlike his famous predecessor, another former Celtic winger, Jimmy Delaney, who also hailed from Lanarkshire, Jinky found it impossible to live by the rules. Yet, for all that his time with Elgin ended in disaster and the wrong sort of newspaper headlines, Jinky's brief love affair in the Highlands was not a complete failure. Indeed, according to Robert Weir, the club's historian, Elgin benefited by having Jinky on their books.

'Jimmy definitely boosted interest in Highland League football,' Weir said. 'Attendances had been steadily dwindling prior to his arrival but crowds shot up by several hundred when he appeared on the scene. It's just a pity that he left under a cloud because the fans in this part of the world were very fond of him. He will always be remembered with great affection.'

It was a measure of that affection that following Jinky's death Elgin produced a special tribute to him in their match programme for the game against East Stirling on 25 March 2006. Its cover carried a photograph of Jinky in an Elgin strip and a moving eulogy by Robert Weir. Proceeds from the sale of the programme went to motor neurone research.

Probably only Jinky could have evoked such emotion twenty-seven years on.

What followed the Elgin experience was an undignified ending to a great career. Almost a year after being dismissed by Elgin, Jinky embarked on his final football journey – with Blantyre Celtic. His career had come full circle, for Blantyre had provided him with a launch pad nineteen years earlier. Mercifully, that return to the Juniors was short-lived. To the great relief of most of his many fans, Jinky spent just eight weeks prolonging the agony. It was no place for greatness.

24

Starting Over

Life after football was not kind to Jimmy Johnstone. It can be argued that many of Jinky's problems were self-inflicted, but it is also true that fate conspired against him, often in the cruellest way imaginable.

Jinky's generosity, coupled with his failed business ventures, most notably his investment in a pub, meant that there was no nest-egg to cushion the blow of his ended career. After nearly twenty years of earning a very comfortable living from the game he graced in a way few others have managed to do, Jinky found himself facing the stark reality of having to make his living in the real world.

His days as a big spender were over. Instead of investing a sizeable chunk of his earnings from football – as much as £300 a week at his peak with Celtic – Jinky frittered away most of his cash. He reflected on the realisation that he could have been a millionaire had he not been such a soft touch whenever he encountered someone claiming to be down on their luck. According to Agnes Johnstone, Jinky would have given you his last shilling. Unfortunately, over the years he loaned thousands of pounds to would-be friends, most of whom failed to repay the favour. Publicans, too, had cause to give thanks for Jinky's contributions.

For several months, Jinky pondered his future in a mood of

growing apprehension. Many of those who had been so keen to enjoy his friendship when he was at the peak of his powers, for the sake of the reflected glory it brought, shied away from him now that he was no longer a star at Celtic Park. Indeed, there were some who must have experienced difficulty looking at their reflection in a mirror when Jinky's life eventually unravelled.

With what small cash reserves he had dwindling fast, Jinky cut out the booze in an effort to put his life back on track. He rejected the idea of 'signing on', even though he was perfectly entitled to claim unemployment benefit. The prospect of taking his place in the dole queue was not one that appealed to a man whose pride remained intact. But pride and principles do not put food on the table, and Jinky grew increasingly concerned by the lack of job offers.

Then, just when it seemed that he would have little choice but to visit his local Labour Exchange in an effort to find work of some sort, Jinky got the break he so desperately needed. By chance, he was introduced to a prominent Glasgow building contractor. The introduction was made by Sean Fallon, Jock Stein's assistant, at a Celtic Supporters' Club dinner in honour of the manager. Frank Lafferty, a Celtic fanatic, took to Jinky straight away, inviting him to be his guest at a subsequent boxing evening.

The businessman had been unaware of Jinky's plight, but when he learned of his guest's need to find employment, Lafferty was quick to come up with the offer of a job.

Jinky described the moment as one of the most significant of his life. But his initial euphoria was soon replaced by a feeling almost of dread. How would others perceive him in the role of handyman/labourer?

There was also a touch of irony associated with Jinky driving a lorry, delivering building supplies to construction sites all over Scotland. He was, after all, the world's worst driver, according to most of his Lisbon Lions team-mates, one of whom claimed that Jinky managed to be involved in three minor bumps on one occasion when the pair made the comparatively short journey from Celtic Park to Glasgow city centre.

Jinky admitted that initially the experience had brought him down to earth with a crash. But in some senses at least it proved invaluable in highlighting the harsher realities of life.

'At first, I must admit, it was a crushing blow to my ego,' he confessed. 'I was instantly recognised and inevitably asked the obvious question: "What are you doing here, wee man? You should have been a millionaire by now."

It was a long way removed from his days living in the lap of luxury. He admitted that his extravagant lifestyle was in stark contrast to that of his new workmates. But now he was one of them. To him the past was just that: history. Jinky said: 'I pulled no punches and told my workmates the truth. My wife and kids still had to be provided for, so here I was earning an honest living.'

Inevitably, there were those who felt sorry for Jinky, a complete stranger to manual labour. But he did not welcome their pity. Instead, he embraced his situation with a stoicism that spoke volumes for his character and down-to-earth approach to life. He enjoyed his workmates' earthy humour and spirit of camaraderie, even when he was the victim of their antics at times.

Yet this was a very different lifestyle compared with the one that Jinky had enjoyed during his playing days. Rising at six in the morning and often not arriving back home until early evening, he admitted that his limbs ached from digging holes with picks and shovels. It was back-breaking work carried out in all sorts of weather and designed to test even the toughest among his new workmates. But Jinky survived.

He also retained his links with football when he spent a year working in Kirkcaldy, digging test holes for gas pipes on the seafront of the Fife town, where his former Rangers rival, Willie Johnston, owns a public house. Inevitably, visits to the Port Bar became a regular custom during lunch breaks.

Johnston recalled: 'Jimmy was a regular visitor and more often than not he would end up belting out songs on the karaoke machine. He wasn't a bad singer either. To be honest, I think he spent more time in the pub than he did on the job. But he was a great wee guy who only ever wanted to have a laugh and enjoy himself.'

Jinky lasted three years before he parted company with Lafferty, following several scrapes. According to Billy McNeill, one of them involved him forgetting where he had parked his van after a tea-time session in a pub.

'Frank Lafferty loved Jimmy,' said McNeill. 'He was a great Celtic man himself and was like Jock Stein in some senses, the way he tried to nurse Jimmy along. But Jimmy continued to get up to mischief and eventually Frank had enough.'

During his spell of labouring, Jinky coached Celtic's under-16 and under-18 sides on a part-time basis for two years, also assisting former team-mate Bobby Lennox to oversee the progress of the reserve team. Jinky's talents as a coach were highlighted by the level of success enjoyed by the youth sides and the second string. Both the under-16s and under-18s won every competition open to them. Indeed, the latter side's achievements in winning the league, League Cup and Scottish Cup, as well as the prestigious BP Cup, bore glowing testimony to Jinky's ability to impart his knowledge of the game to young players coming through.

Another former team-mate, Davie Hay had become manager of Celtic, and it was he who approached Jinky about assisting Lennox to run the reserve team. The new partnership hit it off straight away and the reserves won both the league and Scottish Cup. But resentments were building in the background, or so Jinky saw it.

It was not uncommon for the reserves to play against the first team at five-a-side, and inevitably Jinky was keen to be involved in these games. It was like stepping back in time for him, and he loved the chance to once again display his skills. But after a few weeks, following a meeting of the coaching staff, it was suggested to Jinky that he should no longer take part. He was convinced that the directive was born of jealousy. Jinky was convinced that someone on the permanent staff thought he was after their job, a suggestion that he himself strongly denied, insisting that he was not bothered about securing a permanent position at Celtic Park.

Jinky eventually left the club under a cloud. Having made a

pact with Hay to stay clear of alcohol, Jinky broke his word on several occasions and was eventually asked by the manager to leave. It broke Jinky's heart but he insisted that he did not bear any grudge, adding that he was already giving serious consideration to his position because of the internal strife which had overshadowed his return to Celtic.

Jinky was also mystified by Jack McGinn. Jinky believed that McGinn had something against him. He was never able to identify the cause of a perceived snub, but McGinn, he claimed, had never made any attempt to acknowledge his presence.

Following his spell working for Lafferty, Jinky tried his hand as a salesman, flogging satellite TV dishes. The job paid well, and Jinky's profile ensured that he had a steady turnover of customers, yet it was a huge comedown for a sporting legend.

But for all that he struggled to make his mark as a businessman, Bertie Auld holds the view that Jinky could have been very successful in life without football. Auld, who became very close to Jinky in the final years of his life, insists that his Lisbon Lion teammate was full of bright ideas.

'Jimmy was a clever wee fellow and he was forever coming up with schemes to make money,' said Auld. 'I remember one time the pair of us were struggling financially and were agreed that we needed to do something to improve our situation when Jimmy suddenly hit on the idea of going into the scaffolding business.

'We were having a drink and bumped into this fellow Jimmy knew from his days working with Frank Lafferty. The chap was a foreman with a building company and he mentioned that he was on the lookout for scaffolding. Quick as a flash, Jimmy told him he had a contact who could supply exactly what he was looking for. What we didn't realise at the time was the job in question involved renovating multi-storey flats in Kilmarnock, and that was just a wee bit out of our range.'

Jinky tried his best to support his wife and family, but as his drinking increased it became progressively more difficult for him to hold down a steady job. Eventually, he turned increasingly to religion in an effort to turn his life around.

Jinky had for many years sought sanctuary at Greyfriars Monastery, just a short walk from the home he had bought at Birkinshaw in 1977 following his brief spell with Dundee. He found that chatting to the Benedictine brothers in the tranquil surroundings of the monastery offered a form of escape from his problems. A deeply religious man, Jinky had discovered the retreat towards the end of his career with Celtic and attended confession there.

Happiest when he was among his 'ain folk', Jinky still lived barely a mile from his previous home in Viewpark and only a short distance from the house where he had been brought up in Old Edinburgh Road.

But by the early 1990s Jinky's life had fallen so completely apart that he might not have survived but for the love and support of his wife Agnes and his children. Out of work and almost out of hope, he was prepared to sell his most treasured footballing mementos – to enable him to buy drink.

25

Battling the Booze

By his own admission, drink took Jimmy Johnstone down a lot of roads. Jinky eventually sought the help of Alcoholics Anonymous in his long-running battle with the booze when his life reached crisis point.

It was in the summer of 1993 that the full realisation of his condition struck Jinky during a trip to Ireland with his fellow Lisbon Lions and convinced him that he had to tackle the problem head-on. Jinky revealed in a newspaper interview that it was only when his close friend Jim Craig pulled him aside and virtually begged him to stop drinking that he finally listened.

In Dublin, the pair were attending a supporters' function, but Jinky confessed to hardly knowing where he was because he had been hitting the bottle hard. Yet he listened when Craig told him he had to do himself a favour and get a grip on his life – or face further humiliation. Craig's words hurt but they had the desired effect. It was at that moment Jinky realised enough was enough after living in another world for so many years.

'I sat and thought about all of my problems in life and it wasn't hard to see that there was one common denominator – drink!' Jinky recalled.

'All my money problems were caused by my drinking and I had upset everyone in my family by being selfish and irresponsible. I was a disgrace and that's when I finally realised it. The truth hit home. Most people enjoy going for a drink but they have a few at the weekend and by Monday morning they are back at their work, living their lives normally. Not me. I didn't know when to stop and when I had reached a certain stage I couldn't stop.

'All the bad things I had done in my life came flooding back to me and I knew I had to sort things out. But it took Jim's words to finally make me come to my senses and try to start a new life.'

Following his decision to attend weekly sessions with Alcoholics Anonymous, Jinky claimed that for the first time in years he could see clearly and function properly.

He also had reason to be grateful to Glasgow businessman Willie Haughey. Virtually penniless and in utter desperation, Jinky tried to sell his collection of football medals, including his European Cup winner's medal, to Haughey, turning up at his office one day in desperate need. 'I couldn't have got any lower,' Jinky later confessed. 'I was up to my neck in debt and I just didn't know where to turn to next. It was an awful time in my life. The booze took me into dark areas for a long time and I couldn't handle it. Things just got worse and worse. I was losing everything.'

Haughey, a former Celtic director, saw it as the desperate act of a man trying to sell a lifetime's achievements in a wooden frame. Haughey, a compassionate individual who has donated much of his wealth to charity and various worthwhile causes, considered it a tragedy when he recalled in his mind's eye the sight of Jinky in his pomp twenty years earlier, turning full-backs inside out.

Jinky revealed: 'Willie told me to have respect for myself and for others. It was he who helped me set about rebuilding my life. My family also stuck by me and I owe them everything. It took me an awful long time to turn my life round but getting it right eventually gave me the greatest pleasure.

'It is still hard for me to think about what I did to my family and the people closest to me. They all suffered, especially my wife and children. My wife is the loveliest girl in the world and the best thing I ever did was to marry her. But I put her through some terrible things and I don't know why she stayed with me, although I really appreciate the fact that she did. She should get a medal.

'When I was drinking I just wasn't a family man at all while my children, Eileen, Marie and James, were growing up. I didn't do all the things a father should have done. Instead of taking my kids to the pictures I would go to the pub or take a carry-out to a friend's house.

'I missed birthdays. I never went to any of their Christmas parties, not did I go to communion with my family. That was because I was either too hungover or out drinking again. They would come home from a party or important school or church event which I should have been at and I would have sobered up by then. I could see the disappointment in their eyes and I felt awful.'

Billy McNeill recalled: 'Jimmy would go off the drink for ages and then something would happen and he would be back on it. Off the pitch, Jimmy was a great personality, full of life and mischief. He was a real character; cheeky, funny and, at times, downright mad. Most times he didn't create a problem for anyone other than himself. But Agnes had to put up with a lot.

'Fortunately, Agnes had the personality to be able to handle Jimmy. Without Agnes, Jimmy would have been in dire trouble and he would have been the first to acknowledge that.'

But ready as he was to admit that he had been the architect of his own downfall, behaving in a manner that was totally unbecoming in a man who was idolised by thousands, Jinky insisted that it was as if he had been taken over by an alien being when he hit the bottle.

'I am ashamed of anything I did to hurt others,' he said. 'But I am not the person in my mind who did these things. They were drink-driven and alcohol-related. That is not an excuse. But I believe that I am a reasonably nice person and a generous guy. But I was a different person in drink – it was like the devil taking me over.'

Bertie Auld witnessed Jinky's benevolent nature many times. 'He was the kindest wee guy in the world,' said Auld. 'He would never pass anyone down on their luck. If he saw someone struggling he would go and buy them a couple of cans of beer, even a complete stranger. He would say to me: "Bert, there but for the grace of God."'

There was sometimes a humorous side to Jinky's drinking, although Agnes must have struggled to raise a smile. Auld recalled how Jinky would telephone him pleading for his assistance in carrying out a ruse to fool Agnes. 'He would tell me that Agnes had locked all the windows and doors so he couldn't get out for a drink. Jimmy was effectively "grounded". So he would ask me to phone back and tell Agnes that we had an engagement – attending a supporters' club function or whatever – and ask if he had already left. Agnes knew nothing about this supposed engagement, of course, but she immediately relented, thinking that Jimmy was letting people down, and the next thing he would turn up at the pub as we had planned.'

Billy McNeill remembered how shortly after he had undergone triple heart bypass surgery in 1997 the Lions were invited to Las Vegas by one of the North American Supporters' groups to celebrate the thirtieth anniversary of Lisbon. Having been given medical clearance to attend the event, McNeill was advised by his doctors to take things easy. His fellow Lions were also anxious to ensure that their captain did not overtax himself.

McNeill said: 'Jimmy was especially attentive. One evening we were invited to one of the many casinos and ended up having a few drinks too many. Jinky, never the best at holding his drink, became increasingly emotional and eventually there was just the two of us sitting on high stools at the bar, with the wee man telling me what a great bloke I was.

'Jinky always fancied himself as a bit of a singer, and the next thing I knew he was holding my hand and telling me he was going to do a Bon Jovi number, especially for me. Bon Jovi? I had never even heard of them. Undeterred by my show of ignorance, Jinky launched into song What the local made of our touching scene I hate to think, but we certainly attracted a few strange looks.'

That same year the author had the privilege of co-hosting an event attended by the Lisbon Lions. Six readers of the *Scottish Sun* newspaper had won a competition to have lunch with the Lions, and Jinky made their day. He posed for photographs, signed autographs and chatted with his fellow guests as if he had known them all his life. Jinky's charm offensive highlighted the view held by the majority of his team-mates that he was the most popular of their group.

'Jimmy was probably the best liked of all of us,' said McNeill. 'He was an entertainment in himself, and I am not talking about his ability on a football pitch.'

Unhappily, while Jinky's enduring popularity with the Celtic fans put him in constant demand to attend various supporters' functions, his former employers took a dim view of his antics when he was employed as a match-day host at Celtic Park for a brief period, and his services were eventually dispensed with after he made the mistake of having one drink too many.

But, by the mid-1990s, having brought some semblance of order to his life, Jinky found employment for a time in financial services. His innate charm, wit and ability to win over just about anyone made him a natural salesman. 'Can you imagine that cheeky wee face looking up at you? How could anyone have refused him a sale?' said Bertie Auld. 'But I don't think Jimmy particularly enjoyed the job.'

More than thirty years after Celtic's European Cup triumph, Jinky was once again in demand, and his talents as a singer led to him featuring on a recording of 'Forever Celtic' by the Mourne Mountain Ramblers, in company with two of the new generation of Celtic stars, Henrik Larsson and Jackie McNamara.

There had even been talk of Jinky becoming a movie star. Hollywood legend Robert Duvall 'discovered' Jinky by chance after becoming hooked on Scottish football while watching recordings of the winger at his peak during Celtic's European Cup run. Duvall was so impressed that he named his pet dog Jinky.

The star of *The Godfather* also made Jinky an offer he hoped that he could not refuse – a role in the movie he was planning, *A Shot at Glory*, the story of a small-town football team who defy the odds to reach the Scottish Cup final. Duvall had cast himself in the role of manager, based loosely on a Bill Shankly figure. An approach was made to both Jinky and his close buddy and former Old Firm rival Jim Baxter, another larger-than-life character, to play cameo roles. For whatever reason, Jinky rejected the offer.

But Duvall did meet with Jinky over dinner at a Glasgow restaurant, and by all accounts rushed up to his guest, threw his arms round him in a welcoming gesture, and declared: 'I can't believe I've come five thousand miles and here I am next to my hero.'

Duvall later claimed: 'Jinky was the greatest character I ever met. After four or five hours drinking I put him in a cab and told the driver: "Treat him good because he's like Jesus Christ." The driver replied: "No, he's better than Jesus Christ!"'

26

The Cruellest Blow of All

The last five years of Jimmy Johnstone's life were undoubtedly the most remarkable. The courage he had shown as a player was replicated many times over as he fought the toughest fight of his career. Although still prone to occasionally falling off the wagon, Jimmy Johnstone approached the millennium in optimistic mood, having conquered at least some of his demons. But then in November 2001 came the cruellest blow of all, in the shape of the dreadful news that he was suffering from motor neurone disease. It was effectively a death sentence.

The diagnosis was made by Celtic doctor Roddy MacDonald after Jinky complained about a weakness in his shoulder and cramps in his arms and legs. He had been training at Celtic Park when he started to feel weak and could not control his hands and arms properly.

Motor neurone disease destroys the nerves that send signals from the brain to the muscles. When the muscles fail to respond they waste away through lack of use. For someone who had wands for feet and who would not have looked out of place in racing silks, it was the cruellest blow of all.

Before he fell sick, Jinky had regularly run four miles round Strathclyde Park and was remarkably fit for a man of fifty-seven. He had also been behaving himself in a way that had earned him new-found respect. He thought at first he was suffering from arthritis. When informed of the seriousness of his situation one of the first questions he asked was, had his drinking been responsible? It was not a factor, he was assured.

One by one, Jinky informed his former team-mates, some by telephone, others in person. Bobby Lennox, who had been closest to Jinky during their playing days, remembered receiving a call. 'Jimmy phoned to say that something would be appearing in the newspapers and he wanted me to know beforehand to lessen the impact. But nothing could have prepared me for the shock.'

The official announcement that Jinky was suffering from an incurable disease was made to 60,000 fans on Sunday 25 November, just before the Old Firm match at Celtic Park. A stunned silence followed, and Celtic's subsequent 2–1 victory had a hollow feel to it.

Almost from the moment he was told of his condition Jinky pledged to remain upbeat and positive. He admitted that at first he felt down when people said the disease was incurable. But he quickly regained his fighting spirit. 'I don't know how long I have got, but I am not finished yet,' he declared. 'Some say days, months, others years. If it is up to me it will be years and years.'

Celtic manager Martin O'Neill, mindful of the part the Lisbon Lions had played in putting the club on the world map, had encouraged the directors to make greater use of the men who had won the European Cup. Previously, those overseeing the club's fortunes had largely ignored the opportunity to utilise the Lions' standing in a public relations role. But, increasingly, Jinky and his team-mates' profile rose.

It was a measure of Jinky's widespread popularity that he received a flood of letters of support from ordinary fans and personalities alike. Sir Alex Ferguson, Arsène Wenger, Terry Venables, Sven Goran Eriksson, Berti Vogts and Lennart Johansson were among those from the football world who rallied round the stricken winger. Prime Minister Tony Blair and colleagues Gordon Brown and John Reid also expressed their support.

Jinky's first intimation to his close pal Bertie Auld that he was unwell was delivered out of the blue when the pair of them were making their way to Jim Craig's father's funeral. 'We had stopped to ask directions from a fellow, who instantly recognised Jimmy, when he suddenly turned to me as we drove off and said: "Bert, I have been to the doctor's and he's diagnosed motor neurone." There was no big build-up, just a statement of fact.

'I had heard of the disease, of course, but I hadn't a clue as to the seriousness of Jimmy's situation, so I replied: "F— me, Jimmy, I always thought you were a Mercedes man!" I wished afterwards that I hadn't said that. But Jimmy being Jimmy, he just laughed.'

Just a fortnight after being given the shattering news, Henrik Larsson beat Jinky's club record of sixteen European goals when he scored in a 1–1 draw with Valencia at Celtic Park. Instead of bemoaning the fact, Jinky reacted by lavishing praise on the Swedish striker.

On Sunday 8 September 2002 the view long held by many that Jinky had been the most gifted player to wear the Hoops was confirmed as fact when he was named 'Greatest Ever Celtic Player' at a glittering awards ceremony in Glasgow. Jinky topped a poll of Celtic fans worldwide and was duly presented with his award in front of three thousand of them.

Six of Jinky's Lisbon Lions team-mates – Ronnie Simpson, Tommy Gemmell, Bobby Murdoch, Billy McNeill, Bertie Auld and Bobby Lennox – were included in the 'Greatest Ever Celtic Team'. Danny McGrain, Paul McStay, Kenny Dalglish and Henrik Larsson completed the line-up alongside Jinky.

John Greig, voted the Greatest Ever Rangers Player, expressed the view that it was a marvellous honour for Jinky to receive and one that his former rival thoroughly deserved. But Greig wondered if Jinky felt entirely comfortable with the accolade.

'Jimmy played in the best Celtic team ever and was an integral part of that side's success, but football is a team game and you need good players around you, so I suspect that he was perhaps a little embarrassed to be singled out. I know I was,' said Greig. 'But I cannot think of a more worthy candidate. Jimmy's loyalty to Celtic and his affection for the club and its fans was such that he never wanted to leave to better himself financially.'

Jinky's view was that Larsson would have been a more worthy recipient. 'I sat beside Jimmy that evening and he could not believe it when he was announced as the Greatest Ever Celt,' said Bertie Auld. 'He kept saying to me beforehand that it must be Henrik. He was a huge fan of Henrik because he thought he was a wonderful player and a tremendous entertainer, and he was genuinely shocked to be chosen ahead of Larsson.'

Jinky said: 'I couldn't believe it. I don't believe I deserved the award because I just went out and did my best. But the award showed just how much people appreciated me though, and I am grateful.'

Denis Law, who has always bemoaned the fact that Jinky was denied the opportunity to grace the World Cup stage in West Germany in 1974 because of attempts to appease the 'blazers' at the SFA following the infamous Largs boating incident, said: 'At least the fans recognised Jimmy's brilliance when they voted him the Greatest Ever Celtic Player. When you consider the impressive list of players who preceded him, and those who came later, it was some accolade.'

Jinky's induction into the Scottish Sports Hall of Fame in 2002 represented another notable landmark in his life story. Celtic's decision to open a new restaurant at Celtic Park and call it 'Number Seven' was another sign of Jinky's enduring popularity.

His willingness to offer himself up as a guinea pig in an effort to help other sufferers of the disease also won Jinky many new admirers.

An example of his desire to find a cure for MND was his backing of Professor Ian Wilmut, leader of the research team at the Roslin Institute near Edinburgh that famously cloned Dolly the sheep.

When he learned in 2004 of the team's application for a licence to clone human embryos for stem cell research, Jinky offered himself as a guinea pig, explaining: 'The professor is not interested in cloning human beings and neither am I. This research is for curing diseases like mine, not for cloning, and I am convinced it is an area where a cure can be found. These scientists may be on the brink of wiping out these degenerative illnesses.'

But Jinky's sense of humour had certainly not deserted him in adversity. Commenting on the notion of human cloning, he quipped: 'Imagine two of me. Big Jock would go daft, wherever he is, although the Celtic supporters might like that.'

Jinky also travelled to Turin to consult a specialist on the disease who was involved in stem cell research. He visited America, too, to discuss his condition with experts in motor neurone disease. By then Jinky's knowledge of the disease was quite remarkable. Auld, who accompanied him on several hospital trips, revealed: 'Jimmy was able to speak in depth about his illness. I was often amazed by his level of knowledge. He didn't just sit there nodding his head, he really did know what the specialist was talking about.

'The only time I saw a negative reaction from Jimmy was when I took him to see his specialist at the Southern General Hospital near the end of his life. The specialist asked Jimmy if he realised just how ill he was and how advanced his condition was. I was sitting behind Jimmy and I saw him raise his hand and heard him say that he didn't want to know.

'It was the first time I had seen Jimmy put up a shield. Afterwards, as we drove home, Jimmy asked me if I had heard what the doctor had said. I lied that I hadn't listened to their conversation and there was no further mention of it.'

Jinky had lost the ability to sign autographs, such was the effect of his condition on his arms and hands, but his faith was undiminished. 'I just get on with it and try to be positive,' he said. 'I have dark days but I snap out of it. I also say a lot of prayers, because I believe anything that happens comes from the man upstairs. He gave me this, and I don't know why, but maybe there's a reason for it.'

Jinky's voice remained intact, and he sang a lot. His talents as a singer persuaded Simple Minds frontman Jim Kerr, a big Celtic fan, to record 'Dirty Old Town' with his hero in 2004 to raise funds for research into MND. The venture proved highly successful, raising thousands of pounds.

Shane MacGowan, of the Pogues, was also inspired to pen a song in tribute to Jinky entitled 'Road To Paradise'. The recording was another winner for charity.

Even Manchester United got in on the act when the club selected Jinky's version of 'Dirty Old Town' as their official ringtone. The gesture raised tens of thousands of pounds, and when Celtic produced charity wristbands featuring the words 'Jinky – Greatest Ever Celt' the response was such that the club sold six thousand in less than a week.

Jinky took his fund-raising role seriously. But there was never any shortage of humour either. Bertie Auld accompanied him on his trip to Madrid in 2003 to meet Alfredo di Stefano to record a scene for *Lord of the Wing*, the film dedicated to his life and his fight against motor neurone disease.

Auld will never forget the moment when Jinky and di Stefano came face to face at the Bernabeu Stadium. Although Jinky had lost much of the power in his hands by then and was starting to struggle, the pair embraced warmly, two superstars united for several moments. On the return flight Jinky enjoyed several glasses of red wine and began singing. His fellow passengers enjoyed his efforts but he was eventually asked by an air hostess to stop.

Auld took up the story: 'Our flight had been diverted to Edinburgh for some reason I can't recall, and on landing Jimmy informed me that he needed to go to the toilet. I asked if he wanted me to accompany him but he insisted he would be fine. But when Jimmy still hadn't returned ten minutes later I became concerned and went to check on him. When I arrived outside the toilets I heard this commotion. Jimmy was all right pushing a door open, but he was unable to pull, and the second one opened out the other way, effectively trapping him between the two.

'Once we were inside Jimmy turned to me and said: "Listen Bert, you'll need to help me out here." I asked what he meant and he replied that I would have to hold his manhood because he was having trouble due to the lack of feeling in his hands and, no doubt, the effects of alcohol. I wasn't keen, I can assure you, but eventually I agreed to help my pal out.

'Picture the scene, there's the pair of us standing at a urinal in a public toilet, me directly behind Jimmy, who has the front of his tracksuit bottoms pulled down, and I am holding on to the most personal part of his anatomy. Jimmy was giggling away and I remember saying to him that he had better not be having me on the way he seemed to be enjoying himself. I also commented that it would be just my luck for someone to walk in at that moment.

'Lo and behold, the next thing this guy appears and gives us a very strange look. I tried to explain that Jimmy was my pal and the guy replied: "Aye, he would need to be."'

When the premiere of *Lord of the Wing* was held in April 2004, three thousand packed into the Clyde Auditorium in Glasgow to watching the screening just days after the death of Ronnie Simpson, Celtic's goalkeeper in Lisbon. Jinky had considered cancelling the event as a mark of respect to his former team-mate but was persuaded not to on the grounds that Simpson would have wanted the evening to proceed as planned.

It was obvious then to all who saw him that Jinky was gradually losing the fight to stave off the advances of his wasting disease. But despite his physical decline, he remained mentally very sharp and addressed his audience at the Auditorium in a moving way that reduced many of them to tears.

Billy McNeill wondered how he would have dealt with the ravages of a disease that affects 120,000 worldwide, and remarked that he never once heard his former team-mate moan about his misfortune. Jinky handled his situation magnificently, according to McNeill, and continued to set himelf targets because of his desire to do as much as possible in the time he had left to help experts investigate the causes of the disease and perhaps even find a cure.

'Jimmy was a very religious man and never lost belief that there would be an answer eventually,' said McNeill. 'He fought like a tiger, but I wondered if he knew deep down that he wasn't going to survive. But he wanted to leave a legacy behind for others who contracted the disease and give them hope. He never just accepted his lot and he was never afraid to ask questions, or allow himself to be used as a guinea pig.'

McNeill added: 'Eventually I came to admire Jimmy for his dignity in a way that is difficult to explain. I remember once going to visit him and he fell off this wee seat he had. Jimmy couldn't stop laughing. Agnes was also a wonderful companion for him and she was able to laugh along with him. She was a rock. But the latter stages of Jimmy's life were difficult. It was unfair the way the illness kicked in. But Jimmy was never what you would call lucky and he did not deserve what happened to him.

'But the Lisbon Lions were lucky to have played with such a wonderful footballer and a lovely little guy with an incredible personality.'

Bertie Auld visited Jinky three or four times a week and was astounded by his former team-mate's bravery. 'Jimmy never lost his ability to laugh,' Auld said. 'Any time I called to see him in the latter stages of his life I would make up stories to amuse him and he would giggle away. His eyes would light up and his wee belly would heave with laughter.

'Jimmy was a great pal and I hated seeing him in such a state. But what a shot in the arm he was for others. Spending an hour with him was like being given a blood transfusion. You came away feeling ten times better.

'I think Jimmy also appreciated the fact that he had the chance to show his family what they meant to him and how much he valued the fact that they had stood by him during the tough times in his life. His grandchildren all called him Jimmy and the sight of them running into a room and cuddling him was moving. It was a different type of hero worship to the sort he had been used to as a player.'

Tommy Gemmell recalled: 'Whenever I went to see Jinky I used to come away thinking there was something wrong with me. He would laugh and joke as we recounted old times and behave in a thoroughly unselfish manner. There was never a hint of self-pity. Jimmy faced up to his situation without a murmur of complaint. He was a wee tiger – on and off the park.'

It was an index of Jinky's standing in the game that he became the first living person to have a Fabergé egg created in his honour when Sarah Fabergé, great-granddaughter of the Russian Imperial jeweller, was moved to produce the unique work after viewing *Lord of the Wing*. A limited edition of nineteen eggs was produced, to commemorate Jinky's achievement in winning nine league championships, four Scottish Cup and five League Cup honours, in addition to the European Cup.

In July 2005 one of those eggs sold for £47,000 when businessman Willie Haughey, who had been so supportive of Jinky during his battle with alcohol, purchased the first of the collection commemorating the former player's league championship triumph in season 1965–66. Celtic shareholder Dermott Desmond and Sir Alex Ferguson were among the buyers of the remaining eighteen eggs made to mark Jinky's work in raising the awareness of motor neurone disease.

But the one thing that could not be bought at any price was a cure for Jinky's condition.

27

The End

Jinky fought to the last. Shortly before his death on 13 March 2006, he was banned from receiving Copaxone, a drug used to treat sufferers of multiple sclerosis, which Jinky believed could have eased his suffering. The medication had been tested on other motor neurone patients in the USA with positive results. But doctors at Glasgow's Southern General hospital rejected Jinky's plea because of 'ethical issues', as it had only been licensed for use by those with MS.

Jinky's frustration was deepened by the belief that his acting as a volunteer might bring benefit to others. Through a friend, he said: 'What is ethical about denying a dying man a chance of life? The system is letting me down.'

But the man who had won so many personal duels on the football pitch achieved one more victory just hours before he passed away at his Lanarkshire home. Jinky smiled when he was told that doctors had relented just forty-eight hours before he died. But it was a bitter irony.

Bobby Lennox will always treasure his final meeting with Jinky. Although desperately ill, Jinky's sense of humour had not deserted him. 'I told Jimmy that I was having a pacemaker fitted and, quick as a flash, his eyes darted to Stevie Chalmers and he quipped: 'Does that mean we have to call him Gerry from now on?'

'That was one of the last things I heard Jimmy say. I am glad it was humorous because I laughed with Jimmy throughout my adult life. My memories of him will always be of the little jack-in-the-box chatterbox, cracking one-liners and hee-hawing uncontrollably.

'For me the warm, funny wee man away from the football park, who could light up any room, transcended the truly phenomenal player who dazzled on it. His spirit and sense of humour were unquenchable.

'Almost from our first meeting at Celtic Park Jimmy and I became each other's shadows, we did everything together. We shared a love of a sing-song at the back of the bus on away trips. The other players gravitated towards us because Jimmy was such a great chanter and a great comic. What a voice he had, and what an ability to learn all the words of songs only the day after hearing them on the radio.

'We always roomed together, whether it was at Seamill or in foreign parts, and I was fortunate to have such a good pal. He was also a wee man who displayed remarkable courage and dignity, remaining chirpy to the end.'

Stevie Chalmers said: 'Jimmy loved the other Lions and would have done anything for any one of us. He was so happy to see the boys when we visited and was always saying how much we meant to him. He always felt there would be a cure for his illness and he believed that right up to the end.'

Bertie Auld recalled the last time he saw Jinky. 'I visited Jimmy on the Friday prior to his death and he looked better than he had done for some time. There was almost a sheen to his features. But I did notice that his voice had suddenly grown weaker, which I found strange because, for all that his physical appearance had deteriorated quite noticeably, his voice had stayed strong up to then.

'As I was leaving Jimmy asked me to join him on the Sunday so we could watch Celtic's match with Hibs at Easter Road together. I think Jimmy enjoyed my company when there was a match on

TV because of my antics. I have a habit of jumping up and down and he found that amusing.

'Regrettably, it had snowed overnight and I was unable to get my car out of the driveway at my home in Strathaven on the Sunday morning. I phoned Jinky's wife Agnes to explain my predicament and offered to jump on a bus instead. But Agnes told me not to bother as Jimmy had decided to stay in bed. She also assured me he was OK. But the next morning, at 7.30, my wife Liz took a call from Agnes to say that Jimmy had passed away.'

Auld also told a heart-warming story highlighting the impact Jinky had on others suffering from the same disease:

'A couple of months after Jimmy died I was in Majorca on holiday and I was sitting on a wall outside my hotel in Palma Nova when I spotted a couple and their child walking towards me. I could see that the fellow recognised me, so I said hello and his wife asked if her husband could have his photograph taken with me.

'I noticed that the chap seemed to be suffering from some sort of paralysis down one side of his body and I imagined he had suffered a stroke. So I asked what had happened to him and he replied: "I have the same illness as my idol, Jinky Johnstone."

'That comment emphasised just how much Jimmy had done to highlight the disease. It was as if the fellow I spoke with had taken strength from his example and it seemed to make his condition easier to live with in a sense.'

It took Denis Law thirty years to fully appreciate Jimmy Johnstone's brilliance. Law played alongside Jinky eight times in a Scotland jersey over a period of ten years from the mid-1960s. Yet, the Manchester United legend – the last survivor of the great triumvirate of Law, Baxter and Johnstone – admitted that he was not aware at the time just how outstanding Jinky was.

'It was only a couple of years ago when I was watching a DVD of Jinky that I realised what a truly great player he was,' said Law. 'I was aware, of course, that he had been special, but even I was taken aback by his remarkable skills, especially when I saw his performances against Leeds United in 1970.

'The wee man was breathtaking; world-class, and there have not been many Scottish players you can say that about. Jinky was a joy to play with. You never knew from one minute to the next what he was going to do but, of course, neither did the opposition.

'I think it was his devil-may-care personality – the Jack the Lad in him – that made Jimmy the player he was. He oozed personality and fun. He also possessed courage beyond belief, so it didn't surprise me when he battled against his terrible illness in such a courageous and determined fashion. It was typical of him.'

Davie Hay was cast in the role of Jinky's 'minder' when the pair were on international duty immediately before and during the 1974 World Cup, rooming together for five weeks. It gave him an opportunity to get to know Jinky in a way few others did. Hay was also one of those who had tried to 'rescue' Jinky during the infamous Largs boating incident before the squad left for West Germany.

'It was very unfortunate that Jimmy didn't play in the finals, because he deserved the chance to appear on the world stage,' said Hay. 'It was a tragedy that a player of Jimmy's calibre and ability was denied the opportunity.

'Yet, for all that he must have been hurting deeply, he never once complained or caused any unrest in the squad. Mind you, I am sure our opponents were relieved, especially Yugoslavia, considering the way he had destroyed Red Star Belgrade a few years earlier.'

Jinky was in his pomp when Hay established himself in the Celtic first team in season 1969–70. 'Playing right back I was very much involved with Jimmy on the pitch and he was always available to take the ball,' said Hay. 'Playing directly behind him I also saw just what a great player he was.

'I never perceived any shortage of self-belief in Jimmy. If he had issues away from football he never gave the impression that he lacked faith in his ability. But he had humility. He never portrayed himself as a superstar in any shape or form, even though he was one.

'But he was always a bubbly character. He was also a genuinely nice guy and was generous almost to a fault. It just happened to be

Jimmy's misfortune that if there were any misdemeanours he was invariably the one who got caught. Maybe it had something to do with his mop of red hair making him stand out from the rest of us.'

When Hay became Celtic manager in 1983 his decision to bring Jinky back as a coach led to raised eyebrows in certain quarters within the confines of the club. As Hay remembered: 'The young players respected and appreciated Jimmy. The problem was that he still wanted to show off his tricks in training. Sometimes I had to remind him that he was supposed to be supervising training, not participating in it.

'Unfortunately, when things didn't work out some took delight in saying that they had warned me in advance, although I never regretted asking Jimmy to assist me. But I do regret not seeing a lot of him towards the end of his life. On the last occasion I did visit him he was still the same bubbly character. He had changed physically of course, but his personality remained intact. He was still cracking jokes and having a laugh.'

Another of Jinky's Scotland team-mates, Eddie Gray, the former Leeds United winger, claimed that he was every bit as talented as George Best. 'They were also very similar in personality,' said Gray. 'Both were surprisingly quiet and shy and neither was comfortable in the company of relative strangers. Maybe that explains why they turned to drink.'

Gordon Strachan, manager of Celtic, revealed: 'Growing up I had two real heroes, George Best and Jimmy Johnstone, and I am a Hibs fan. That tells you something about the impact Jinky had on me. No matter where you go in the world everybody remembers Jimmy Johnstone. He was an incredible man.'

Strachan's predecessor at Celtic Park, Martin O'Neill, said: 'I met Jimmy with the rest of the Lisbon Lions when I first came to Glasgow. He made you feel as if you were his best friend – but you still felt in complete awe of a footballing genius. He was wonderful company, sometimes teasing everyone in sight, yet at other times deflecting the conversation away from himself and his legendary exploits.'

Celtic's other famous number seven, Henrik Larsson, admitted: 'At first I did not realise what an honour it was to wear the same number of jersey as Jimmy. But by the time I left Celtic I knew exactly why it was so special.'

Jinky's skill and popularity won over even his English rivals such as Sir Bobby Charlton, whose first memory of Jimmy was in a preseason match at Celtic Park when Manchester United lost 4–0. He recalled: 'I thought he was a cheeky little so and so, the way he turned our full-back inside-out. But any footballer looking at Jimmy would have to be in awe of him. He was an absolute nightmare to play against but the English respected him tremendously, despite the fact that he tormented us to hell.'

Eusebio, of Benfica and Portugal fame, revealed that Jinky had tried to persuade him to become a Celtic player. 'I am sure I would have scored many more goals with Jimmy supplying the crosses,' he said, 'because he was one of the best players in the world and a lovely man.'

Jinky's friends in the music industry remembered him fondly. Rod Stewart said: 'I visited Jimmy at his home just a few months before he died, and his body was in tatters, but he was still in great heart and was still wearing a smile.'

According to Jim Kerr, of Simple Minds: 'The likes of Henrik Larsson will always be looked on as a god but Jimmy was one of us – born and bred. We come from a small country and Jimmy showed us we can punch above our weight. Jimmy gave you the feeling that you could be born and bred in Scotland and still conquer the world.'

Even those from the world of politics were moved to express their admiration for Jinky. Gordon Brown declared: 'He was one of

Britain's greatest players and he will be remembered not just for his football, but for his brave fight against motor neurone disease and his dedicated campaign.'

Scotland's First Minister, Jack McConnell, saw Jinky as an inspirational footballer and a real Scottish hero, a man who always played with pride and passion – an opinion shared by John Reid, who added: 'Jimmy was a smashing entertainer and a great human being. He was a delight to watch and a privilege to know. Jimmy gave sheer pleasure to millions way beyond the tribal limits of club football.'

But perhaps Jinky's Lisbon Lion team-mate Tommy Gemmell summed up the player best when he said: 'Jinky could have played in any team in the world – club or international.'

Jinky's passing was felt most profoundly by his wife, three children, six grandchildren and one great-grandchild. But they were not alone in their grief. Their pain was shared by tens of thousands of football fans, many of whom turned Jinky's funeral into a wonderfully moving celebration of his life.

The solemnity of the occasion was relieved by smiles and laughter, just the way Jinky would have wanted it. For, as Bertie Auld emphasised, he was the people's champion – a man with an aura, but one who remained humble for all that.

Auld also considered that Celtic should have made Jinky an ambassador for the club. But it hardly mattered that he was never officially given the title. To the vast majority of Celtic fans Jinky was the epitome of what they believe their club to be – a football institution that transcends class differences.

They were able to take the boy from his working-class roots in Lanarkshire and turn him into a star, but luckily for Celtic, and for Scotland, they couldn't take the simplicity and sincerity out of the boy.

The tears and cheers as Jinky was taken on his final journey past Celtic Park said it all.

JIMMY JOHNSTONE STATISTICS

James Connolly Johnstone, born Viewpark, Uddingston, 30 September 1944.

Career: St Columba's Primary and St John the Baptist Secondary schools. Signed for Celtic 1961. Freed by Celtic 1975. Signed for San Jose Earthquakes 1975. Signed for Sheffield United 1975. Signed for Dundee 1977. Signed for Shelbourne 1977. Signed for Elgin City 1978. Signed for Blantyre Celtic 1980. Retired 1980.

Diagnosed with motor neurone disease 2001.

Named Greatest Ever Celtic Player 2002.

Release of *Lord of the Wing* 2004.

Died 13 March 2006 at Uddingston.

JINKY

Appearances/Goals

CELTIC

	League	League Cup	Scottish Cup	Europe	Total	Goals
1962/63	4	–	1	–	5	1
1963/64	25	2	4	7	38	10
1964/65	24	10	1	4	39	4
1965/66	32	8	7	7	54	14
1966/67	25	10	5	9	49	16
1967/68	29 (1)	8	1	5*	44	10
1968/69	30 (1)	7 (1)	6	5	50	9
1969/70	27	4 (1)	4	9	45	11
1970/71	30	9	8	4	51	19
1971/72	23	8	2	5 (1)	39	10
1972/73	21 (1)	7	6 (1)	3	39	10
1973/74	13 (2)	7 (2)	2	6	32	8
1974/75	15 (6)	7	–	2	30	8
	298 (11)	87 (4)	47 (1)	66 (1)	515	130

* Includes three matches against Racing Club of Buenos Aires for the World Club Championship. Figures in brackets are substitute appearances.

SAN JOSE EARTHQUAKES 1975/76 – Figures not available.

SHEFFIELD UNITED

	League	FA Cup	Total	Goals
1975/76	6	1	7	1
1976/77	5	–	5	1
	11	1	12	2

DUNDEE

	League	Total	Goals
1977/78	2 (1)	3	–

SHELBOURNE

	Appearances	Goals
1977/78	9	2

ELGIN CITY

	Appearances	Goals
1978/79	18	2

HONOURS

League championship   Nine championship medals for seasons
1965/66–1973/74 inclusive.

League Cup   Winner 1965/66, 1966/67, 1968/69, 1969/70 and
1974/75.
Runner-up 1964/65, 1970/71, 1971/72, 1972/73 and
1973/74.

Scottish Cup   Winner 1967, 1971, 1972 and 1974.
Runner-up 1963, 1966, 1970, 1973.

European Cup   Winner 1967.
Runner-up 1970.

Full International Honours – 23 caps
1964 v Wales and Finland
1966 v England and Wales
1967 v USSR and Wales
1968 v Austria
1969 v West Germany (2)
1970 v England and Denmark
1971 v England, Belgium, Holland, Portugal
1972 v Northern Ireland, England
1974 v Wales, England, Belgium, Norway, East Germany, Spain

International goals

1966 2 v England, Hampden

1969 1 v West Germany, Hamburg

1974 1 v Belgium, Bruges

Also represented Scotland at Junior, Under-23 and Scottish League levels.

SELECT BIBLIOGRAPHY

Campbell, Tom, and Potter, David, *Jock Stein: The Celtic Years* (Mainstream, 1998).

Campbell, Tom, and Woods, Pat, *Dreams and Songs to Sing* (Mainstream, 1996).

Campbell, Tom, and Woods, Pat, *The Glory and the Dream* (Mainstream, 1986).

Crampsey, Bob, *Mr. Stein* (Mainstream, 1986).

Docherty, David, *The Celtic Football Companion* (John Donald Publishers, 1986).

Healey, Jeff, *Lord of the Wing* (ACFTV, 2004).

Jinky. The Jimmy Johnstone Story (Freemantle Home Entertainment Ltd, 2003).

Johnstone, Jimmy, *Fire in My Boots* (Stanley Paul, 1969).

Johnstone, Jimmy, and McCann, Jim, *Jinky ... Now And Then* (Mainstream, 1988).

McCuaig, Margot, *Jimmy Johnstone, A Bhoy's Life* (2006).

Macpherson, Archie, *The Great Derbies: Blue and Green, Rangers versus Celtic* (BBC Books, 1989).

Wilson, Brian, *Celtic: A Century With Honour* (Willow Books, 1988).

INDEX